D1082667

An Interpretation
of Universal History

by JOSÉ ORTEGA Y GASSET

SOME LESSONS IN METAPHYSICS

THE ORIGIN OF PHILOSOPHY

THE REVOLT OF THE MASSES

MAN AND PEOPLE

MAN AND CRISIS

WHAT IS PHILOSOPHY?

MEDITATIONS ON QUIXOTE

HISTORY AS A SYSTEM

CONCORD AND LIBERTY

MISSION OF THE UNIVERSITY

THE IDEA OF PRINCIPLE IN LEIBNITZ AND THE EVOLUTION
OF DEDUCTIVE THEORY

AN INTERPRETATION OF UNIVERSAL HISTORY

VELAZQUEZ, GOYA AND THE DEHUMANIZATION OF ART

PHENOMENOLOGY AND ART

HISTORICAL REASON

JOSÉ ORTEGA Y GASSET

An Interpretation
of Universal History

TRANSLATED BY MILDRED ADAMS

W · W · NORTON & COMPANY

New York · London

Published simultaneously in Canada by Stoddart,
a subsidiary of General Publishing Co. Ltd, .
Don Mills, Ontario.

W. W. Norton & Company, Inc., 500 Fifth Avenue, New York, N.Y. 10110
W. W. Norton & Company Ltd., 37 Great Russell Street, London WC1B 3NL

Copyright © 1973 by W. W. Norton & Company, Inc.

First published in the Norton Library 1975

Books That Live
The Norton imprint on a book means that in the publisher's
estimation it is a book not for a single season but for the years.
W. W. Norton & Company, Inc.

Library of Congress Cataloging in Publication Data

Ortega y Gasset, José, 1883–1955.
   An interpretation of universal history.

   Series of lectures on A. J. Toynbee's A study of
history.
   1. Toynbee, Arnold Joseph, 1889–   A study
of history. I. Title.
CB63.T680713   1973   909   73–10

ISBN 0-393-00751-0

ALL RIGHTS RESERVED

Printed in the United States of America
   2 3 4 5 6 7 8 9 0

Contents

Preliminary Note

The prospectus that announced the creation of The Institute of the Humanities promised an inaugural course of twelve lectures, to be given by its founder and entitled, "Concerning a New Interpretation of International History. (Exposition and Examination of A. J. Toynbee's work, A Study of History.)" But the course as given (in 1948–49) went much farther than that announcement, for the "examination" consisted principally of a critique of Mr. Toynbee's work from the point of view of Ortega's own doctrines, together with the unfolding of his personal ideas about the science of history and the progress of peoples—in particular the Romans—with frequent side excursions, meant to be systematic, into the crisis of the present time.

As stated on page 225, the central theme of these pages becomes "the analysis of life established in illegitimacy . . . of which the two gigantic examples are the declining days of the Roman Empire and the period in which we ourselves are living." To the modern crisis, Ortega brings a basic analysis and a program of reform for intelligence by which contemporary life might emerge from the confusion it now suffers.

In preparing this book for publication, our work has been to collate two texts, the original manuscript as edited for the lectures of this course, and the stenographic version of the course as given. Each of the two versions contains passages which are lacking in the other; on the one hand, the lecturer while speaking was moved to amplify his prepared text; on the other, such additions are lacking elsewhere in the manuscript. In general, we have kept to the stenographic transcription, but we have also added parts of the manuscript in which omissions in the text as spoken could be explained only by lack of time. At the beginning of each lesson we have set headings meant to orient the reader to its argument.

The complexity of the principles set forth in this course, and the amplification of them in the process of its oral exposition, force one to think that only by a most attentive reading can its extreme importance be perceived. In the last lecture Ortega expressed his gratitude to the public for having "endured some of the most dense, most concentrated lectures which have ever been given any-where," and in the place where this occurs we feel the statement to be fully justified.

The Compilers

An Interpretation
of Universal History

I

Toynbee's careers. International information.
Communication. Experience of life.
The Greco-Roman decline.

ARNOLD TOYNBEE was born in 1888. He is a professor of history in the University of London [1] and a director of the Royal Institute of International Affairs. He studied at Oxford, where he became extremely proficient in Greek, which is, as you know, the language of Oxford. He married the daughter of that grand old patriarch of Hellenic studies in England, Gilbert Murray. Then he studied Arabic, and this enabled him during two wars to occupy various posts in the British Intelligence Service, particularly in the Middle East.

Each year since 1926 he has published a volume setting forth the situations of various countries, including the most remote, which serves as a handbook of information in the international politics of England. In 1934 he published the first three volumes of his prodigious work *A Study of History*, and in 1939 another three volumes. We shall make the acquaintance of this great work, and in the course of twelve lectures we shall be reflecting on it. Therefore we can enter into the matter bit by bit, proceeding without haste. Today we will content ourselves with stating certain themes that will later appear fruitful and at the moment will prepare us for entry into

1. Professor Toynbee is now (1972) Professor Emeritus in the University of London [*Translator's note*].

Toynbee's thought; these are inspired by a mode of thinking very different from his own.

You will note that what has been said presents certain
limited data concerning Toynbee—his person and his
life—data which must be defined as external. But human
life is a reality in which everything is internal, including
that which we call external. Thus this series of data is a
list of dry statements behind which are hidden many
things that are abundantly human and full of sap.

For example, the professorship of International History in the University of London, the leadership of the
Institute of International Affairs, and the yearly publications concerned with these matters show us that inter-
nationalism is the profession to which Toynbee has dedicated his life, and that in this profession he appears as one
of England's most eminent figures. Well now, the act
of dedicating one's life to a specific thing is a privilege
of the human condition. The stone, the plant, the animal
are, when they begin, whatever they can be, and therefore what they are going to be. Man, on the other hand,
has, when he begins to exist, no prefixed or imposed
image of what he is going to be, but, on the contrary, he
carries with him—predetermined and imposed—the freedom to choose what he is going to be. And this within a
wide horizon of possibilities. The power to choose,
which, in the universe of being is his privilege, has at the
same time the nature of a sentence and a tragic destiny,
for as he is forced to select his own manner of being he
is also condemned to the responsibility for being himself
—a situation which does not confront the stone, the plant,
or the animal. These, being innocently what they are,
have been dowered with an enviable irresponsibility.

Thanks to his condition, man becomes that strange
creature which goes through life carrying within his being both a culprit and a judge, both of whom are man

himself. Hence the most intimate and at the same time most substantially solemn act of our lives is the one by which we dedicate ourselves to something: it is not mere chance that we describe this action with the word *dedicate*, which is a religious term of the Latin language. *Dicatio* or *dedicatio* was the solemn act in which the city, represented by its magistrates, declared a building to be set aside for the worship of a god; therefore to be sacred or consecrated. And as a matter of fact we ourselves say casually of someone that he has dedicated or consecrated his life to some office or occupation.

Note that we have clarified this point in the human condition by using the most religious of words—*dedication, consecration, destiny*. At the same time, also note how, on the common tongue, those words have lost their pathos and their transcendent resonance, and in continuing and prolonging their existence they have become trivial. This close connection between transcendence and triviality will surprise us again and again as we turn corners in all human affairs.

Thus, when I have been meditating on man's destiny, there always comes back to me—impertinent but irrepressible—the memory of how, during my adolescence in that Madrid which then oozed tranquillity, daily habits, and—let us confess it—a bit of commonness—my home, very influential in the Spanish life of that time, was always full of people who came looking for a little patronage ("*un destino de seis mil reales*"). Younger generations cannot imagine the tiresome frequency with which this matter was then discussed, and the monstrous importance which that concept and the humble reality behind it had in Spanish life. Upon it rested, at the time, no less than the political life of the entire country, because as one could move easily between jobs and no grave problems existed, a change of political party meant only the end of

many *"destinos de seis mil reales"* and the parallel grant-
ing of as many more. In fact, for many a man in that
humble and modest period, a "six thousand *real* destiny"
was the destiny of mankind.

It would be an error to regard this as no more than a
play on words on my part. Better to note that it is not I,
but the thousand-year-old language of our entire people
—even more, of all the Latin people—for, among them,
many coincide in offering us these apparent plays on
words, already become folk sayings, and this makes it
appear that there is more than word-play in them.

Well, then, this Englishman with whom we are going
to deal for a long time is first presented to us as an internationalist—that is, as a man occupied with learning
what is going on in distant countries and informing others
about it. Mr. Toynbee did not invent this occupation. It
is very seldom that an individual invents the occupation
to which he will dedicate his life. That which—using a
concept more dazzling than accurate—we call "genius"
means (and really it means just this) the ability to invent
one's own occupation. Normally, however, the individual
chooses one of the generic forms of existence which the
social milieu about him has prepared, and which we call
posts, professions, careers. As these are generic, we have
in them a previous and concrete picture of how a specific
individual pursues them, and the simple hearing of the
name of the office arouses within us a peculiar sense of
expectation.

There is no doubt that automatically, without need to
reflect, we take on a different personal posture when a
man is presented to us as a poet from the one we adopt
when he is presented as a colonel. It may happen that an
individual's behavior contradicts what the name of the
office suggests: a poet may be inclined to be haughty and
demanding, or a colonel to write verses in secret, but
this seems merely the exception that proves the rule. Be-

cause our life is in fact made up on one side by a collection of expectations and prognostications formed spontaneously within us. Existence would be impossible if we had to confront everything that happens as entirely new, and if we did not have in advance a certain known pattern of behavior allowing us to prepare our own conduct and take certain precautions. We shall see how imperative it is for everyone to have that repertory of expectations very clearly in mind, and not to give himself up carelessly to everything that comes along.

What I have just said is especially valid in the case at hand. It is very important to have a clear expectation of what this description represents—an Anglo-Saxon occupied in informing himself and others about international affairs. In no small measure, the immediate future of the world, and of all of us, depends on what that human type may be. Therefore, watch out! Be on guard!

It would not be strange if many of you asked yourselves in vain what picture that description arouses in your minds. You know what the words say, but that is all. The reason is that, as I said before, such expectations do not spring from whatever reasoning you may improvise, but are formed spontaneously within us by a gradual decanting of experience. Now the internationalist, the profession of gathering and conveying information about international affairs and the character of the various countries concerned, is a recent one, which began to take shape and appearance after the First World War. It is, then, not strange that it has not yet succeeded in printing its features on the mind; many people, on hearing that word, are left with no precise impression of what it means. Therefore, I feel it all the more urgent to call attention to this new profession, this new human type which has already had, and in the future will continue to have, an influence as great as it may be dangerous.

For many reasons which then converged, the end of

the 1914–18 war was followed throughout the world by a phenomenon of which the gravity and importance have not yet been sufficiently recognized. This consisted in the fact that in terms of history, of the way people lived, the planet suddenly contracted, so that people began living together much more closely than they had ever lived before. Each nation felt that all the others, even those most distant, had come close and immediate, so that its own security and well-being depended on what happened to each of those others. The principal cause of this sudden drawing together was the fabulous progress in means of communication. News, men, and things were transported at a dizzying rate from one point on the planet to another that had been hitherto remote. The result was that, in terms of industry and war, all peoples became frontier nations—even more so from the industrial point of view, in terms of obtaining raw materials and in terms of market, did the nations become mutually interpenetrated, so that there is no country for which the others are not indispensable.

For the moment, all this is a most glorious victory for physical science, the creator of contemporary techniques. Without going fully into the question, for it is exceedingly profound, I should like to point out the contradictory character which the element of distance as such has had in human life. The reality is not that man begins by being in the near and immediate, in what we call the "here," in such a way that this is what first exists for him. It is evident that, just as there is no "right" unless there is a "left," no "above" without a "below," so one cannot be conscious of a "here" without at the same time being aware of a "there." Consequently, in order that man may feel himself "here," he needs, in some way or some sense, to be at the same time "there." This is why I said that the reality is not that we are first in the proximate and immediate, so that it becomes what first exists for us, but that the nearby, the object we see in our immediate neighborhood, is presented to us against a background of other more distant things, that is, against the background of a horizon. Thus, this room in which you read is now your "here"; it is vivid as the nearest part of a reality far more ample than any behind or about it; as a place in the immense world, which is the most vast horizon.

Imagine the surprise, the terror you would feel if, on leaving your room for a moment, you should find that this space and this reality were all there was, that there was nothing outside; in short, that there was no "there." This shows that our consciousness of being "here" implies and requires a previous consciousness of that remote horizon; therefore, we are truly in that great distance which is the world, in the "there," and from it we come incessantly to be aware of that which is nearby and to feel ourselves "here." The matter is paradoxical but is evident; man is first of all "over there" in the distance, and only by contraposition with the "there" does the "here" appear. This state of finding ourselves at the same time both "here" and "there," these two opposing ways of being, constitute the contradictory character to which I referred earlier; it makes of space and distance a painful and damaging dimension of human living. This is the hurtful duality of our condition. Mentally we are everywhere, ubiquitous, but our bodies chain us to one place, localize us. Whatever the precise spot in which we are, we keep coming back to it from the horizon, from the world's great far away.

This means that if we are "here," it is because by consent or constraint we have renounced being in some other distant place which constitutes "out there." So that something as simple as "here," as having to be "here," represents in our lives a permanent crippling, a denial of other possibilities, a retraction and a confinement; in a transcendent sense it is that slavery to the soil suffered by the human condition. Fortunate is the stone which rests where its matter lies. But man is that strange animal which, while materially "here," is in reality always coming back from the Universe to the corner where he finds himself, always bringing with him the presence of that Universe. And thus our way of being both in the distant and the "here" entails feeling ourselves separated from them as though we were exiled.

Perhaps this way of putting it may not be adequate. Perhaps we can say that man is a captive in the "here" and an exile from the "there" which is his true fatherland. Hence our relation with the far away, our being in it as a man exiled from his own country still belongs to his country, gives rise to one of the most essentially human emotions which exist; this is nostalgia, which is the feeling of missing the nearness of the distant, the moan of a "there" desiring to be "here," a sorrow at being where one is not. For this reason nostalgia has always been the most fruitful source of poetry, and the mold in which some of the most exquisite human sentiments have taken shape.

Some day, in this Institute, we will construct a history of the passions, for, contrary to what is usually believed, passions also have their history and are not permanent and unchanging characteristics that fail to vary with man's vicissitudes. Passions are born, they develop, and they die; they are triumphant, or they are in stages of withdrawal and defeat. Well, then, some day we will trace the history of human passions, and among them the history of love, which—strange as it may seem—no one has yet undertaken. Then we will see that what we call the love of a man for a woman began, and always has begun, not (as one might think) through enthusiasm for the woman who is close at hand in the same tribe or social class, but, on the contrary, through imagining the woman far away, distant in space or in social rank. Time after time woman has become a beloved in the guise of a *princesse lointaine*, and it is not by chance that when customs bring men and women very close together the amorous sentiment of love becomes volatile, evaporates, and there come into being those strange lackings in love which characterize certain periods.

But let us leave what we can call the essential paradox of the "here" and the "there"; I let myself contemplate it superficially because I believe that we should all be sensitive to the importance, the gravity which every change, large or small, in the relation of man with space has in his life.

As both the idea and the phrase "progress in the means of communication" have neither a poetic aura nor an emotional metaphysical resonance, we run the risk of failing to realize to what extent they affect the very root of existence itself; yet by attaining an almost circular velocity, by almost destroying distance, they have upset one of life's basic factors, and have suppressed if not ended the stupid limitation and servitude from which human existence suffered. But on the other hand, man had long ago accommodated himself to those handicaps; he had so organized his life in its deepest dimensions as to take distance and space into account, and he had even managed to draw from those limitations certain advantages. Man ends by making the best of everything. Therefore I mentioned earlier the fruitfulness of nostalgia in poetry and in love: I could have cited other examples.

That is to say, this near-liberation of man from slavery to the land and the soil, and from the fact of distance which puts far away the things we most need and the people we most want to see—so that in order to reach them we must spend time, of which we have too little, and energy, of which we have not enough—this new freedom means that these limitations have been overcome. But man was used to them. In the face of them he had organized his life and his conduct. Their new absence poses new problems. The fact that people have suddenly come close together, especially in terms of space, does not mean that in vital terms they are any nearer to one another. Quite the contrary. In finding themselves suddenly so close, they discover that this spatial proximity is not accompanied by a like proximity in their manner of being, in ideas and sentiments, in customs, institutions, economics; so that if in the long run our victory over space and distance means a basic benefit, for the moment it will bring great losses and enormous conflicts.

Let us keep in mind this other circumstance: each people was so constituted that it took into account the traditional distances which always separated it from the others. Someday we will see—I hope clearly—how the entity called "people," the entity "nation," signifies "distance." In thus diagnosing the present situation I leave it to you to judge whether or not the diagnosis must be taken as serious.

Now the new profession which I have called "internationalist," and of which Toynbee is today perhaps the most eminent representative, was born as a first result of that sudden approach of the peoples to each other. They began to feel that they needed to know what was happening to other peoples. Diplomatic dispatches which for centuries had been sent to royal courts, dealing almost exclusively with concrete questions of the policies followed by governments, were no longer sufficient. Nor were the correspondents in foreign countries who, in the nineteenth-century way, sent home information only on certain precise and exceptional events, such as battles, earthquakes, or celebrations.

In the last thirty years, especially among the Anglo-Saxons, a type of journalist has appeared who devotes himself to going from nation to nation in order to inform his own people what the others are like; how they feel, think, and wish; what their intimate disagreements are, their hopes and their problems. This work, which later appears frequently put into books, has in the past fifteen years become one of the favorite forms of reading. At the same time it is the principal source on which great internationalists like the Toynbees are nourished. This group, made up of the journalists and the Toynbees, is what I call "the new profession of internationalist."

At first glance one might judge that nothing would seem more desirable than such work, through which people can quickly acquire an adequate knowledge of each other, but I must confess that long and attentive reading of those publications has produced in me a less favorable hope of the internationalist profession. This for three reasons.

In the first place, the facts or events which are reported are frequently false; they are bits of gossip, idle talk gathered by the traveling journalist from persons whose credibility, social status, sense of responsibility he may not know; at other times the facts may not be completely false, but they are practically so; and this is almost more serious, because it makes the lack of orientation even sharper.

Second reason: the most dangerous aspect of these pieces of information does not lie in errors of fact—one must say most precisely that in the greater part of such cases the information, especially in Anglo-Saxon reporting, is, taking fact by fact, of an almost prodigious exactitude. If the "information" which the word itself both promises and states could consist solely in a series of facts which are exact, one would ask no more; but there remains another series of facts which are not put into words; lacking this second group, the first cannot be understood in the structure and perspective within the country from which they stem, so that although they have a certain external accuracy they lack both reality and internal truth.

Third, and this for me is the decisive reason: what I most fear is the enormous faith which those great countries have in that information. This faith implies that they believe it easy for a foreigner, looking from the outside, to go to a country in order to know what goes on within it; this in turn assumes having an erroneous idea of what a people and a nation are, for it ignores the fact that the collective life of a people, a nation, is an intimate—and to a certain extent a secret—matter, very like what those words mean when one says of a personal life that it is an intimacy within itself, and no one who looks at it from the outside can easily come to understand it.

The damage which this type of information will produce—and note that I am not referring especially to Spain—became to me such an obsession that in January of 1937 (I emphasize the date) I wrote a long study which appeared shortly afterward in one of the leading English magazines; in this I went into the matter somewhat more deeply, and later I included it as an appendix to a new edition of my book *The Revolt of the Masses* under the title "Epilogue for the English." There you will see (if you read it) how many things therein predicted have since come true, not to Spain, but especially to England. Unhappily, many more will follow.

Now you will understand why, on the threshold of a course on the great book in which Toynbee will speak to us of universal history, I have appeared to be wasting time by describing to you the expectation which the vocation and profession of internationalist arouses in us. Should we not fear that as Mr. Toynbee belongs to this profession he will be overconfident concerning what he can discover about historic reality, looking at it from the outside as though looking at a phenomenon of nature? Should we not fear that he might minimize the intimate and secret element in every human happening, and fail to take into full account the depth lying in the fact that man in the abstract does not exist, but that every man belongs to a people, and that a people, whether they wish it or not, is made up of individuals? Does not all this carry with it the assumption that the man who minimizes these things may, on the other hand, find human utopias and abstract associations among nations both easy and probable?

This, at least, was the expectation with which I began to read Toynbee's great book. But if I have said that we are obliged to keep our list of expectations clearly in mind, I now add that we must avoid having them turn into prejudices. Those expectations do not assure us that the individual in question—Toynbee in this case—will suffer from those optical illusions to which his profession inclines him. Let us, then, begin this study without a prejudice, but on the alert.

You see that we had only to press lightly on the simple and apparently external information that I gave you about Toynbee—that he was an "internationalist"—to draw forth abundant and even tremendous problems. Now a very few words about the fact that Toynbee in Oxford was a most eminent Greek scholar. I do not know whether this simple phrase says anything to you. I do not know whether it will arouse in you a sufficient degree of expectation. In my judgment this reveals one of the most admirable and extraordinary facts of our contemporary age.

Ever since the eighteenth century, England has maintained hegemony over the Western world. During the nineteenth century she extended this dominance to the entire planet. I think there is no point on earth where she failed to have interests. In order to carry on and direct these affairs, to govern English life as well as her ubiquitous interests, England needed many able men capable of the most concrete struggles with things, situations, and people, in Europe as in Asia, Oceania, and Africa. Now, the Englishman has always been valued as a practical man *par excellence,* and to this characteristic both his progress and his victory have been attributed. How, then, did England arrange to have at her disposal those numerous teams of men whom we might call "directors of affairs"? This is what she did: in every generation, England chose the best lads of the upper classes, and shut them up in Oxford so that they might devote themselves to learning Greek and to practicing sports as the Greeks did. That is all. You will recognize that the fact is phenomenal and more than unexpected. When, in my own youth, I learned this and recognized the extraordinary paradox which it represented, I searched everywhere for an explanation, but failed to find one.

Then later, having a better acquaintance with England's genius (at once magnificent and eccentric), I had to improvise an explanation for my own use; I pass this on to you with due reservations. Nevertheless, I believe that those of you who know the peculiar manner of man whom we describe as "being English," and, in knowing him, get a sense of the whole man and come to admire certain peerless gifts in him (mixed with not a few less pleasant things) will judge my attempt at clarifying that amazing enigma to be entirely credible. Here it is: most educators, especially when inspired by an eagerness for the practical, think that what they must do with boys is to prepare them in the most concrete possible fashion for life as it is, leaving aside all disciplines and

methods which seem merely ornamental, lavish, or su-
perfluous. But it is a fact that the condition of historic
life is one of constant change. History is unending restlessness and mutation. So that if one educates a boy by
preparing him concretely for life as it is today, that boy
will find, when grown to manhood, that life then wears
another face, and that the more practically he was prepared for an earlier way of life, the less well adjusted will
he be for the new present in which he must live and act.
This is what I have called the constitutive anarchronism
of customary pedagogy. It aims the new generation at a
target which, when they reach it, will have been taken
away and put somewhere else.

Whether fully conscious of this contradiction or acting by instinct, England resolves it inversely; for some
years her best youth would be going to live with others
in the age of Pericles—that is, in place of adapting their
education to the present, England projects it outside of
time, for the century of Pericles is an unreal date, an imaginary and exemplary time which soars ideally above all
specific time. Within that unreal Greece, England's
young men are educated in the essential forms of living;
that is, they are trained in pure abilities which allow
them to adapt to the most diverse concrete situations; by
the same token, they are not prepared especially for any
single occasion.

Now, biologists have taught us that a very specialized
organism, with its structure adapted to a single medium,
remains helpless when the medium changes; while a form-
less, organless creature like the amoeba has the power to
create for itself in every situation the provisional organs
that it needs. If it needs to approach food it sends out
from its plasma an extension, or pseudopod, that functions
like a foot; with this it walks. Having once made use of it,
this pseudopod is quietly reabsorbed back into the plasma.

The great biologist von Uexkull formulates this in saying, *"Struktor hemmt Strukturbildung,"* "having structure hinders the creating of structure." I find this English solution to the essential contradiction in ordinary pedagogy a bit of real genius. The practical Englishman, for the very reason that he is genuinely practical, knows that at certain times the most practical thing to do is to not seem so.

Of course this solution, like all human solutions, has its inconvenience and suffers from its limitations. You will see that at times we trip, annoyed, over a certain Greek and especially Athenian pedantry in Toynbee. The University of Cambridge, where he studied the physical and biological sciences in depth, represents a certain concession to the needs of the moment, and in the period now beginning we shall see whether that education à la Grecque serves also for England's very new problems; we will see whether, in the crowded present, the English amoeba is capable of thrusting forward the appropriate pseudopod.

We will now ask ourselves, What is the content of Mr. Toynbee's book; what is it all about? The title, *A Study of History,* seems a bit equivocal. Does this mean that Toynbee proposes to write history in a different form from the one it has taken up to now? To some extent; for what he does is to start from the history books, from the science of history as such, and as it has been understood, in order to produce other effects and elaborations. What he does, then, is to take for granted historic science in its present form, and submit it to a second treatment in order to see whether, in that enormous chaos which is a historic happening, one cannot glimpse rhythms, structures, laws, regularities which allow one to arrive at a clear picture of the shape and features of the historic process. Therefore, it treats of what, thirty years ago, was called the "philosophy of history."

Now to call something the "philosophy of history" is to use a misnomer which started from the fact that people held the most confused notion of what philosophy is and thought that a philosophy could be made out of everything; that, as the man in the street, the good bourgeois, used to say, putting on a painfully intelligent expression, "everything has its philosophy," as if philosophy were like sugar, something to eat with other things; this led him to state that one must "take life with philosophy," as coffee is taken with a lump or two. The great historian Dilthey said that a philosopher of history is a monster, half philosopher and half historian. In fact, there is no such thing as a philosophy of history. Philosophy is a science as special as any other, which has its completely specific themes and problems. One is not discussing that, but trying simply to see if, in the chaotic and confused series of historic events, one can descry lines, features, traits—in short, a physiognomy; there has not been a single period for which historic destiny has not presented something resembling a face, or a set of recognizable features.

Well, now, note that this is something that every man does, at least in his personal life. Man not only goes on living his life, but as he does so, there takes shape within him—spontaneously, without his compliance or premeditation—an idea or a knowledge of what life is. Everyday language has usually coined a phrase for expressing this spontaneous knowledge about human existence which man gathers. It is called "experience of life." Note that this experience of life is knowledge that does not, like scientific knowledge, remain more or less outside the life that possesses it; experience of life forms an integral and effective part of life itself. It is one of the components that make up life. In proportion as man keeps on acquiring it, he keeps modifying his own living. Well, now, men do not acquire that knowledge which we call "experience of life" by reflecting on it, or by a special intellectual effort such as scientific knowledge demands, but it goes on being formed within us automatically, even though we may not wish it. Life goes on clarifying itself, while we live, as if discovering its own reality, and this process of finding out enters in turn into life to form part of it, is retransformed into life, and so on successively. It is the only kind of knowing which is at once, and of itself, living. At the same time it has the inconvenience that it cannot be transmitted to anyone else. It is nontransferable, and each new generation has no choice but to begin its own experience of life at the beginning.

You will recognize that the theme which we have entitled "experience of life" is certainly one of those that flies high. If there are half a dozen of these very exalted subjects, this, which springs from the very root of human existence, is certainly one of them. Therefore you may think that it has frequently been dealt with; but if you go to search, you will find nothing about it anywhere, unless it be a few words of a man who could hardly have avoided it, our admirable and venerable precursor Dilthey.

Things which happen to us go on leaving in us, by themselves, a precipitate which crystallizes into rules, recipes, habits which, joining with others, keep on sketching the profile of what life is. This is not a question of reasoning. Experience of life is irrational, and by the same token its dicta impose themselves on us inexorably, however many may be the reasons that we would like to set counter to them. Here you have the origin of those expectations about the professions which caught our attention earlier. If you want another example, close at hand, remember the idea that forms itself within you about the character of people who are known to you. That picture of the character of others has seldom, if ever, been formed by deliberate reflection; rather, it has been formed as though growing within you by spontaneous generation.

Experience of life presents us with what I call "aspects." The commonest and closest example is this: we all talk of how things are given us in streaks, or spells, how there are good ones and bad ones, succeeding each other in a kind of rhythm. This cycle of the favorable and the adverse is one of those features that give shape to life. There are abundant reasons for denying reality to this image, but they all are powerless to evade the fact that the course of life presents itself to us as having the appearance of streaks of luck. This may not be a reality, but only an aspect, so that is what I call it. But as an aspect it is real, and whether we like it or not, it does influence us.

In this experience of life which goes on slowly forming itself like a snowball, making its own path while it rolls, like the snowball it leaves its path opening behind it, so one finds at about age fifty that a very interesting stage has unrolled behind one. Then and there man has the impression that he now knows what life is; not only that he is familiar with this or that pattern of life, but that, in its totality, it is to him diaphanous, transparent. Once more I repeat that it does not matter whether the content of the experience of life, transformed without our reflecting on it or with only enough reflection to formulate it lightly, is true or not. Well then, to what can that strange phenomenon be attributed? Why does man, at a certain moment in his vital chronology, think that now he knows what life is?

I am not treating this in depth, but as a possible explanation let us say that it consists in this: There is an erroneous tendency to believe that the various forms of life are without limit; for example, that the forms of love may, in their diversity, be infinite; that there can always be new forms of government and political institutions. This is not so. All the patterns of life are limited. If, by chance, a new one arrives unexpectedly, it will be after the lapse of many centuries, and intermingled with forms that are not new. So that at age fifty, at that vantage point of living, man will have experienced all the essential forms of life, and nothing would be left for him but repetition. However, repetition is not living, for living is always a matter of trying; to live fully is always to try to present a first performance. Things must come to us anew; at first sight they must wake in us the illusion that we have not tried them earlier, because when we try them we will find their deficiencies and their failures.

Hence one can define youth by saying that it sees the face of things, while maturity and old age begin to see the back of things. This, which happens with one's personal life, this having touched and listened to the essential melody of the ways of living, has consequences of enormous importance when transferred to the broad social order. Because what I have called the experience of personal living spreads itself—through mechanisms I am not now going to describe—into the experience of the collective life of the people to which one belongs. And even more, behind this experience of a people, there extends the experience of an entire human historic process which is preserved in the memory of our people, or the group of peoples to which ours belongs. And this image or shape of the universal historic process continues to be formed to the end of time, just as is the humblest experience of our private lives, automatically and without the intervention—or almost without it—of our reflection.

In order to give a very close and related example of the content of Toynbee's work, let me say that I have always been surprised to note that in it a certain state of mind has never been described; this is the state of mind which came to predominate and be extended throughout Greek and Roman culture at the moment when these began to decline; that is to say, when they had a very long—a millenary—experience behind them, when they had, in the political spectrum, seen every shade of color, when they had tried every form of government, when they had lived, loved, and suffered all the forms of life.

In the political sphere this began to appear as a document in the third book of Herodotus, in the famous conversation between the seven great Persians, when, the throne being vacant, they discuss what form of government they would give their country. But later this takes on its classic formula in the two marvelous books, numbers VI and VII of Plato's *Republic*, whose reading I recommend to all of you. Other books of the same work lose themselves in materials perhaps too subtle and too little controllable, but these books give space only to an experience of some old Greeks who know the history of the thousand states and cities that had made up Greek civilization.

After Plato, Aristotle models the expression of this experience even more acutely, but he does not reshape it. He discovers nothing new, nor had Plato. And this is what seems strange to me—that no one has noted how the dominating image in the last years of the ancient world had so humble an origin. After Aristotle comes his stupendous disciple Dicearchus, a specialist in politics, who, because of that bad fortune which preserves the unreadable works and destroys the best ones, left us no books. He did, however, give his thoughts a formula, probably the most complete one, which Polybius received from him and in turn transmitted to Cicero; this represents the consequence of all ancient learning, because this man, in spite of being a politician, had incalculable capacity for reflective thought, which you can find in his *Treatise on the Republic*.

This concept of the whole historic process for a thousand years and more had been decanted and precipitated bit by bit into Greek and Roman consciousness. It is composed of three great ideas or images. The first is this: the experience that every government carries within itself its own congenital vice, and therefore it inevitably degenerates. This degeneration produces an uprising, which overthrows the constitution, topples that form of government, and in its place substitutes another, which in its turn degenerates, is rebelled against and replaced, and so on. For a short time there was a discussion of what was the exact line of precedence and subsequence in the inexorable move from one form of government to another. For example, Aristotle argues this point with Plato but finally arrives at a kind of canonical doctrine of political thought which comes to this: the oldest and purest institution is the monarchy, but it degenerates into absolute power which provokes the rebellion of the most powerful men, that is to say, the aristocrats, who overthrow the monarchy and set up an aristocratic constitution. The aristocracy in turn degenerates into oligarchy, and this provokes an uprising of the people who throw out the oligarchs and set up a democracy. But democracy quickly becomes pure disorder and anarchy, swayed by demagogues, and ending by being the brutal oppression of the masses which were then called—I am merely translating—the rabble, *okhlos*, and thence okhlocracy. The prevailing anarchy then reaches such a degree that one of the demagogues, the most successful or the most powerful, seizes power and establishes a tyranny; if this tyranny lasts, it is converted into monarchy; then the institutions come to bite each others' tails and the cycle of evolution begins all over again.

This is what was called the circle, cycle, or circuit of the forms of government. It assumes no belief in any political form, having experienced the faults and errors of all of them, and indeed, in Plato as in Aristotle, all those concrete forms of government, ruled by principles that are clear and evident, are called by Plato *hemartémata* and by Aristotle *hamartémata*—two words that mean simply "errors," "sins and deviation." What does this signify? It means that these men appear, at the end of centuries, to have reached that point of disillusion which is despair of the political.

As man does not give way, even in the face of desperation, to that profound conviction that there is no stable form of government, no constitution which will stave off uprising, revolution, what they call *"stasis,"* it might seem that he ought to resign himself and come to a state of paralysis; but man, as long as he is not sick, is incapable of stopping. It is at this point that the writers of political treatises, Plato and Aristotle, begin. And when we ask Aristotle, as he asks himself, what is the purpose and design of political science, he answers us in such a way that, for a moment, you may think I have lost control and am going to talk to you in the language of the man in the street, whereas I am going to quote Aristotle literally. In fact, when Aristotle asks himself what are the purpose and design of political science, he answers that it is no other than to find the means of obtaining *"anastasia."* *Anastasia* is not, as one might first think, a pretty girl in Madrid, but the opposite of *estasia*. It means "stability."

The reaction to that hopeless opinion about the possibility of political forms consists, then, in imagining a constitution which would have the virtue of reuniting the principles of all the others, so that each would regulate and counterbalance the other; there is in it a little bit of monarchy, and another bit of aristocracy, and another of democracy. In this way it might perhaps be possible to avoid that permanent unease and disquiet which marches across all of history. And this is the second ideal, the mixed constitution, which was to occupy all the thinkers after Plato, who announces it not in *The Republic,* but in his last book, *The Laws;* this he wrote when he was almost decrepit. Later, Aristotle would reason about it in detail, as if it were really a formal idea, whereas it is nothing but a pious desire with which to confront the hopelessness of politics.

At this point, forgive me a personal memory. I was seventeen years old when I made my first trip into the interior of Spain, a thing then unheard of. I did not go alone, but was escorted by an admirable man of fine standing, the first man who had walked the whole length of the Peninsula, step by step, at a time when no one else had done it. He was an artist and a critic of art, but his real value lay in his life. And as life holds elegance to be so fleeting that as soon as it appears it disappears, the worth of the life of Francisco Alcántara can be neither perceived nor appreciated by the younger generation. Therefore I think myself obligated to record his life.

The two of us went to the nearby border district between Guadalajara and Segovia, into that land of pine groves where there are scattered, like beads from a broken rosary, a series of towns with enchanting names—Gálvez, Villacadimia, Los Condemias, Campisábalos . . . In Campisábalos, Alcántara had a great friend, the apothecary. This pharmacist seemed by his name, Morterero,[2] to be destined for his profession. In fact, the Mortereros, father and son, had presided over the pharmacy in Campisábalos since the seventeenth century. The establishment, as we saw it, looked like a pharmacy at the beginning of the eighteenth century. The walls were lined with jars of Talavera ware, and of the best period, which is the end of the seventeenth century. On their rounded sur-

2. *Morterero:* He who uses a mortar; hence a chemist [*Translator's note*].

faces one saw, along with the blue decorations, blue letters which spelled Latin and Spanish names out of the old pharmacopoeia; oil of sweet almonds in one, iron from Madrid in another, in a third, the "toenail of the great beast" [3] . . . In one corner stood a little cupboard full of very small bottles containing poisons. This cupboard was closed with a glass door on which was painted an eye, the famous watchful eye of the pharmacist.

But what most impressed me was to see in the center, as if presiding over that democracy of remedies, a great Talavera jar on whose bellied surface I read for the first time in my life, "*Theriaca Maxima*," a name which would forever after give me a great deal to think about. You know what *Theriaca Maxima* is—when all hope in medicaments had been lost, the doctor decided to put all the principle medicines together in a single potion. At times there were more than seventy of them. This potion was then administered to the sick man, in the hope that one of the seventy, or a spontaneous combination of several of them, would produce the cure not achieved by other means. As you see, this "maximum antidote" was invented in a state of despair about any single medicine. In the political field, the mixed constitution serves the same purpose.

And lastly the third idea, which had to do with the same historic process that the men of Greece and Rome had in view at the time, was this: they remembered, or saw, that the center of power, the empire, ruler of the world, had been moving as though emigrating from one point on earth to another. Indeed, they knew that first there had been the empire of the Assyrians, and that from there the power had passed to the empire of the Persians, then in turn to Macedonia with Alexander the Great; in their time it seemed due to end in the hands of the Roman people. That is to say, the empire as such was

3. Elk's hoof [*Translator's note*].

apparently moving from east to west, as do the stars. This must have seemed somewhat astonishing. The curious thing is that if we pry into history from Roman times up to now, we find that the same thing has been happening—the empire has continued to move from east to west. This is what we call "*translatio imperii.*" It indicates that empire apparently follows a sidereal course.

And this stirs us even more when we see that certain modern botanists tell us that a great part of the arboreal species now characteristic in Europe were originally Asiatic species which developed and lived there; on a day, they drooped and died. The only ones saved were those which had emigrated to Europe, where they were renewed and regenerated. This seems to mean that the plants moved along with the empire. But the sad thing is that many of these European species are now beginning to fall ill. At the moment, one of the most splendid trees in our landscape, the live oak, is sick all over the Peninsula, with an illness which cannot be attributed solely to a specific disease, but which implies a weakness in the ability of the species to face up to any disease. Hence the pain we feel in looking at our oak forests. And I do not believe that anyone lives profoundly in Spain (although he may verbalize patriotically in the newspapers) who cannot fail to feel the melancholy of our ancient oak forests. The *translatio imperii* seems, then, to be a law of the world. Or is it only one aspect which our experience offers us?

This is what we are going to see, as we enter step by step into Toynbee's work, which is merely a chronological setting in order, with all scientific discipline, of the profound and spontaneous experiences of life which humanity has received in the slow decanting of its original destiny.

II

The architectonic quality of Toynbee's
work. What is a leaf? The history of
England. Complete reality. Western
society: its limits.

I MUST REMIND YOU that I announced not a series of lectures, but a course of lessons. And as the lesson is designed
to transmit a body of doctrine which has a certain systematic development, it lacks the freedom characteristic
of a lecture. Today I propose to expound the principal
body of ideas which make up Toynbee's thought, and that
body does not appear clear unless one goes over it from
point to point in a kind of unitary exposition which does
not allow the interpolation of anecdotes or bits of persi-
flage and which forbids every pleasure of image and of
word.

The enormous size of Toynbee's volume makes of it
something like an ocean of typography through which
navigation is long and painful. Facing a work so complicated and so luxuriously leafed, I thought it my duty during the first half of this course to reduce myself strictly
to extracting, with the greatest care, the pure architectonic
lines of the doctrine, and if possible to finding outlines
even more exact than those which the author employs,
and more favorable to his thought, at least as those appear to me.

This implies three things: First, suspending criticism
until the second part of the course, except for one or two
observations which may help to keep the pace without

delaying it; second, dispensing with the vegetative ex-crescences which are superabundant in this work, for although it was accomplished amid the cold, the humidity, and the fog of London, it displays a character which is truly tropic. I do not think that those excrescences ever add anything of importance to the theory, because they are not really manifestations of it, but rather of the man behind it, and especially of the English quality which lies within that man. Our consideration, then, of the body of these outgrowths and the particular analysis of some of them belong in the last moments of this course, when we may occupy ourselves with the work as a book, hence as a literary production, and expressive of a character.

The imperative of clarity—I said many years ago that clarity is the philosopher's courtesy—now obliges me to separate the exposition of the doctrine from a look at the facial features of the work and also at those of the au-thor; much as I regret it, this also must be done.

Arnold Toynbee is an illustrious representative of En-gland, at least in the sense in which the summit repre-sents the mountain standing beneath it. And it is very important for us [today] to find out what there is in the soul of England, so that I could with an easy conscience put aside this opportunity and omit a task which is not only painful but one of the most difficult operations that exist; namely, the attempt—and note that I say only the attempt—to penetrate into the English; but the moment has come when we have no choice but to examine this great Englishman from top to toe in order to see what there is in him, for I fear that what is inside an English-man today is very, very strange . . . I believe that no one of you can anticipate what I have in my mind behind that adjective, and even less can you prejudge whether it is a good thing or a bad one. And now let us begin.

If we want to know what a leaf is, and set ourselves

to look at it, we will soon note that our previous idea of a leaf does not coincide with the real leaf itself, for the simple reasons that we cannot determine where the thing that we were calling "leaf" ends, and where something else begins. We discover, in fact, that the leaf does not end in itself, but continues; it continues into the leaf stalk, and the leaf stalk in turn continues into the branch, the branch into the trunk, and the trunk into the roots. The leaf, then, is not in itself a reality which can be isolated from the rest. It is something that has its own reality insofar as it is part of something that is the tree; compared to what we are calling a leaf, the tree now takes on the character of a whole. Without that whole the leaf is not comprehensible, not intelligible to us. But then, when we have noted and taken into account that the reality of the leaf is to be a part, an integral part of the whole tree, and when we see it born in the tree, and find the function that it serves in the whole, when our mind (in a manner of speaking) leaves the leaf and goes to something bigger—to that whole which is the tree—then and only then can we say that we know what the leaf really is. To such a degree is it a part that when, in place of contemplating the leaf as a tree leaf, we separate it from the tree, we say that we have cut it or broken it—expressions which declare the violence that we have caused both tree and leaf to suffer. Further, when we hold the leaf isolated in our fingers where it may seem a whole—given, I repeat, that one could decide where the leaf ends and the leaf stem or the branch begins—when in our fingers it can be considered a whole, at that moment it begins to be not a leaf but merely a bit of vegetable detritus that will soon end by disintegrating.

This relation of part to whole is one of the categories of mind and reality without which that great operation called knowing is not possible. This allows us to generalize and to say that all the things of the real world are either parts or wholes. If a thing is a part, it is not intelligible excepting insofar as we relate it to the whole to which it belongs. If a thing is a whole, it can be understood in itself without doing more than perceiving the parts of which it is composed. This holds good for all the orders of the real. For example, it also holds good for that reality which is language. If I now say the word *Leon* [1] by itself, it is not intelligible to you because you cannot determine whether this means the city of Leon, one of the Popes who bore that name (in English, *Leo*), the famous African wild animal, or one of the lions which stand at the entrance of the Cortes in Madrid.

The word by itself cannot be understood because it is a part of a whole, as the leaf is of the tree, part of a whole which is the phrase, as the phrase in turn is part of a whole, a conversation or a book. The word alone is, as you know, always equivocal, and in order to make its meaning precise we need, apart from the perspicacity which life teaches us, an entire science, and one of the most suggestive and interesting of those with which the Institute of the Humanities must occupy itself: the science of interpretation, or hermeneutics. The principal task of this science is to know how to determine to which sufficient whole a word and a phrase must be related in order that their meaning will lose its ambiguity. This whole, in which the word becomes precise, is what the hermeneuticists and grammarians call the "context." Well, then, every real thing which is a part must have its whole, its context, so that we may understand each other. Nevertheless, one doubt does arise: taking the tree for what it is, from its roots up, it seems to us to be a whole—what biology, with certain misgivings which we can omit, calls "an organic individual"—but the fact

1. In English, *lion* [*Translator's note.*]

is that the tree in order to live, needs earth and atmosphere; therefore it becomes unintelligible if we exclude these two new factors.

Will we then find that the whole tree, in its turn, forms part of a new and more authentic whole, namely, the tree plus its environment? We are not going to discuss the question, which is more complicated than it may seem, because the part of it that now concerns us is clear. As a matter of fact, this new and more complete whole formed by the tree and its environment is not truly a whole, for the simple reason that although the tree needs both the earth and atmosphere, those two have no need of the tree. Tear out the tree, and earth and atmosphere subsist—and do not bring up the argument that if all the forests of a region were destroyed the climate would be modified and both earth and atmosphere would change, because we are now talking simply of felling a single tree, and it is obvious that this would not modify either the earth or the atmosphere. Those two are not, then, integral parts of a new whole, for they are only the surrounding and external medium on which the tree is going to live, and only in that role are they biologically intelligible—that is, when studied from within the tree, from its internal constitution.

Let us now transfer all this onto the plane of historic reality. We want to know that reality which is England. I choose this example because it is the one chosen by Toynbee, and he in turn chose it not out of patriotism but very skillfully, because if there has ever been a nation which has lived to itself, independent of the others and dependent on its own substance and resources, it would be England. There has been much talk—and England herself repeated it for many years with an insistence not entirely free from complacence—about that country's "splendid isolation." She appeared as if encastled in her surly and recalcitrant insularity. Well then, can a history of this England be written if she is considered a single entity, something intelligible in itself? Not without referring it, of course, to other peoples, but treating them only as a simple external medium such as were the earth and the atmosphere in our study of a tree? Or, to put it even more strongly, can one know the historic reality which is England without turning to anything else? Does England, in itself, constitute an intelligible unity?

This is the theme which serves Toynbee as his point of departure, and which I myself have treated since my earliest writings. The man of science, and in particular the historian, cannot be capricious in choosing the perspective from which he looks, because he claims to see a reality, and it is the format of this reality which he decides from that point of view. Otherwise he will see not a reality, but only a fragment torn from a reality, and he will run the risk of describing an amputated hand as if it were an organism. We must not content ourselves with a first vision of things, or with that first visual field.

Note that we must do with England exactly what we did with the leaf, and remember that it was no reflection of ours, but the leaf itself which guided our glance to the point where we were seeing the entire tree. With historic reality we must do something similar. What is called provincialism and small-town isolationism is only the confusion between our visual field and the reality which we claim to see; it is a belief that the world is no more than what we are seeing, and in history it is vitally important that we avoid confounding our visual field with the figure of reality, for our visual field is almost always determined by accidental causes, and, thanks to this, it does not often coincide with the structure and extension of the reality which we want to discover. So, on the contrary, it is necessary that we compel our visual field to coincide with the structure and format of reality, and for this let us take all due precautions.

Well, then, according to Toynbee the history of England cannot be constructed from the English point of view, for although this, among Western nations, is the one which has most lived to itself, although being an island and isolated, it is only part of something more extensive. It does not constitute what I call a solid reality, and what Toynbee skillfully calls "an intelligible historic field." The whole problem of the science of history consists in placing the reality of which one speaks in the intelligible historic field to which it belongs. That history of England cannot be constructed by relying exclusively on her own reality. The proof of this lies in the fact that England does not come to an end in itself, but is always shown in her history to be a fragment of something larger; of this we must take a panoramic view if we really want to understand what the history of the English nation has been and what it is today.

The proof of this can be obtained simply by contemplating the seven great chapters in which the history of England can be summarized. The first covers her conversion to Christianity, which can be dated from the Synod of Whitby in 664; because up to that time the English showed a certain propensity, influenced by the particularism of the Irish Christians—the Irish of those days—to set up a separate church which would have been a far-Western Christianity on the "Celtic fringe"; this would have been modeled on Eastern Christianity of the still-existent Nestorian sect, lost in Central Asia, and because of its religious peculiarity out of communication with the rest of the Western world since the eighth century. The second chapter is the complete establishment of feudalism, produced thanks to the invasion of the Normans, which was like the penetration of the British

Isles by the European continent, and united those islands with western France for generations. The third chapter is the Renaissance, by which England was submerged in the atmosphere of letters, arts, and sciences originating in Italy. The fourth is the Reformation, which, coming from the north of Europe, impregnated England. The fifth is the overseas expansion, into which England was forced by Portugal, Spain, and Holland. The last two chapters include the establishment of the industrial system and the parliamentary regime, which appear to be England's two most original products and which, according to Toynbee (and I leave the responsibility to him), are completely unintelligible unless they are explained as a peculiarly English reaction within the European community.

The detail which provides proof of all this interests neither Toynbee nor you nor me. For what we are going to say, the evidence which his simple statement gives us, is more than enough—except for those two last chapters, for which, I repeat, I leave the responsibility to Toynbee, and which, in the last instance, would not change the question; that statement allows us to declare that England is only a part, that she has her reality as a fragment of a great whole in which she lives with all the other European nations. Because, let us note, England is a society with the same characteristics as Spain, France, Germany, and Italy. We call these societies "nations," and as societies they seem to us of a very different type from the province, the region, the village, or the tribe. They are societies of a distinct species, the species we call "nation." But we see that these "nations" are in turn only part of a very much broader society which includes a multitude of them; this broader society will be perforce a society of a type and species different from the national unit; this we must explain as "an intelligible historic field," or, in my terminology, a solid reality in which to place the history of any single nation or of a thing within nations, as, for example, the biography of a man.

So we find ourselves facing the methodical and strictly scientific need of having to seek out that society of a new species whose members are the nations. For this, I suggest we follow the same process we used with the leaf: letting the thing called "nation"—in this case England— when contemplated in space and time guide our observing eye and bring it to the authentic whole of which the nation is a part. Keep very precisely in mind what it is that we seek. It is to find the area or circle of human things on which we must count in order to get the highest degree of intelligibility, the maximum clarity as to what the reality of England is. Everything outside this compass that does not improve visibility must be considered merely the external surroundings and the means within which that reality we call England lives, but we will not count it as an integrating part of England. We cannot linger along that line.

Let us proceed first with regard to space. The task is made slightly complicated because one must distinguish different dimensions of historic life. However, I think this will offer no difficulty. If we ask what is the "intelligible historical field" of the English economy, let us go back to the time when Toynbee was writing his book, and we will find that that field was without limits, because it included and covered the entire planet, and there was no place even in the most distant isles of the Pacific Ocean where England did not have interests.

If, however, we take her political institutions, we note that the area of participation is much narrower. English law, in fact, has little or nothing to do (except on abstract points) with Chinese law, Russian or African law; on the other hand, and in good part, it proceeds from principles common to the European and neo-American peoples. Note that the community of juridical principles refers to an area less broad than that of the economic, an area which embraces the British Isles, the European continent excluding Russia, the whole American continent, and the English domains in Oceania and South Africa. If, now, we take the cultural dimensions, we observe that one must draw the same geographic figure, for the coincidence is perfect; and if we refer to the religious order, we find that England is included in the Christian world, of which the principal body occupies an almost identical space except for a small piece which detached itself and entered into a community with Russia; this fragment has been called the region of orthodox or Byzantine Christianity—that is, Greece and the Slavic countries. The Christians, at times very numerous, who live in enclaves in other parts of the world, are only minorities which do not define the society in which they are found, apart from the fact that in most cases their conversion is very recent.

There is, then, a lack of coincidence between England's economic space, which, as I said some years ago, covered the whole planet—this was the first case of an effective worldwide being which ever existed—and its cultural, religious, and juridical areas of participation. But it is very clear that those remote spaces where England engages in economic activities are to her only what the earth and the air are for the tree—external media in which it operates and by which it is fed; they are not an internal medium within which England lives side by side with others, and to which in essence England belongs.

In reality, then, the origin of England's economy, her creative force, is not within that unlimited area, but is within the same spatial boundaries as the juridical, religious, and cultural circles of this new kind of society, a society to which we can now give a name—we shall call it "Western society." Note that this community, containing certain principles of thinking, feeling, and wanting which are common to all, is not a matter of mere coincidence produced among groups that differ among themselves, having mutual relations or contacts, but it originated in an effective living together. Furthermore, this living together has been made possible in turn by a unity of principles in what is called "society"; note this well, not a state, but a society.

Well, then, this very broad area to which England belongs represents the territory of a great society, Western society, a society of which all these other nations are integrating parts. We noted that the apparent worldwide extent of the English economy was not in fact so great, but that the origin of that economic vigor was in fact located within this "Western society." And as a matter of fact, nothing of that Western society is without limits; all of it has its frontiers. We only have to look beyond them to find, close to our own society, four other great ones, seeming at least to be of the same type, each one composed of many nations. One of these is the Islamic society, the world of Islam which runs from Pakistan to the farthest edge of Morocco, and in Africa extends almost to the equator; another is the Hindu society, in the tropical regions of Asia; then the Far Eastern society of China and part of the Pacific; and, finally, that strange society which we have called Christian Orthodox or Byzantine, made up of Greece and Russia, with its outside limits occupying a region which is closest to Europe.

It is curious to note that when Toynbee wrote this book, especially this part which must have been written toward the year 1931 or 1932, he included neither in the first line nor the first plan the fact of communism (this

is common among English authors of the period). Therefore, in the second edition, he had to add certain notes
explaining why he had earlier talked so calmly of that
Orthodox religious character as typical of the Greek and
Slavic world.

At this point we must try to find the characteristic attributes which define this new society. For this purpose,
once we have contemplated its extension in space, let us
glance at its development and its vicissitudes in time.
What do we see? Let us leave aside all that is still mere
colonization, for it is evident that the contact of our
own society with those other primitive societies which
we used to call "savage" is not properly a matter of living
together but of an intervention.

Since the sixteenth century, Western society has performed for itself an enormous expansion which includes
the discovery of the New World, and the creation within
it, during four succeeding centuries, of societies seeming
at first glance to be of a type similar to ours. Although
Toynbee believes this type to be completely similar, I
reserve for another occasion my own opinion on the
matter. But the fact is that since that date, and going
back to the eighth century, in which Charlemagne, that
full-bearded emperor, was ruling, the *principal body* of
Western society has occupied the same geographic space
that it fills today. Only in the eastern part of Europe did
there still remain, at that date, certain regions beyond
Saxony which were assimilated later. This means that the
history of Western society is in makeup ascribed to a
region of the globe that runs vertically from Scandinavia
to the Mediterranean and horizontally from Scotland to
the Danube. That geographic figure we can call the system of frontiers which limit the Western nations in
space. Now we must ask ourselves about its frontiers in
time.

As to the future, we can determine nothing, because the historic world to which we belong, that Western society in which, to use St. Paul's phrase, we live and move and have our being, is not yet finished. We do not know what its limit in the future is. It is the hope of obtaining some light on the vague and reverberant future that moves us to undertake this great operation in history, because—as we will carefully observe at another time— history, which is our occupation with the past, springs from our preoccupation with the future. So there is a way of occupying ourselves with something that consists in preoccupying ourselves with it. And as we will see, every human occupation originates inevitably in a preoccupation, because human life is always attentive to what is to come, and excited over it. Well, then, the peculiar manner in which the future and the things to come occupy us is that they preoccupy us. All history is born of the rebound of our curiosity, which, anxious about the near and the distant future, stirs us to discover the past. To remember, to turn the face backward, to look at the past is not something spontaneous which happens by itself. It occurs because—having no sure means of coping with the enormous uncertainty of what is to come (you remember Victor Hugo's phrase to the Emperor Napoleon, "The future belongs only to God") in the face of the terrible and constantly oppressive indecision which the future is, we search about us for whatever means we have for confronting it, and the arsenal of our means lies in what has already happened to us. So we turn our glance backward, for the very reason that the first thing to do is to look forward. But however effective may be the prophecy and the prediction which our study may give us, it is clear that the end of our civilization will be known as a fact only by an individual of another civilization of the same species, but different from ours, who may live in future centuries. As I said before, the only thing that we can do is to look backward in order to see if we can find another society which borders on our own; that is to say, look back to discover the end of our civilization in the past, that is, at the point where it begins.

In order to abbreviate—not words, but syllables—I have managed to sum up in the following form what I have had to say up to now.

It was in Charlemagne's empire that our European society appeared for the first time in almost exactly the same format and figure that it was going to have, except for the expansion of another kind which is represented by the discovery of America. That is, if we go backward from today to the end of the eighth century, we can follow in strict continuity the existence of our historic Western world; in saying this, we recognize the uninterrupted identity of its substance, its personality.

Let us look still farther back, behind Charlemagne. What do we see? Well . . . the first thing we see is that we do not see, because what is presented to us is the spectacle of historic chaos. Western society, whose persistence we were following backward, disappears from our sight. In its place we find the ruins of a society, the detritus of institutions, the volatization of a state, the involution of culture until it falls back into the most crass ignorance; and so much so that going back from the Carolingian period to the one that precedes it, we find knowledge itself to be exceedingly elemental. There were no roads, estates remained isolated one from another. Everyone warred with everyone else. In every corner one man ruled one day, another tomorrow, and and the next day no one ruled.

In short, there were almost four centuries of absolute confusion, produced by the invasion of the barbarians. The image of European society which we had been recognizing with perfect continuity becomes blurred, disappears, vanishes like those Australian rivers which in the infinity of desert spaces cease to exist. This is what Toynbee calls a period of *interregnum,* that is, a period in which there is no government, either of persons or of principles.

Nevertheless, in this all-embracing chaos there are two elements—but only two—which we recognize as we go backward from the Carolingian period. One is those barbarians, the agents of that confusion who would be the renovating force whose first construction would be the empire of Charlemagne. Now, Charlemagne was merely one of those barbarians decorated with a bit of polish. Those barbarians themselves became our kings, our captains, our sages in medieval times and in the Renaissance. Our own Cid Campeador was one of those barbarians, a barbarian who had decided to re-barbarize: for if, as has been said, we Spaniards are always more Papist than the Pope, this good Goth, the Cid, wanted to be more Gothic than the Goths themselves. In his conduct and ideas he defended a Gothic archaism which had been abandoned everywhere else, and from which the reigning king, Alfonso VI, and his court felt themselves very distant.

This situation and this hyper-Germanic and therefore excessively, healthily barbarous temperament of the Cid appears in him as in no other European figure of the time. And it has been an error (which I impute to no one) not to study the figure of the Cid by placing him in his historic field, which was the marvelous eleventh century, one of the most marvelous centuries of Europe. Remember that it was this century in which—and almost at the same time—the first Gothic church was built, the first *chansons de geste* were sung, the first songs of the troubadours were contrived; in short, it was the first moment of authentic productive creation in which Europe would give voice to what she is.

The other element in the aforementioned chaos which

we recognize is the Christian Church. This, in the fifth, sixth, and seventh centuries we find extended and dominant throughout all the Western area. The barbarian peoples were being converted to it. The Church was like a common and universal basis of life. It was, says Toynbee, a universal religion.

In those centuries of interregnum, the fifth, sixth, and seventh, we have, then, lost sight of and contact with Western society. If now, in our imaginary backward trip, we install ourselves in the fourth century after Christ, putting our feet down in London, Paris, Rome, or Madrid (that is, in the grove of trees which later would be Madrid), we awake to find ourselves in a perfectly organized society, enormous in size, solid and dense in its common living together, a society which is called the Roman Empire. But we would soon note that this society is completely different from the Western society in which we find ourselves today, and whose former life we have been tracing backward. Neither our ideas nor our values nor our points of view help us to understand that historic reality which we call the Roman Empire.

But let us not lose the thread of retrospective continuity! We were saying that in the confusing centuries of the interregnum we continued to recognize and to follow backward at least two elements of our own society, the Christian Church and the barbarians. In the fourth century, which is where we now imagine ourselves to be, both elements also exist. Does not their permanence indicate that although our Western society has gone through almost four centuries of confusion and blurring of outline, it continues in the society which is the Roman Empire as the leaf continues in the branch? Let us see. But of course, to see in history is, at the moment, to see with the eyes of that time. And now we have become Roman citizens who see the world from London—(Londinium)—from Caesar Augustus—(Zaragoza)—or from Rome.

We are, for example, Roman Senators, not of course, in the Senate's best days, but nevertheless members of the Roman Senate, which is no small position. And as such, we look at the landscape of our imperial society in order to recognize those two elements which claim to guarantee historic continuity between Roman society and our own.

But we cannot do it. The Christian Church is there, certainly. Beyond any doubt the barbarians are there. But with what different characters from those which they have for us today! They are unrecognizable. To us, as Roman Senators, the Christian Church appears as a confused, dangerous, unpleasant complex of beliefs, rites, uses which are held and practiced by groups that are already numerous, but belonging chiefly to the humblest classes. Christ, a figure not yet clearly pictured, is the strange God of the lower regions of the world—that is, of the Greco-Roman world. He is, above all, the God of small foreign colonies made up of artisans, money changers, and beggars who have come from Syria to live in the great imperial cities and are called Jews. That complex of beliefs and rites was born out there, in the poorest section of the periphery which the Roman Empire reached, in Palestine. That is to say, the religion which, at the end of the Roman Empire, during the interregnum, would be a universal religion, triumphant, official, powerful, emerged from the *internal proletariat* of Roman society; it was therefore something which—in the eyes of a Roman Senator toward the year 300—had not the slightest importance in the historic reality which was the Empire.

In a similar way the barbarians were there, or rather, *out there*, in a vague distance beyond the limits of the Roman Empire. Their constant warrior restlessness, their continuous pressure on the outline of the Empire, made it obligatory for Rome to elaborate a permanent army which was spread from the coasts of Britain, passing through Batavia (that is, Holland) and along the Rhine and the

Danube. This is what was called the *limes*, the defensive line of the Empire's frontiers. *Frontier* means something like a "profile," and the profile is always in everything the most threatened, most exposed, and therefore the sector that must be defended. Hence we Spaniards always have a blow prepared for anyone who comes too close, and without permission, to our profile.

There, in fact, the barbarians were, but they did not belong to Roman society; they were Germans, Scythians, savage peoples wandering in the forests of the Septentrion or on the steppes of Asia—they were *other* than the Roman Empire, miserable beings who represented an absolute far away; they were the external proletariat of Roman society. Their reality was so blurred, so unapparent and without substance in the Roman world, they seemed so remote, that Verlaine could symbolize the Low Empire in those famous verses:

> Je suis l'Empire à la fin de la décadence
> qui regarde passer les grands Barbares blancs.
> . . . .
> Là-bas on dit qu'il est de longs combats sanglants.

"I am the Empire at the end of its decadence who sees the great white barbarians pass. They say that out there, far away, great bloody battles go on." But before long those barbarians would break through the frontiers, pocket the Empire, and destroy it.

We have found two important things: one, that in our backward trip toward the past, there comes a point at which we lose sight of our Western society, that is to say, a point at which this society comes to an end. Beyond this point, we see an interregnum of confusion, and then we find ourselves in the midst of the Roman Empire, of another marvelous civilization which we have entered at its final stage; that is to say, we are present at the way in which a civilization ends.

Is it an accident, or a law of history, that every civilization reaches a point in which it must set up an Empire, a universal state which means power among all nations, and that this universal state is inundated from the subsoil (at a certain period literally inundated by subterranean peoples coming from the catacombs), by a religious principle which originates among the internal proletariat of that civilization; and that while this religion is swelling and filling the spaces of that universal state, the barbarians —that is, the inferior peoples which surround the frontiers of that civilization—burst into the state and destroy it? Is this a particular case, or the law that governs the end of all civilizations?

In order to answer this question we need clearly to investigate each of the civilizations which up to now have existed and succumbed. This obliges us to determine what and how many civilizations have existed up to now. Once we have done this, we can ask ourselves how these civilizations originated, how they were born. Undoubtedly some of them proceed from others, and have with them a relationship which we can call maternal and filial. But there have been other civilizations without precedents. Which of these have been the factors and the causes that motivate this great creation which is a civilization, and, more in general, every great historic creation?

Once we see this, let us scrutinize the normal development, the process of formation of those civilizations; then we will ask ourselves the lamentable question—How is it that they declined and succumbed? Once this is done, if our study gives us any light, we will look at our own future and ask ourselves, What can we hope? What is going to happen with our own civilization? You will recognize that the theme is dramatic, and more than a little rich and filled with interest.

III

The "case" of England. Review. The Empire. The Mediterranean and the *limes*.

I STATED EARLIER that in the first part of this course, dedicated to setting forth Toynbee's thought, I considered it obligatory to limit myself to extracting the purely architectonic lines of his doctrine, suspending criticism (except in rare cases) until later and dispensing with the vegetative excrescences with which the book abounds. Having to state the starting point of the Toynbee theoretic trajectory, I saw myself forced to fulfill completely this ascetic imperative, because Toynbee's point of departure is not as heavily botanical as the one I used, mine having a certain garden sweetness in which, taking a leaf, I invited you to contemplate it and to reflect on that contemplation.

Toynbee's point of departure consists in directing a general censure at contemporary historians (except for the most recent ones, whom he does not care to name) because they each write the history of their own nation as if it were an independent and autarchic entity, both of these being things that nations are not, either in reality or for the purposes of knowledge. His censure is not limited to a criticism of this procedure as a scientific method, but he then adopts a tone of formal accusation, because in his judgment this intellectual defect has its roots in a moral vice, the most serious vice of the contemporary age, namely, nationalism.

Remember that, when he uses this word, Toynbee is not referring in particular to those political activities which, expanding the usual meaning of the word, have been called "nationalist"; but he makes it a synonym for the spirit of nationality, so that not only nationalist political activities, but the simple fact of being a nation, that is, the being national of the individuals who make it up, is for him almost a crime. At least he characterizes it literally as a sin, and is even pleased to seek in the Koran the name of a similar sin in order to reinforce his anathema. Thus the Koran calls it *Schire;* as our collaborator in the Institute of the Humanities, the great Arabist Emilio García Gomez, explained it, this means, for the Moslems, every association of another being, whatever it may be, with the unique person of the one God; therefore, something like polytheism, but with the notation that, as the religion of the one God is, for the Moslems, the universal religion to which all men should belong, this *Schire* or polytheism implies secession, sectarianism, particularism.

This shows that for Toynbee, to be a nation is something like being a collective particularism. The idea seems a bit extravagant. It surprises us to stumble on a thing like this in so huge a work and with such international pretensions, for one would not assume that Toynbee, on the first page and to justify in some manner his *ex-abrupto*, would make an attempt—however moderate—to distinguish the different historic realities which have been called "nationalisms"; nor does he offer us an idea of what a nation is that we can half swallow, but he contents himself with defining the spirit of nationality or nationalism—the same in this definition—as "the spirit or tendency which induces people to feel, act, and think about what is part of a given society as if it were the whole society."

It is not easy for an alert reader not to feel annoyed

and almost personally offended at the impact of these first pages, composed in a bad intellectual—or better, a pseudointellectual—style. I will avoid facing up to them as I ought to, for they are examples of those excrescences to which I referred earlier, excrescences not only because they are unnecessary and inopportune, but for a more serious reason, in that amid many of them, with an air of arbitrary solemnity very common among English writers of the last twenty years, Toynbee throws in our faces certain private beliefs of his own, an act as little compatible with a scientific discussion (assuming that this is one) as with a courteous conversation.

The theoretic attitude, the method which is knowing, consists in a combination of clearsightedness and doubt: it starts with a previous admission of all the possibilities. Thanks to this, theorizing is—not by accident or by polite addition, but in substance and shape—always a matter of taking account of the next thing and its possible discrepancy. Faith—and do not think now only of religious faith, but rather of all the other innumerable things in which we believe—faith, on the other hand, is an attitude that is closed within a man, therefore intimate and, moreover, blind. Its importance in human life is enormous, much greater than that of science.[1] But for this reason the expression of a faith demands certain precautions in interhuman affairs. It is not right to throw our faith in this or that in the face of a passing neighbor, because its attribute as an intimate thing makes of it a personal secretion with which we soil the other person. To declare our faith at close range is to spit it out, and thereby to degrade it, vilify it, and transform it into an insult.

But this is what Toynbee does in the first pages of his book. Without giving us time to draw a first breath, he

1. On this, see my study entitled "Ideas and Belief," *Obras completas*, Vol. V.

throws in our faces his very personal hatred for the idea of nation and his somewhat vague belief that we do not know anything else to substitute for it. With this it follows that anyone who, for a quarter of a century, when no one in England would suggest it, made the peoples of Europe see that a historic turn would come very soon in which it would be a matter of life or death for them to rise above the principle of nation as the ultimate constituent form of collective life—such a one could not walk with the author's antinationalism a single pace. This is so because, for the very reason of not being nationalists, we do not want to load our shoulders with an idea of nation which is as ridiculous, inconsistent, and improper in a man of science as is the one emitted by Toynbee, on the very threshold of his great production.

I have some authority for saying this, because Mr. Toynbee, so successful in teaching us so many things, cannot, as I have just suggested, teach me not to be inconveniently a nationalist. This is a more serious matter. It has to do with the most serious problem that faces the world, and one which, for more than a quarter of a century, weighed down my person and my life because I saw it coming. It is the gravest problem in the entire world today, because it is perhaps the only theme that ferments on both sides of what is called the Iron Curtain. Hence, when I see someone approaching it frivolously I feel as terrified as one who watches a child handling a machine gun.

This whole course carries as a sort of counterpoint the preparation for this theme. In the first lecture I began to suggest the first note that would have to be sounded so that it would become fully mature at the proper moment. One day in these lessons you will recognize that the theory of "here" and "there" which I set forth in the first lesson was not a side issue, but that, in addition to being

the fundamental metaphysical theme, it is the foundation
for a deep comprehension of the present situation. Hence
I have hesitated about whether, in the prologue of this
course, I ought to renounce my own mandate, which
recommended that I leave criticism aside and omit those
excrescences, although this implies hiding from you the
author's less attractive side. But if I did this, if I went
straight to the matter, then the prologue would have to
be long and continuous, because it would have been
necessary to do the following things:

First, to engage in a criticism *au fond* of Toynbee's idea
of nation and to counterpoise another which is more
fitting—a thing which, as you will see, would in itself be
simple and easy, but which requires considerable preparation.

Second, to show—and note that my words are hard—
how false it is to argue that during the time to which
Toynbee alludes, the science of history developed inspired by nationalism in any sense of the word. To affirm
and sustain this by itself, as he does, is a frivolous error.
If we remember Niebuhr, Ranke, Fustel de Coulanges,
and Mommsen, this appears to border on insolence; the
science of history created in the nineteenth century by
these men was made by their treating of nations which
were not their own; even more, of nations which were
not then even existing. Can one talk of the Roman nationalism of Mommsen, of Fustel de Coulanges? And as
for Ranke, he was, if anyone in the world has ever been,
the man of universal history; he wrote several books on
the subject, one after another, and when he wanted to
treat a particular theme he entitled it *The German-
Roman Peoples*, showing in the unguarded quality of the
title his willingness to jump the frontiers of all nationalist
criticism whether Mr. Toynbee likes it or not.

Third, all this would lead to an attempt to explain to

myself and to you how this behavior, scientifically and humanly incorrect as it is, characterized by an unpleasant mixture of impertinence and inconsistency, could be possible.

After all, the thing is not new. There is a whole fashion running the length of English history in which the fusion of these two ingredients appears, and in each period it has a name. Mixed impertinence and inconsistency are what constituted, for example, the behavior that in 1800 was called "dandyism," one of the most typical of English forms. And it is convenient to note in passing, because I am going to use something that I will add later—that dandyism can only be explained and only makes sense as the badly-brought-up behavior of an individual within a society that is extremely well brought up. All the wit of dandyism lies in the pleasure of breaking through this regime and this power of good rearing. For example, the Prince of Wales, an enthusiastic admirer of Beau Brummel, the great "dandy," the arbiter of elegance (although he was not rich), went to visit the latter. He arrived very happy with his new cravat, and he asked the fashion expert, "Mr. Brummel, how does this cravat look to you?" The latter with his genial disdain did not even turn his head to look at it, but answered, "Not bad. A little like the one my valet wears."

But unfortunately this kind of behavior, as I said before, is now very frequent among English writers, and particularly when they talk about the idea of nation. So that we would have had no remedy but to make an effort to enter with a certain analytical violence into the intimate centers of the modern English soul, a difficult matter which, as I said, I will leave for the end, for before groping into those recesses, I would have to say to the person who wrote that first page, "Mr. Toynbee, that is not *good manners.*"

Is it true that good manners are being lost in England? And if they are being lost, what is taking their place? Without a minimum of good manners, society has never been able to exist, whether as a people, a tribe, or a nation. They are like social bumpers which, when inserted between individuals, ease the pressure between those who constitute society and make it less rough and difficult. Hence there has never been a society which has not had a minimum of good manners, under penalty of coming apart, of disappearing automatically. But it is a fact that England has not been content with this minimum; it was her glory to have created a refined treasure of good manners, prodigious and exemplary. Does she now want to renounce this, abandon it and leave it to perish?

This would be serious for England and for all of us; contrary to what some trivial irresponsibles mutter, it does not seem that people, East or West, agree that England ought to break down. Rather, some of us think—and my words carry no dogmatism, nor do they pretend to persuade, but they are a qualification which I need to make in order to give my ideas a certain chiaroscuro—some of us think it would be a great convenience to have England continue to exert her guiding influence in the world, an influence which no longer, as formerly, depends on her power, but is an influence of a new kind which might consist in seeming not to exist. Therefore that loss in behavior patterns would be very serious, and the more so because that regime of good English manners, until very recently one of the clearest and sweetest notes in the world, has always been noted and praised but has never been explained.

It has been assumed somewhat frivolously that this refined and complicated code of good manners was an addition which England put into her previous existence as a luxury. But is there not room for an opposite suspicion? Can one not think inversely that England did not create a system of manners because she was a great people, but, on the contrary, that she managed to become a great people, and even simply a people, thanks to the fact that she was known to be creating that repertoire of good manners? The result would be not that England would forcibly have had to go on dressing up the artifact of her good manners, but that—given the kind of people that Englishmen are as individuals—without this she would not have been able to endure as a people, as a stable and sane society.

I do not say that it is this way. I limit myself to imagining this as a mere hypothesis which it might perhaps be convenient to take into account. At least it explains by contrast why other peoples have been able to survive with a repertoire of exceedingly bad manners, because certain of their individuals, spontaneously and by themselves, were socially better endowed. This is, for example, the case of the Spaniards, who enjoyed an elevated regime of good manners for only a little more than a century, in the period which they lived in full form. What must be said about the tremendous defects of the Spaniard has nothing to do with this. They are little capable of solidarity, and therefore Spanish public life usually has gone badly; but on the other hand, like it or not, for this is something over and above will power, they have a certain native fund of elemental sociability which is lacking in other human castes. Hence it has always been so difficult that there should be a state in Spain, but, on the other hand, it is impossible that there should not be *tertulias*.[2] And everything that goes with this—the network of relationships between individuals, the tapestry of

2. A *tertulia* is a gathering of friends, often repeated, for the purpose of conversing about a specific question of mutual interest [*Translator's note*].

friends and "best friends" which, however held in jest, is the authentic basis which has always upheld Spanish life—supplying the deficiencies of the state and of all collective forms.

Inversely, the Englishman is unhappily not capable of *tertulias* and is, fortunately for him, most capable of public collaboration, and if what I was saying a moment ago about the origin of English good manners, though in the form of a question, be not forgotten, if it had in it an antipathetic aspect of paradox, it must be due to the vagueness of the notion of what society is and its relation to the individuals who make it up. Thanks to this, people have not noticed that the virtues and vices of an entity are frequently different from and even contrary to the virtues and vices of its individuals. Thus it may very well happen that nothing seems less like England than an Englishman. Figure, if there is any truth in this hypothesis, how serious it would be for England to lose the exemplary treasure of its good manners.

There you have the overwhelming program of affairs which we would have needed to mobilize if we had wanted to face up as we should to these first pages of Toynbee.

On the other hand, with what was said it will be enough for you to have in mind certain less pleasing peculiarities of the author; at the same time we have avoided any untimely entry into those matters which will later be opportune. Now they would come as if motivated by one of what I have called excrescences; in the second lesson, leaving those excrescences aside, I could set forth Toynbee's thought, and above all his starting point, with strict fidelity and even more vigor; this shows that his *ex-abrupto*, more than being an *ex-abrupto*, was also a hindrance.

Let us now resume our exposition. As this is a trajectory of ideas in which each one leads to another, it will be well to refresh our memories by a brief sketch of what has been said. I began by noting that every thing in the real world is either a whole or a part. If a thing is a part, it is unintelligible until we track it back to its whole, as the leaf of a tree is not understandable without being referred to the entire tree; nor is a word understood without being included in a phrase and the phrase interpreted by reference to the complete conversation in which it appears. On the other hand, the thing which is a whole is made intelligible simply by going over the parts that make it up. In the same way, historic comprehension demands that we not study human reality by taking it merely as chance drops it into our visual field without knowing what we are talking about, but that it be placed in an "intelligible historic field": that is, it must be an effective whole, a solid reality. The evident reason for all this lies in the fact that the thing, when it is a partial reality, does not end in itself, but continues in another thing, and to begin by isolating it is to run the risk of cutting it off, leaving outside what is perhaps its most important part.

From my earliest writings I have repeated to the point of boredom that whoever wants to see a brick must look at its pores, and therefore must bring his eyes close to it, but whoever wants to see a cathedral cannot see it as he sees a brick. This demands of us a respect for distance. Every single thing, if we want an optimum vision of it, demands of us a specific distance. Not to recognize this condition is to wish to deceive oneself. If your valet is not a great man, it is because of his inconvenient proximity. Similarly, the nearsighted historian who does not know how to keep clear of details is incapable of seeing a genuine historic fact, and we take pleasure in shouting to him that history is that manner of contemplating human things from a distance great enough so that one need not see Cleopatra's nose.

Note that this does not imply any disdain toward meticulous erudition, without which one is ashamed to say (as one is ashamed to say everything that is obvious) that history is impossible. But if it is certain that without erudition history is not possible, one must say no less energetically that erudition is not yet history. Good erudition must not be confused with what I call "erudite-ism" which is a baneful vice into which Spanish intellectual life has fallen, and note that *baneful* here refers to the funereal task in which we busy ourselves with a corpse. Erudite-ism is not sane and indispensable erudition, but the stupid idea of believing that erudition today, or the simple accumulation of information, may be the constituent form of intellectual life; this latter ceased to have meaning after the end of the eighteenth century, at which time the disciplines of the humanities entered a new intellectual phase in the form of science, which, I repeat, is not merely erudition, nor the simple accumulation of information, but is theory and construction.

Well, then, according to Toynbee—and it goes without saying that the idea is not solely his property—a nation does not constitute an intelligible historic field, not even in the case of England, his homeland, despite its being the most separate, the most "*señera*" among western nations. The etymology of the word *señera* in well known. It is the short version that the people made out of the Latin word *singularis*, "singular"—what is or goes alone; as in wild country there would always be a wild boar that went by himself, far from the herd; he was called *singularis*, and from that comes the French word *sanglier*, which our neighbors use as the name for the wild boar.

Well then, although England is the most individual, the most *sanglier*, of nations, her history cannot be con-

structed from an isolated point of view, cannot be local-
ized within itself. Nations are societies of a specific species, among other attributes; this characterizes them as
being essentially parts and only parts of another much
larger society, in which various of them live side by side;
this is what Toynbee calls a "civilization." This surely is
an intelligible historic field, that is to say, it can be known
and understood from within itself; England, like France,
Spain, Italy, and so on, are parts of the great historic subject which is "Western civilization." Certainly Toynbee
does not explain to us how those nations were formed,
nor even how they live and exist within the scope of
Western civilization. But let us leave the question now.
For him, a civilization is a certain living together of peoples which extends across a specific space in the planet
and which has both a beginning and an end in time.
Hence, in order to define a "civilization," what we must
do is to fix its limits in space and determine the dates of
its temporal beginning and end.

The limits of occidental civilization which come from
America run through Iceland and, passing through Scandinavia to and including Poland, drop to the mouths
of the Danube, cutting off a part of the Slavo-Balkan
peoples; they then enter the Adriatic, and running along
the Italian and Spanish peninsulas, go on back toward
America. Having determined the geographic limits of our
civilization, we discover that four other present civilizations exist on its borders. One of these is what Toynbee
calls the Christian-Orthodox civilization which occupies
Greece, a part of the Balkans, and the whole Slavic region of Russia. Another is the Islamic civilization, which
occupies an entire part of Asia Minor up to Pakistan and
on the other side runs across Africa to the equator. Next
to this is the Far Eastern civilization of the present China
and its neighbor; this has its principal field in China and

in what Toynbee will call the Japanese offshoot in the Japanese islands. And last, the Hindu civilization in the tropical and subtropical regions of India and Indonesia.

As for what sets limits in time, I said that we could not be precise about our civilization as far as the direction of the future is concerned, for as long as we who are that civilization are still here, it has not ended. Even more, in spite of what we have said, and what we ourselves, reflecting, may think about an eventual collapse of our civilization, in our hearts we find an automatic belief— like every belief, not founded on reason—by virtue of which we hope that our civilization is not going to decay. Perhaps it is proper for every civilization, as for every genuine love, to believe in its own eternity. I doubt that there is any Western man today, even the most pessimistic, who may think over and over again that for this reason or that our civilization is going to succumb, who really believes it. Because believing is a very different thing from thinking. Thinking is able to think everything; it is enough to want to think it. But believing, or not believing, is outside and beyond our free will. We think the scientific truth, that is to say, we consider that a certain idea has certain precise attributes which oblige us to include it in the great intellectual construction which is the system of theories. Scientific truth persuades our intelligence, but this does not imply that we believe it.

But now it is not a question of believing, but of reasoning, and what we must do is to force ourselves to obtain the clearest possible notion of these enormous realities which are civilizations in order to find out whether, by their very essence, they are all consigned to death, or whether by good fortune it may happen that one of them, perhaps our own, has the grace of permanence.

With respect to our own, for the moment, we look only backward. In that retrogressive journey which we began rapidly, we went on recognizing its identity through its changing aspects, back to the eighth century, in which we found it wearing the shape of the Carolingian Empire. In fact, it was Charlemagne who, on creating his empire and inspiring what has been called the "Carolingian Renaissance," set up for the first time the space and the soul of our civilization. And it is not bad to recall that Charlemagne hammered out this empire with his sword, which in its work was terrible, but in its name was amiable, being called *la joyeuse*, "the joyous." It is nice when swords, as they have to be swords, manage to carry names that are tender and promising.

If we follow farther back than the Carolingian Empire, if we penetrate into the eighth century, we lose all trace of our civilization, and in place of it we find what is the opposite of a civilization, a historic chaos, a world destroyed by the invasion of the barbarian peoples, especially the Germans. There are three centuries of what Toynbee calls "interregnum." But if we follow a little farther back and reach the fourth century after Christ, we will again find ourselves amid a perfectly constituted civilization: a universal state, the Roman Empire; a mandate, the *Pax Romana*, which is built on an immense portion of the planet; and a universal church which has spread over that whole space and which originated in the depths where the internal proletariat of the Greco-Roman empire lived. That *Pax Romana* was broken; that universal state was torn to bits by the eruption of elemental peoples, by what Toynbee calls a *Völkerwanderung*. Toynbee usually gives his general historic categories the names of events in particular histories. Thus every migration of less cultured people who fall on an old civilization he will call *Völkerwanderung*, using the name which German historians employ euphemistically to designate what we call "barbarian invasions." Whether this terminological propensity of Toynbee's is compatible or not with the essence of historical reality, and therefore with the historian's science, is a matter that we will discover bit by bit.

The fact is that still farther back than the Carolingian Empire and the three centuries that Toynbee calls "interregnum," we feel our feet cross the chronological frontiers of our Western civilization and find ourselves within another civilization at whose destruction we are present. This is the Greco-Roman civilization. Let us go on, doing there the same thing we did with our own civilization. Let us begin by asking ourselves what are its limits in space, and then we will have a geographic configuration of the Greco-Roman civilization which is as follows: it starts from the British Isles below Scotland, which it did not actually reach; goes down through the Low Countries to the line of the Rhine and the Danube; on the other hand, it reaches the north coasts of the Black Sea; in its period of greatest expansion it enters Bactria, India, and then runs through the whole high portion of Arabia, including Syria; finally it slips across the whole north end of Africa, coming to join once more with the British Isles, and including France and Spain.

As you see, this configuration is very different from that proper to our civilization, and yet there is a part which is common to both. But that part is for the moment minor, and, moreover, it is characterized by the fact that its similarity in shape alone is merely an "almost" likeness, and that "almost" is very important. Our civilization has added to what were the limits of the Greco-Roman civilization in the Rhine and the Danube all of Germany and all Scandinavia—that is to say, the whole north of Europe, the *limes;* with this the military frontier line and terminal of the Roman Empire now becomes nothing less than the central line, the axis line, of the geographic configuration proper to our civilization. In truth, the fate of that line is exceedingly mysterious and magical. Because if from a point of view which we might call geometric its variation has been the greatest it could have been—for it moved from being a limiting and extreme line to being an axis line, a central line—on the other hand, its historic function continues to be identical from then until the present date. The history of this line is curious, and its destiny is, I repeat, mysterious. What is it that lies behind this strange fate? This demands a certain preparation.

For the Greco-Roman man, *empire* and *emperor* meant a very precise function: the command of the army. In the civil life of Greece and Rome nobody commanded—you will presently understand me; the idea of authority was not associated with the idea of command. To command is to impose on other men the decision adopted by the will of a single person. Hence the verb *mandar* ("to command") which comes from *dare manus, manus dare;* and *manus* certainly means "a man's hand." But a man's hand insofar as it is the agent of force in the struggle, insofar as it represents power when facing will or duty. Hence *manus dare* means, in one sense, "sending army forces," for *manus* since the most primitive times of the Latin peoples has belonged to the military vocabulary, and *manus* means simply "belligerent force," the troops. *Manus dare* means "to send troops," and at the same time, as happens so often with words, it means the opposite: "to surrender" those troops. Hence also the minimum tactical entity of the Roman Empire was called *manipula* ("a small troop"), from the same root as *manus.*

The chief of the army gave orders in accordance with his will and responsibility to the forces under his auspices; that is to say, "he commanded." On the other hand, the civil magistracies of Greece and Rome were very different; far from giving orders proceeding from personal will, the Greek and Roman magistrate was not a person; he began by depersonalizing himself, and his entire function consisted in seeing that the law was fulfilled, in carrying out the regulations. He had no will, and hence Cicero, in his treatise *De Republica*, would say that the magistrate was living law. Well, then, the army was the only public function in which, by the needs of its activity, the Roman permitted a man to personally dispose and order. That is the empire and that is the emperor, the chief of the army. And as the army is not, or ought not to be, in public places, in the Agora and the Forum, but out there where it is fighting (and it fights above all on the frontiers where the enemy threatens), it is on the frontier that the army will be, and therefore the function of the empire and the emperor. Hence the line, the *limes*, of the Rhine and the Danube would be, for the whole history of the Roman Empire, the imperial line *par excellence*.

But let us leave this matter suspended here in order to take up again the explanation of the geometric change in the position of that line, together with the survival of its historic function.

During the Greco-Roman Empire the center of life was the Mediterranean. It is, in truth, an interior sea, a sea amid the land, and all life circulates from one coast to the other. If we wanted to represent geographically the vital dynamism of those centuries of Greco-Roman history, we would have to draw a series of arrows which would start from the interior of the land, but direct their heads toward the coast; on reaching the coast, they would not stop there, but would cross the sea and go on to the opposite coast. This means that whatever depth of territory back from the coast the Roman Empire acquired, Greek and Roman life was always a coastal existence, whereas our history, especially around the sixteenth century, is a land history made on horseback. Remember the thousands and thousands of leagues which Charles V still had to ride. Ours, then, is a history of horsemen and a whole glorious cavalry. On the other hand, life in the ancient world was entirely made by ships. Hence the entire existence of ancient man would be full of preoccupation concerning vessels.

The Greek legend which is perhaps the oldest, and one almost purely mythological, is the voyage of the ship of Argos in search of the Golden Fleece, the voyage of the Argonauts. And the tale which was most frequently told and told again the ninth and the eighth centuries B.C. at the end of Greek adolescence is the story of the wandering ship, the ship of Ulysses in the Mediterranean, sailing from coast to coast, from Calypso to Circe; the poor man had not only to submit to great storms, but to something more serious: he had to face the graces of all the enchantresses of the Mediteranean. And, likewise, when those Greeks set themselves to dreaming, they would dream of ships capable in themselves, without a pilot, of bringing the sailor safe to port. These are the mysterious ships of the Phoenicians, and when one begins to study them, there on the coast of Ionia, in Miletus, a society of men emerges presided over by Thales, which calls itself the "Forever Sailors" (*Siempre Navigantes*); these celebrate their scientific sessions in a boat on the high seas. And thus, in one way and another, the idea of the ship enters into the most profound and moving depths of the ancient soul. Hence its cult of the ship and of opportunity, for *opportunus* means nothing more nor less than the way which leads us surely to the *portus*, or port.

Well then, in 1937, some three years after the first three volumes of Toynbee had appeared, the great Belgian historian Henri Pirenne published the book which he had thought about all his long life, a book called *Mohammed and Charlemagne*. In it he argues—and I am going to neither accept nor reject his doctrine, because the part which interests us at present is true enough—that it is a mistake to date the end of the ancient world, of Greco-Roman civilization, at the time of the barbarian invasion. They could have caused as much disturbance as you like; could have given the historic life of that period an appearance of chaos; but the truth is that they did not change in the least the historic *corpus*, the geographic configuration, the anatomy of the territorial existence of that civilization. The barbarians invaded Greece, they invaded Italy, they invaded Spain, but they did not stay there; crossing the Straits, they ran across North Africa. That is to say, they were a new element which, mixing with preexistent people who were now worn out, would, without modifying the geographic structure of the old world, continue the life of that *corpus* without, for the moment, suppressing it.

The true modification—and this time it is radical—happened, according to Pirenne, when in the eighth century the Moslems, the Saracens, that is to say the orientals—and it is curious that the Moslems should have given that name to themselves, a name which as you know they now detest—conquered the whole of North Africa, split the Mediterranean in two, and absolutely cut apart the traffic from coast to coast. This is a really radical modification. The anatomy of the historic configuration is now different, and hence—at least this is one of the historic causes—a new civilization is born. Because from this moment, when the Mediterranean ceased to be the center of life for the interior world and the place from which the life of one coast gravitated to the other, the structure of existence had to change completely, and the vital dynamism which we represented earlier by arrows going from the interior to the coast must now be represented by drawing the arrows in an inverse direction: now they would leave the coasts and go inland, toward the *hinterland* which is the North. The whole of European history has been a great emigration toward the North. And hence, with the anatomy of the historic *corpus* changing completely, the line which earlier was frontier will now be converted into the axis and center of the new body.

On dying, Charlemagne had only one of his sons left, Ludovico Pio. When he in turn died, he left three sons, and following the very old custom of the Franks, he divided his estates among them. To Louis, the German, he left the East; to Pepin, the West; but to the oldest, Lothar, who was going to inherit the imperial title, he left Lotharingia, a state with a very strange shape which has always disturbed and surprised historians. He left Lothar a strip of land which goes from the Low Countries along the Rhine to Italy. Why? Was this strange resolution a mere whim? Again and again because of that lack of respect which every modern man feels toward the past, it has been thus considered. The past, which does us the favor of carrying us on its shoulders—and thanks to that we are not ourselves the past—has the bad luck that the present always disdains it; because it rises above it and is carried by it, the present always believes itself superior to the past.

As a matter of fact, when we contemplate that strange strip which goes from the Low Countries along the Rhine to Italy, we are surprised to find there the two imperial capitals—the capital of the Roman Empire which Charlemagne wanted to resuscitate with his empire, and the capital of that empire itself, Aix-la-Chapelle. Those are the two imperial cities. But even more—that line, which was the imperial line, the battle line, the line of command of the Roman Empire—is going to continue up to our own day being the line on which all those who have wanted to command in the West have had to struggle. All the great battles for European hegemony have been fought there; Charles V had to fight there; and even Philip IV, in those days of such terrible asthenia for our empire—a period of weakness about which I may someday say something—the soldiers, almost bloodless, went on having to fight along the line of the Rhine. Even more, at the present time—I say it deliberately—one of the things which are now discussed in the world is what is happening on the Rhine; thus the line that was previously the imperial frontier continues to be the central axis of history. See how, having changed its geometric situation, it has conserved its historic function, its imperial function.

IV

Domi et militiae. The Roman Empire,
an abnormal state. A halt: the
Institute of the Humanities
and the science of history.

IN THE PREVIOUS LESSON we began a journey that moved
backward: starting from the present we went toward the
past until we discovered in the eighth century A.D. the
beginning of our own civilization, Western civilization.
Continuing back we found ourselves in the Roman Empire, at whose overthrow we had been present a bit
earlier—that is to say, we had entered into the ambit of a
civilization different from our own, the Greco-Roman
civilization.

We immediately performed the same operation with
this which we did earlier with our own, and this is the
first datum which must be acquired about a civilization in order to define it: the determination of its geographic figure, its historic space. We saw that the space
occupied by our civilization coincides in part with that
of the Greco-Roman civilization. Provisionally, we did
not include America, which less than two centuries ago
was solely a colonial fringe of our world, and then we
noted that the difference between the old world and
our own consists, on the one hand, in the fact that our
civilization added to the Roman Empire the continental
portion which is beyond the Rhine and the Danube,
the northern lands, the northern regions Germany and
Scandinavia, Scotland, and Iceland; while on the other

hand it lost the Mediterranean, the Near East, and North
Africa, which the Moslems had conquered during that
same eighth century. These two facts—the change in
space which they represent, a spatial annexation on
the one side and on the other a spatial amputation—
would not in themselves mean anything important, but
only an overflow of the same geographic figure from
some latitudes to others.

The important thing in this shift in space is that it
automatically made it necessary to invert the direction
of the existing vital dynamism, and therefore it created
a historic body having a different anatomy. In the Greco-
Roman world the center was the Mediterranean, and life
went from lands in the background toward the coast;
here the Latin sea, far from dividing those coasts, united
them and sewed them together. Antiquity, I said, was a
coastal life.

Remember that throughout North Africa splendid
cities were built, neither more nor less Greco-Roman than
those on the other side of the sea. The deserts of Algeria,
Tunisia, Libya, and Tangiers are sown with their egre-
gious imperial ruins. Thus the enthusiastic traveler, moving nowadays through those melancholy places, comes on
a day to the walls of solemn and shuttered stables, the
surviving vertebrae of an aqueduct, the broken curves of
mutilated arches; and asking the guide what that city was
called, he hears it carries the name of a city with more
sex appeal than any city had ever carried: it was called
Volubilis. It is the city in which, without knowing it, he
would have wanted to live forever.

With the loss of the Mediterranean the new life which
would become European life had to invert the direction
of its dynamism, and now it was the Far North which
would draw from the coasts toward itself and, as it were,
suck in their sap. Centered as it was in the Mediterranean,

ancient history is a meridional history; ours, on the other hand, gravitates toward the North, toward the Septentrion; European life and history are predominantly a septentrional existence. *Septem Triones*, the seven sea-calves, is what the Latins called the seven stars in the Great Bear, which helps us to discover the North Star in the stellar landscape.

The different anatomy of the two worlds is revealed to us in the change suffered by the line of the Rhine which, from being the border and frontier line of Greco-Roman civilization, became the central line and the axis of our own. Toynbee expresses this change by saying that what was a rib of the Roman world has by our civilization been made its vertebral column. But this formulation is more ingenious than accurate, for, as we will see, that line, despite its basic geometric or purely geographic change, has continued to keep in both historic bodies its own organic function, that of being the imperial line, as it continues to be even up to the present time.

To rule, we said, is no other than to command, and to command is, as our Suarez would say, for one man to impose on others the decision of his personal will. Well now, city, *civitas*, "state"—to the Roman these words meant an ambit in which no man imposes his personal will. Only in the city did authority rule, and authority is the law which is the same for everybody, law anonymous in its origin and anonymous in its content. The Roman (readers of Cicero will surely remember this) feared or hated nothing so much as a legal disposition— the sentence of a judge is not a legal disposition—in which the slightest reference to a specific person, whether for or against, would have been included. This is what they called privilegium, "privilege," a word that has come down to us charged with the hatred which the Latins put into it, a curious persistence that is more like a new

shoot, because in the Middle Ages, which was in everything an inversion of antiquity, the best and biggest grace
of a law was that it would be a "privilege."

The Romans, who did not digress, did not invent
utopias, who looked at reality with heads that were clear
and hard, made a basic distinction between the civil hour
and the military hour, the citizen's life and the military
life, distinguished *domi* from *militiae*, "at home" or "in
the army." And both forms of life conceded at heart and
without affectation what was expected of them. Military
action, strategic behavior cannot be foreseen, cannot be
made to follow rules. In the din of battle or in the con-
vulsions of discipline, luck depends on the sudden decision which a man makes on his own account and at his
own risk. Therefore they created the figure of head of
the army, and with the crude and exact frankness which
they used in naming things, they called him without any
disguise *imperator*—"he who commands."

It is well known that the superiority of the Roman
army over all the others, particularly the Greek, lay in
the unlimited powers, the absolutism granted to the chief
of the army. In Book III of his *Civil War* Caesar himself
compared the powers of the legate with those of the
imperator, saying that the former had always to submit
to what was prescribed; on the other hand, the latter
must solve all questions in absolute freedom; *libere ad
summum rerum consulares debet.* (*Imperar* came to mean
"command" because it used to be *im-paro*, that is, "take
the necessary means," "make whatever preparation an
urgent moment demands." Therefore it has the same
double meaning as our word *ordenar*, which is "to plan
an order that will be effective in those cases" and to
"impose that order.") But of course those exceptional
powers did not begin to exist until the moment when the
general put his foot on the farther side of the line in

which the territory of the city ended, which was called the *pomerium;* that is to say, outside the walls, or later, beyond the first military milestone outside the urban area. In order to symbolize the rebirth of these exceptional powers the official body stopped at that spot, and into the bundles of staves carried by the lictors who accompanied the general they put the axes of the executioner. The *imperator,* in fact, had the power of life or death over his soldiers. In this he alone exercised authority, and authority is impersonal law.

By popular election one citizen stood out from all the rest to see that this was fulfilled. His personality disappeared, and that man was transmuted into an automaton of legality; in other words, his human reality was taken away from his person, and in the vacuum which was left there was installed the anonymous entity that is the law. As the depository, the base, the container of the law, that man was given advantage over the rest. He was made *magis*—more than the rest; he was made *magister* and *magistrado* ("magistrate"). The *imperator,* on the other hand, was not a magistrate; to a certain extent he was just the contrary; we would say that he was one commissioned to or charged with carrying out a need; namely, the surgical operation which is called war. Far from being a *magister,* he was rather a *menestral,* a *minister.*

This comparison is the shortest form which I have found for making visible and, so to speak, palpable the absolute change, the complete tergiversation—and note that *tergiversation* means "to turn a thing completely upside down"—which the Roman Empire represents in comparison with Rome's entire earlier past. The state that we call the Roman Empire came to take root in this very transitory and contingent imperial institution, an institution which is not even a magistracy, which is the complete opposite of any civil and therefore state-made authority, which is a momentary and abnormal office, emerging only, and while, the occasion demands it. It is useful not to forget this, so that we can put it into relation with something that I am going to say in the next lesson.

It is extremely revealing that Augustus, when for the first time he came to found the new imperial authority, conscious of the extreme Roman sensitivity in regard to law and the legal fundamentals of every public action, should seek, in order to support his exercise of an unusual power, to take refuge in the two most peripheral, most extravagant, and most abnormal powers that there were in Roman public law: the tribunate of the plebs and the *imperium militae* or chieftainship of the army. Nor was the tribune of the plebs a magistrate—he was much less than that. The tribunate of the plebs is the most unorthodox, original, and irrational institution that has ever existed. The tribune could not do anything; he could only hamper, prohibit, and veto. He was obstruction itself consecrated as an institution, and I say "consecrated" formally, because in fact the person of the tribune was sacred. And yet this unorthodox and irrational institution was the most effective one that ever existed, for apart from its inestimable services during the Roman Republic it was—together with the *imperator*—the cement which held together the most illustrious state in the annals of humanity, the Roman Empire.

It is revealing, I said, to see what Rome was, not only with respect to the past, but perhaps even more so with respect to our own future.

But for the present let us leave this end open. On the other hand, let us emphasize how what has been said makes it clear that that most illustrious state, which Toynbee calls "universal" and which is going to serve him as a prototype for his thesis—according to which all civilization reaches a moment in which it is constituted as a universal state—that illustrious state which was the Roman Empire was an abnormal state, abnormality consecrated as normality, the state's pathology accepted as health. Perhaps Toynbee does not see this, because Toynbee does not see anything in history which is decisive. What I have just said cannot be seen except from within civilizations, but he is accustomed to contemplating them from without as one contemplates the mountains; and thus he makes the soul of the tourist which God has given to the English go wandering through the vastness of history.

I have the impression that the history of the Roman Empire is still to be told, and that the reality which it was has never been understood. Mommsen, one of the few geniuses that have ever been in the historic science, and of whom I am very admiring, stopped at Roman history when he reached it. He says that he lost the manuscript that dealt with it when he was on a trip, but we know perfectly well, though we have not seen that manuscript, that its contents could not be guessed at. Mommsen, who understood the Roman Republic superbly, did not see the figure of Caesar clearly; not by chance but because of the conditions of the time in which he lived he was blind to that new and strange historic physiognomy which is the Roman Empire; this was true up to the point in which not even in his finest achievement, his study of law and institutions, did he succeed in interpreting the new political body in its figure as a state. New documents and later analyses have demonstrated this. And the ultimate reason for this blindness, even in such a genius, must be seen in an inopportune and bigoted idealism which does not accept the fact that historic reality, apart from passing disorders, can be constitutionally sick and defective. This is the vice of intellectual optimism which we inherited from the Greek philosophers, with which Hellenic paganism infected the Scholastic thinkers, which the humanists of the fifteenth and sixteenth centuries revived in Europe, which the rationalist philosophers of the eighteenth century sanctified under a kind of progressivism, and whose cure or correction is the most urgent and important reform that must be made in the contemporary mind. Because it should be emphasized that this is perhaps the only decisive theme among those in which St. Thomas Aquinas and Voltaire, for example, go hand in hand.

This does not mean that I think the opposite vice—intellectual pessimism—is the truth. At the very moment one is falling perilously into this new vice, and this is happening because human minds are not being educated so that they can be equally open to optimism and pessimism. No one has imposed on intramundane reality the obligation to end well, as is obligatory in American films; no one has the right to demand of God that He prefer to make human history a sweet costume comedy in place of letting it be a tremendous tragedy. One must let God stay in the infinite breadth of His free will. How much more profound than that inveterate and perfectly arbitrary philosophic optimism, so badly founded on reason—and I refer to Plato and to Aristotle—how much more profound is the geographic definition which the Christian religion gives this world when it says that the world is a vale of tears!

From a certain period forward the *imperator* acted most of all along the line of the Rhine, because that was the frontier and the place of danger. But we see that the change in that line into a central axis line did not prevent its continuing to be, throughout all the later centuries of Western history, the imperial or command line. Along the territorial belt which runs from the Low Countries, the length of the Rhine, to Milan is the region where all those who for twelve centuries have wanted to command in the Continent have had to fight. And it is not by chance that the only emperor whom the Spaniards had the luck to have, the last of the great ones, Charles V, had as his inheritance the very territories of Flanders, Burgundy, and Franche Comté. In order to be master in Milan, he had to fight Francis I, because, as he said, "My cousin Francis and I are in entire accord about Milan; each of us wants it for himself." That is to say, Charles V possessed all that strip which Charlemagne's son, Ludovico Pio, apparently arbitrarily, willed to his oldest son Lothar, under the name of Lotharingia, which in the process of phonetic evolution has come to be *Lorraine*, meaning, in this latest form, a meager portion of that long region—meager, but still being fought for as late as 1918; that strip which apparently is decisive in Western history, because this explains to us what Toynbee failed to explain.

But if I reiterate that statement, it is to add something of the greatest importance which I did not say earlier and which explains why, in our civilization, the imperial line is not a frontier as it was in the ancient world, but a central line and the axis of the anatomy of our historic body. In effect, once Lothar received Lotharingia, the Orient and the Occident in Europe were separated, and they never came together again. Lotharingia acts, then, as an isolating element, a factor of distance between the two sides of the continent, and this results in the initiating and maturing within Europe of two profoundly different ways of being men, the French on the one side, the Germans on the other; or to put it another way, that separating strip is the cause of the formation of two great continental nations: France and Germany.

And remember now that in talking of the "here" and the "there," I said that some day I would explain how every nation in one of its facets is actually "distance." There has been not even a shadow of an explanation, but you will have recognized, in an urgent and exemplary case, how the simple fact of distance, of separation, suddenly gives birth to a pair of nations, and not weak ones at that. But if I have not explained why distance is nation, this fact does explain something important: namely, why the imperial line in our civilization is no longer a frontier but a central line; the reason is that the historic body of our civilization has a double-lobed anatomy. Its torso consists of two principal lobes, France and Germany, and this inevitably necessitates a line between them, a line at once of equilibrium and of pressure. But the Greco-Roman world was not like that. This fact, in turn, makes clear to us a new reason to invalidate the image Toynbee presents, wherein what was a rib came to be a vertebral column, because if the line of the Rhine was a rib in the Roman body, this seems to assume that Rome would have its vertebral column on the other side.

Would Toynbee tell us where? Not at all. Rome had no vertebral column, nor was its anatomy bilobar. This is one of the profound differences between that civilization and our own, but this anatomy cannot be seen unless it is looked at from within, and Toynbee prefers not to look at civilizations from the inside. Then one notes that the Greco-Roman civilization is of a different species from our own. Rome is an invertebrate organism having no lobes. Toynbee's theory, then, encircles a great historical error: the disregard, or the ignorance of, a profound structural difference between the two civilizations.

I must interrupt myself to say that when I was previously comparing the magistrate and emperor, I did not mean to state that the Romans would ever call the *imperator* formally the *minister*. I took advantage of this comparison between the *magister* and the *minister*—the one being more and the other being less—and I applied it artificially, and therefore fraudulently, to the relation which the Romans felt and lived between the *magister* and the *imperator*. But this was, of course, with the intention of producing in your minds a shock whose effect corresponded completely to the truth, because it made you see what was the effective attitude in which the Romans lived within the Republic. And if I called what I just finished doing a "fraudulent" action, you will understand that this too is out of a pure luxury of veracity, for I could have remained silent and taken refuge in the great authority of Mommsen, who, in his history of *Roman Public Law* (a work never superseded, and for which there is no substitute), said textually on page 45 of Volume II, "The emperor's title was accepted as an inferior distinction"; therefore it was not a *magis* but only a *minus*.

I made this purely technical remark so that it may serve as an example in other cases, because it would go very well in the style of those who are incapable of genuine science—I refer above all to the science of history—or at least of those who run back and forth in scientific businesses, boasting of being scrupulous, thinking how they could give weight to a bit of nonsense if, on hearing me say it, they hurried to point out that in the juridical and administrative terminology of Rome the *imperator* was never described as a *minister*, ministerial. And it is clear that in the historic sciences there are points and themes in which exactitude of detail is indispensable, and the scientific operation consists facing up to these; but in all the others proper scientific behavior is the opposite: namely, to eliminate the trifles which are not opportune, and *thanks to this*, thanks to their very omission, to make sure that what is important remains clear and definite.

What is now important is that we recognize how those

two institutions, the *imperator* and the *imperium*, went on living among the Romans twenty-four centuries ago. It is not my way to say anything merely as a simple way of saying it; when I say now that the continuance of this distinction is what is important, I want it understood that whether we pay heed to it or not, it is highly important to see clearly what, in that remote period, the word *emperor* or *empire* meant to the Roman who heard or pronounced those words. Because a few centuries later those words denote the monumental historical fact which was the Roman Empire; this, according to Toynbee, is the universal state, and with or without Toynbee it is evident—some of us said this a quarter of a century ago—that the world seems to be moving toward the formation of something like an empire, a universal state or various universal states in which we would all be subjects. The Roman *Imperium* is the prototype of the universal state and the only one we know fairly well from the inside out. So that what may seem merely like an erudite joke, this *magister* and *minister*, implies something which life gives us both individually and collectively. Such, gentlemen, is the preeminence of history over all the other sciences.

History, say what you will, is always a matter of men in the present talking about ourselves, men of today; because we were made in the past, we continue being in that past, although in the peculiar fashion of having been that past. Thanks to the fact that each one of us continues to be the child that he was, in the form of having been that past, you are able to be what you now are. Otherwise you would be nothing or would continue being that child of long ago. History always talks about us: *de te fabula narratur.* The question is whether we know how to tell it, and whether we know how to listen to it. So do not believe that the present situation, so important to us, in which for various reasons the whole human past comes to a sharpened point, can be defined with a few words or be clarified with fewer than many explanations. For it must be noted that above all the tremendous happenings, the catastrophes, and the present disasters which give events that overwhelming appearance that afflicts men today, there must be added a fact in which one cannot take refuge, because it is a negative fact, a defective reality: the peoples of the West were accustomed as we are to the vicissitudes which fate flings, but they were also accustomed to having men who for better or worse managed to explain, define, clarify, to explain the causes and the perspectives of those happenings. Those men were genuine intellectuals, and that was their most human mission.

I do not attribute any undue importance to the intervention of the intellectual in the march of history; I know it is very little, and if I had time to talk at length, I would have to say it is minuscule. But the volume of vitamin substance is also minuscule, and yet our bodies cannot live without it. The peoples of the West were accustomed to that vitamin-like function of the intellect which is worthy of the name, and which goes on putting clarity into their comings and goings. Western man has never known how to live without clarity or out of clarity. Therefore, as they come from the deepest depths of the European soul, Goethe's words speak to us:

> I declare myself of the line of those
> Who out of the darkness aspire to light.

Well, then, for the first time after ten centuries, in the last fifteen years or more, European intellectuals have grown silent, and that task of making clear what is happening as it happens has remained unfulfilled. And this at a time when emerging events were so tremendous, and wearing such new faces, that the concepts acquired in the contemplation of the traditional historic fauna had no value for them—at least at the moment. This is not the time to specify why the intellectuals have been silent; let it suffice to note that this has happened everywhere and that the cause of their silence, though wearing a different disguise in every place, is identical. But the result of this is that those tremendous happenings, that anguish concerning what is occurring, has been doubled by the new anguish produced by the darkness, the obscurity in which it all takes place. People are torn by suffering and, submerged in darkest night, do not know where their hurts come from or where they are going. In 1935 I could say publicly, "We do not know what is happening to us. And that is what is happening—the not knowing what is happening." Or, if we want to find relief in a humorous simile, let us remember that picture exhibited in a Bellas Artes exposition in which the whole canvas was daubed with black and on the frame the title read, "Struggle of Negroes in a Tunnel."

I too have been silent for the whole time and very basically—because I could not speak in Spain, outside of Spain I did not want to speak.

Some day, I will show why I fell silent. It is not interesting to hint at the sacrifice which such a long silence represents, but I must say that if I never had difficulty in making my fellow compatriots understand that I know this or that branch of learning—the proof of this lies in the apparent lightness and popularity of almost all my writings—I wanted to demonstrate that I know that perhaps the most difficult science of all does not exist. But now I think that the moment has come to end that silence and to begin a new work, initiating it in Spain, although it does not refer only or even principally to Spain, but to the whole Occident and even to the whole world. And I would like to do it because I think that Spain has something to say—not much, perhaps but something—which is important to other people about what is happening in the world; and this because, with Portugal, we Spaniards are the oldest people in Europe and have "seen them in every color," because we are the old Chinamen of Europe who have accumulated the most ancient and succulent experience. As Gracian said, "Time is a great teacher for the old and experienced." Hence Spain has the duty to say its say without petulance, for the quantity of its pretension is very limited; and the desire of contributing to fulfill it is one of the reasons which has led me to plan this Institute of the Humanities.

The Institute of the Humanities is an institute of history, but by *history* I understand the study of human reality from the most remote past up to and including living men. Therefore, there neither is nor will be any theme in our Institute which has not some dimension of actuality. Nor do I admit that there may be science, and much less historic science or a discipline of humanities whose theme does not reach more or less to the men now living. But what does one think science is? Science is not a lymphatic ornament, or a mere chess game, nor is it an inert water wheel; it is human life itself, taking account of itself. At one and the same time it is the transparency of the idea and the trembling of the viscera. The task, then, is both dramatic and arduous. It has to be fulfilled. Step by step and calmly.

So I ask patience, and especially in this first course (which will show what will follow, if it follows) when you see me stop sadly at some theme or perform apparent evolutions like the flight of a swallow, do not judge prematurely that I am leaving the subject, because in truth I will be settling you more deeply within it. In this manner it will always be necessary to´ be able to count on your benevolence in enterprises like this, which will be limited by the deficiencies in my learning and by scarcities of time. Because I intend to make history seriously. But this seriousness does not consist either in a grim face or a rude one or in perpetual solemnity. Rather it is compatible with a certain gayety and lightheartedness. That seriousness is not a matter of collating old manuscripts; going through papers in the archives; publishing, with a careful review, the ancient texts. All this, as I have said, is most important, is indispensable. Men who are busy with it merit our gratitude, our respect, our admiration, and if they do their work well, they have a right to expect us to say of them that they are serious men; but what one cannot say in such a case is that what they make is—seriously—history. Because history is a good understanding of what those documents are and of the human realities to which these documents allude, and this mental activity assumes the possession of a whole assortment of difficult theories, some fundamental and others supplemental, with which those worthy men are not acquainted and which they conscientiously ignore, so much so that they do not even miss them. But without those theories there is no history. Hence history is still an adolescent science which frequently babbles. But as it is, under another name, the science of man, and as man is entering an extremely critical period so far as his fate is concerned, we have the duty of making an energetic and peremptory effort to transform it into an adult science.

This is the central proposal which led me to initiate our Institute of the Humanities. Thus the fundamental, the basic doctrine in all history, is the general theory of that strange reality which is human life; human life which is always the life of someone, and more precisely, is always my life—the life of an I which is I, or you, or he; therefore the theory of human life is, for the moment, the theory of personal life. But within our personal life we find not only other individual persons like ourselves, who do not pay attention to a discipline different from that one, but we find them together in a group, which is different from each of them and from all of them together; this is the group that we call a society or a collectivity.

Spain is no single Spaniard, nor is it the series of all the Spaniards taken individually; it is a reality different from each one of them, and with which each of them finds himself both outside and inside that reality. An example of this latter is language. From infancy the Spanish language is, of course, imposed upon us. With it we must make do, not only in order to talk to the others, but even to think in the deep solitude of our conscience. That language comes to us imposed since infancy by our social surroundings. No single individual created it or is responsible for it. There it is by itself, whether we like it or not, just like the mountain ranges of our peninsula. (I know very well the ones which I have passed many times in order to think my personal thoughts in Spanish.) The same thing would have happened to me with any other language which might have been my mother tongue. This is simply one example to make clear how different from the person is the reality of the society or the collectivity. Therefore, to the theory of personal life there must be added a theory of collective life, a theory of society; it is not now urgent to make clear the change in meaning which the word *life* undergoes when it shifts from meaning "personal life" to meaning "collective life," but it is important to say that without a perfectly clear theory of social or collective phenomena, anything that can remotely merit being called a science of history is impossible.

Next autumn, if this Institute continues its existence, I would like to offer a course,[1] in which we put, clearly and precisely, some transparence into these concepts which usually wander vaguely about our heads, concepts of society, the collectivity, people, customs, the state, the nation, public opinion, usages, disuses, and abuses, peace, war, revolution. Do you think history can be written seriously unless we have terribly clear ideas about these human realities? I assure you that the immense majority of historians—and now I am not referring to Spaniards—have not believed it to be their obligation, or that it is incumbent upon them to dedicate a fraction of a second to meditating on these concepts which they are constantly employing. If this is not a scandal, may God come and see it, and after seeing it, judge whether or not I am right in being uneasy about the historians.

1. This promised course was given in 1949–50 and published in the volume *El hombre y la gente*. See *Obras completas*, Vol. VII. Translated into English as *Man and People* (New York: W. W. Norton & Co., 1957) [*Translator's note*].

V

"Naturalities" and "humanities." About the realities which make up history. *Imperium* and *imperator* before the wavering glance of the historian. Illegitimacy.

I HAVE TRIED to make clear how important it is for men of the present day to have an adequate understanding of what the Roman Empire was and therefore what the words *imperium* and *imperator* meant to the Romans. Such a statement sounds at first ridiculous. When people are weighted down by wars and revolutions, without houses in which to live, without adequate food, standing prisoners for desperate hours and hours in lines in front of offices or shops, or before the stop signs of streetcars or buses, the process of inviting them, on top of all this, to occupy themselves with what the Roman Empire was and what *imperium* and *imperator* meant is one of those mad things that we intellectuals do; this is why the man in the street judges that being an intellectual is to be a bit touched in the head. Yet today it is not the intellectuals but the journalists and politicians outside of Spain who talk for hours about the United Nations, which is nothing less than the attempt at a universal federation, a world state or—more moderate and measured—a European union with some aspects of a confederation. Well now, there is not the slightest doubt that if the Roman Empire had not existed, it is extremely improbable that an idea so impulsive and apparently fashionable would have occurred to any of these men (apparently men of no particular acumen). The pure truth is that the Roman Empire has never disappeared from the Western world. For certain periods it remained latent, under the river bed, as if absorbed within the earth of the many European nations, but at the end of a certain length of time the intent of empire always began to sprout afresh.[1]

Remember that in our trip backward, when we were discovering the beginning of our civilization, we found it in the Carolingian Empire, which was consciously and deliberately an attempt at the restoration of the Roman Empire; going to the other extreme of time, that is, to-day, we find the idea of a universal state to be the central theme of the latest attempt made by a European to rein-terpret universal history, which is Toynbee's work; this is once again nothing but the Roman Empire, now be-come an obsession within the excellent head possessed by this professor. Therefore, the effort to become well acquainted with these matters is by no means extravagant.

Everything converges, then, to make that great his-toric phenomenon the central theme of this course. We will have to face up to it successively through various of its phases; the first that appears is the idea of *imperium* (in lower case) and the twin idea of *imperator*, because if we do not understand thoroughly how these two words were part of Roman life, we will later understand no better what the Roman Empire was, even though we said some important things about it in the previous lec-ture. Meanwhile I am going to use myself as a sober and simple example in order to show you how, in my judg-ment, one must think in history or, reducing the expres-

1. This is a first-rate theme for any young historian who has the wit to see it—the history of the Roman Empire after its official disappearance, that is to say, the history of how this proud his-toric figure survived after it ceased to live.

sion to the limits possible at this moment of the course, what the first and chief thing is that one must know, or count on, in order to study a human theme in a truly historical form.

Fortunately, the phrase "natural history" is becoming obsolete, and the word "history" refers exclusively to the history of human things. Thus, facing the great intellectual system of the "naturalities," there appears the great intellectual system of the "humanities." Science accepts that specific character of history along with the science of biology, physics, and mathematics, not through any courtesy insofar as the intellectual activity is concerned, but because the reality with which it deals —in this case or that a human thing—has in itself a real structure which is historical. The primary meaning, then, of the word "historical" is the one it has when referring not to the manner of being of a science, but to the way of being of a thing. The triangle and the dodecahedron do not, as objects, have a historic texture, and hence one cannot write a history of them, but must create the very opposite of a history; namely, a form of mathematics, which we call "geometry." The triangle is not historic because within its essence, within what makes it up, what I prefer to call its "consistence," time does not intervene. The mathematical triangle does not contain within itself anything that is temporal; it is immunized by time. It is always equal to itself. And the equilateral triangle of which Archimedes thought twenty-three centuries ago in Syracuse is the same for a modern boy in Alcobendos to whom his professor is teaching geometry.

The physical world, on the other hand, is within time. Its way of being is to exist in the now, the present, but the now and the present are instantaneous; we have no sooner finished naming them than they have fled, have ceased to be a "now" and a "present" and have been converted into a past, into something that no longer is, but was. When a moment has passed, the physical world ceases to be what it was at that moment, and for it is substituted another physical world which exists in a new "now," a new present, or, to put it another way, the physical world changes, and that is what being in time means.[2]

Whatever the present world, the physical world may be, depends on what it was in the previous present which is now the past. But this relation between the present and the past of the physical world which leads us to say that the world of the immediate past is the cause of whatever the world may be in the immediate present—hence the relation between cause and effect—is a pure hypothesis about the reality of that world which our minds project.

In fact that past, that world of the immediate past, forms no part of, is not in the present world. It is our intelligence that assumes that if there had not been that previous world, there would not be this present world.

2. The physical world is pure present and hence pure instant in such a way that Descartes considered its conservation in the series of instants to be unintelligible if he did not assume that at every new instant God created another world, which otherwise would have succumbed to going into the past at the previous instant. We are not now interested in how much of truth and how much of error there is in this Cartesian idea; according to it, the conservation of reality would be continuous and incessant creation. True or not, this idea of God as a rhythmic and tireless creative pulsation is magnificent and moving. But it is evident that the idea of time would not have occurred to us, we would not distinguish between past and present, if the physical world did not change, if it were not modified. If things remained identical with themselves, like the triangle, if the physical universe were an immense universal paralytic—or, as our grandparents would have said, a palsied world—there would be no difference between the now and the before.

We can say the same of the physical future. The world of today will be succeeded by another one tomorrow, but that future world as such is not in the present. Only our mind, which anticipates, puts into the present world the little tail of a future world which is not yet in this one. Hence neither the past nor the future would form part of the present world, and this is what I want to emphasize; that the present world is only the present. Its reality exists only in that which is solely present; its past is absolutely past, or in other words, its past absolutely is no longer, and the future absolutely is not—all of which allows us to conclude that the physical world has a past and a future, but does not contain them; they do not form part of it.

If, unlike the triangle, the physical world exists in time, so—different from the physical world—human things are not only in time, but time is in them. A nation, a man, a world, a gesture also exist in a present. Insofar as the present and the now are concerned, they exist in both, but in their present the past resounds and the future vibrates; that is to say, these periods of time are not outside of those but, on the contrary, form part of them. So human things not only have a past and a future, like the physical world, but also in their present they are made up of past and of future. If we want to understand of what they consist, we have no course but to talk of their past and their future, to define them by showing those two organs of theirs which function within them, which give them their present being.

But let us stop talking in general terms, which are always somewhat abstruse, and operate with an example which we must choose most simply, although it may be a bit absurd and have no poetic aroma; besides, it is extremely well known by linguists. A thing, a human action is the kind of fact which we Spaniards call the "liver," the "guts," in order to name it as part of the viscera of our body. One tries to understand that reality, the humblest and simplest act—I choose it for this—the mental act we perform when we give that rude, loud sound in naming those viscera. For the moment you will recognize that the link between that word and the thing it designates is enigmatic, unintelligible to us. Why is this so? We did not invent that word *guts*, we found it there in our surroundings, before our entire present, before we existed; in fact when we use it, it comes out of that past into the present, forming part of the present as we use it. So that if we use and pronounce this word again and again, without taking account of the link between its sound and the thing it designates, it is beyond question that in its present there persists a past, namely, the word *hígado* ("liver," "guts") which forms part of that past and is integrating it. Well now, when this happens, when a thing, however small, is a present portion of our personal life and at the same time a past, we have a clear case of a constituently historical reality.

But we still have not said why the word *hígado* ("liver," "guts") is a past, though we indicate something important when we say that before using it we find it "there" in our surroundings, as something therefore that preceded us and came out of the past. And note that the same thing happens with words that surge forth in our own time. The hateful word *haiga* [3] which I ask you not to use because its invention reveals a soul full of sly resentment at lacking one of the shining vehicles, then one tries to make amends by demonstrating that one knows how to conjugate the word *haber* correctly—I repeat

3. In Spanish the word *haiga* is a popular corruption of *haya*, the subjunctive of *haber*. It can be construed as meaning "a would-like-to-have." It is used as a slang term meaning "automobile" [*Translator's note*].

that the first time we meet the word *haiga* we find it there in the past; no one of us invented it, we do not know who did or where; it has a past that goes back before our time, a very short one surely, but a past. It being very short, we have been told the word's origin, because many people know that it began in a joke. But you can be sure that if this sad word should unfortunately endure, twenty years from now no one will have the slightest idea why an automobile is called a *haiga*.

To say the word *hígado* ("liver," "guts") is at once a present and a past. What does it have of the one or the other? What it has of the present is clear: this consists of the utilitarian use which we make of it when we say to a friend—in order to excuse our bad temper, our black bile—that we are feeling "liverish," or to the doctor when he is diagnosing us; or when, in praising the energy of a man engaged in difficult affairs, one says that he "has guts" (note the plural); or as in certain arguments, when, for example, one of the contestants for a chair of theology was dressing down his rival with innumerable and white-bearded syllogisms, I heard an unknown beside me say, "He made a bird's liver out of him." This is the present use of the word.

What the act of saying this has in it of the past is that, being a human act, something we do without knowing why we do it, we are not the conscious and responsible authors of our own action; hence we ignore completely why we call that organ *hígado* ("a liver," "a gut"). We do it, then, on account of someone we do not know, someone who is not present in us. We say it because we have heard it said, because it *is* said, just as when we greet someone we shake hands because it *is* done, or as we believe the sun will shine tomorrow because this is believed. It—the causal agent of all this—is an impersonal entity of which we know nothing, except that it was he (or she) who performed the act of saying "guts" before we did, and that it is he who imposed it on us, if we want people to be understood. So that we find ourselves facing a curious phenomenon. This or that one on account of whom we say the word is present in that he acts within us, but he is there in a very strange manner, namely—he is present in the character of being absent, in that we do not see him, nor do we know why it pleases him to call our viscera "guts."

Well then, that act of considering in the present something that is latent, distant, which is, at the moment, absent—that something is the past. The part of it that is present to us is its effect on us, but the thing itself remains hidden—the past is "the man that throws the stone and hides the hand." We live the greater part of our own life on account of that great absent force which is the past; we call it that because it no longer is, but was; that is to say, it went away, it absented itself. So that the word (*hígado*, "guts") has its face, its frontal aspect which we see and which is its present, but fastened onto this is its dorsal aspect, its back which we do not see; and this is its past; we see only what it contains. We realize that this past is constantly coming forward to the actuality in which we use it.

This happens throughout our entire life, and in the lives of all men who have ever been; our life goes incessantly pushed *a tergo* by the past; like a magic wind from the sea it blows the past across the back of our existence, moving us to actions which we perform, but of which we are not the inventors, nor even do we understand them. Hence, as we are seeing, man and everything human in him is historic reality; it is literally true that he is, at the moment, made up of the past, because one of his parts, what we have called his back, consists of the past, the most effective past.

As this is the content of historic reality, it offers no

doubt about what must be done in order to know it; hence no doubt about what constitutes historic science. Holding fast to our example, let us say that one is trying to understand the human act in which, in order to designate viscera, we pronounce the word *hígado* ("guts"). That human act is unintelligible because we do not at the moment see what link there could be between the thing and the name. We do not see that link because the word comes to us out of the past, and the reason for that link, the motive which created this verbal usage, is absent, back there in an unknown fold of the past, in a time which has been lost to us. If we want to understand our own most humble act, which is to say "guts," we have no recourse but to dedicate ourselves to hunting out that lost time in which the expression originated; we must give ourselves *à la recherche du temps perdu*, which is one of the ways in which the science of history is defined.

And in turn, of what does that task consist? Of this. Out of our own life, which is the absolute present, and taking advantage of whatever data there are—that is, footprints, traces, remains, signs that we can gather—we must go on reconstructing the series of present moments which that word had; the total of these forms is its past. We must, then, re-present ourselves, go back to resurrecting those dead presents, and this means that we need to revive for ourselves those forms which have ceased to live. All history is the revival of what seemed dead. As Hegel says pathetically in the beginning of his *Philosophy of History*, "When we cast a glance at the past, the first thing we see is only ruins." These ruins are the data, the material which we must reanimate; for this we must be capable of going back to live on our own account those ancient lives which have vanished; we must repeat what has already been lived by others.

In this sense history is clearly repetition, a task that is

never easy, as anyone knows who has desired to repeat the emotion felt on a voyage, or to repeat a love affair. In trying to do this he discovers sadly that the thing repeated, for the very reason that it is repeated, has become something else again; its original grace has lost its virtue. History is so difficult a task for the very reason that it is repetition. But we do not give enough importance to that term, about which certain recent thinkers raise so confused a clamor in restoring a concept of the Danish philosopher Kierkegaard, who was writing a century ago. Heidegger was the first who renewed the Dane's idea in talking of *Wiederholung*, a word which in modern German means in fact "repetition."

But Heidegger, like every genuinely great thinker— and beyond question he is one—on saying a word does not have in mind merely its present meaning, but also its whole human past; that is, its etymology, and etymologically *Wiederholung* means "to go back to take something that has been left more or less at a distance"; hence "to search" for it. But the so-called existentialists, who are now noisy as jackdaws in France (twenty years late in regard to Heidegger, and more than thirty with respect to me) now spill their clamor over into the philosophy of life; they think that by using the term "repetition" without its etymological resonance they can repeat Kierkegaard, not noticing that the Danish word which the latter uses means "recovery." Well, then, history is the recovery of lost time, of that part of modern men which is our past; this we are, but it is unknown to us, for we have in fact lost it, and it is absent in the depths of time that has gone.

Let us apply all this to our example. We have lost the meaning which was in the word *hígado* ("guts") when applied to our viscera. One tries to get this meaning back again; that is, on calling viscera "guts," we would like to know why we do it. The great task of recovering, which is history, has created many admirable techniques toward this end. One of them, the most advanced and most perfect, and the one that allows us to reach out to enormous distances in time, is linguistics.[4] Linguistics has formulated general laws which we can very often apply to concrete problems that come up; it resolves them automatically. One of these linguistic laws murmurs that the greater part of Spanish words come from the Latin, above all from vulgar Latin, and that a sufficient number come from the Greek, reaching us by way of Latin. In most cases, this law allows us at one jump to connect the modern Spanish word with the corresponding Latin word, and therefore to put ourselves back into a past that is twenty centuries ago, and in principle to include all the intermediate centuries. Unfortunately, in our case this law, if applied immediately and automatically, fails us. Because *hígado* ("liver," "guts") is in Latin *iecur*, a word which has nothing to do with our word; nor does the Greek serve us; it calls *hígado hepar*, whence the term *hepatica* used in medicine. It is impossible for us to benefit from the convenience of the sudden jump which the linguistic law often facilitates. What to do? There is no other way but to go back step by step.

And then we discover this series of the appearances of the word: *hígado, figado, ficatum*. The task is simple. Going backward from the present *hígado*, we find in the fourteenth century, for example, the word *figado*, and back in the third or fourth century, when something like Latin was still spoken in Spain, we find *ficatum*; and if we go on back to a more normal Latin, we find a word

4. Widely represented in our Spain today by the school of a very great master of science—of science, not of inert erudition—who is called Don Ramón Menéndez de Pidal. [Don Ramón died after this book was written (*Translator's note*)].

which differs from *ficatum* simply by a change of accent.

On reaching *ficatum* we have left all the stages of the Castilian language and gone back into Latin—as the other day, on arriving in our backward journey at the fifth century, we left our own civilization and moved into the Greco-Roman age.

Well now, *ficatum* has nothing to do with our viscera; it means something which has been seasoned or dressed with figs, something in which figs play a part; so *ficatum* becomes *hígado*. But on facing that word the Latinist resolves the question immediately. *Ficatum* is a culinary term. One of the dishes popular in the taverns and houses of the Latin Mediterranean and among Helenic people was the *hígado* ("liver") of an animal cooked with figs, and this was naturally called *iecur ficatum* or, in Greek, *hépar sycatón*. Now we can apply a general linguistic law which ends by explaining to us why we call our viscera "a dish made with figs," which has nothing to do with them. That law is that every language has what I call (remembering the pipe organ) different registers in which it is spoken. There is the solemn register, which Sancho Panza called talking in opposition; and there is the register of burlesque language, of talking in jest, which leads us to use names and comic terms for things. This is what the English call "slang" and the Portuguese *calao*, which is not the *caló* of the gypsies. We ourselves, like the French—and this is lamentable—lack a name for this way of talking, which is perhaps more common in Spain than in any other country.[5]

Well then—and note how in any one of these themes,

5. I hope we can manage to baptize it in the colloquium which our Institute is dedicating to idioms, and in which on last Tuesday Don Julio Casares, director of the Lexicographic Seminar of the Royal Academy, made a contribution as magistral as it was pleasing. Idioms are, as a matter of fact, always *slang*.

apparently so dry and purely technical, we touch humanity, strange and inexplicable human realities—for reasons that have never been known, because, absurdly, they have never been sought, men have always had the puzzling inclination to talk jokingly of their viscera. The fact that man jokes about his own internal organs seems to me a great, vexing, and mysterious thing, but it ought not to be so when no one that I know has emphasized it suitably or occupied himself in scrutinizing the reasons for it. Remember the number of burlesque names that Spanish men give the head—*cholla, calomocha, calabaza* ("pumpkin"); the lungs he calls *bofe, liviano, chofe,* and so on. Signs of verbal jesting are also found in making plural what is singular, or using a word in the diminutive. And so the Latins said, as we do, *iecur,* "liver," "guts"; the French call the brain *cervelle,* the diminutive of *cerebro, cerebellum.* The spleen is called *pajarillo,* as in the anecdote citing *higadillo.*

This inclination, as normal as it is confusing, led the Latins to give the liver, in jest, the name of a dish, which included the noun *iecur* ("liver") and the adjective *ficatum* ("dish made of figs"). Then the noun was eliminated and there was left only the surprising and comic adjective as a name for that organ which has made people suffer so.

What should we call an intellectual operation by means of which we manage to describe, to make clear, to find out what a thing is, what is its being? Reason, of course. But in order to discover the meaning of that word *hígado* we performed only the very simple intellectual operation of narrating something that happened, as if we set ourselves to tell a story, although a true one. From which it can be deduced that narration is a form of reason in the most superlative meaning of that word—a form of reason to be compared with physical reason, mathematical reason, and logical reason. It is, in fact, *historical reason*, a concept that I coined many years ago. The matter is as simple as saying "good morning." Historical reason, which consists neither in deducing nor inducing, but frankly in narrating, is the only kind capable of understanding human realities, because the context and structure of those realities is historical, it has the character of history.

Enough of this for now; in order to continue I would have to withdraw what I just said—namely, that historical reason is the form of reason, along with the others, because the truth is that historical reason is the foundation, the base, and the assumption behind physical, mathematical, and logical reason, all of which are only particular and specific examples, and deficient abstractions, of the first one. But it will be better to leave this obscure for most of you because it is an . . . excessive subject. Better that you charitably consider this unsaid, except for the young ones, because they and their sons and their grandsons will, whether they wish to or not, have to busy themselves a great deal with "historical reason."

Now let us continue.

From what was said one can infer that all human reality, because of its historic character, consists in coming from something in the past and going toward something in the future. Hence it is in substance a movable reality—I am not talking of the superhuman—only a "coming from" and a "going toward." Hence the eye of the historian—that is, the science of history—cannot look at its object fixedly, staying quiet with it. Whenever we look at anything human with a quiet eye we fix it, stop it, freeze it, or crystallize it, we make out of it a mineral, we dehumanize it. On the other hand, in order to see a specific thing—a face, a gesture, a word, a work of art, a man, a nation, or what Toynbee calls a civilization—the historian's eye must move unceasingly, swinging constantly from the past to the future, the future to the past. To what point in the past and in the future this oscillation should reach is a question which in every concrete case will have to be determined. We are going to see all this with the same clarity with which I hope we have finally seen the previous example. Only now the example we face is not ridiculous, it is one of the most meritorious ones that exist, it is the great theme of the *imperium* and the *imperator*.

As historic reality is always most concrete, is a here and a now, human life and all that is in it are the inexorable necessity of having to be here and having to be now—living is always shooting off at arm's length. Let us try to understand precisely what the Empire and the emperor were for the Roman toward the year 190 B.C. I choose this date because it is the culminating moment, we would say the high noon, of Roman history. Nine years earlier, after a terrible struggle in which she was at the point of giving up, Rome conquered and smashed her great enemy Carthage, and with it the man who was probably the greatest genius, the almost superhuman warrior of all time, the one-eyed Hannibal. After this victory, which was followed by other, easier ones over Greece and other peoples, Rome enjoyed a period of sweet living which would last a very short time. This momentary sweetness can be symbolized by the most illustrious and outstanding Roman of the time, Scipio Emiliano, one of those marvelous men who are a marvelous delight. Anyone who wants to get acquainted with his appearance may see a sketch of his portrait, very short and condensed, included in my prologue to the *Treatise on Hunting* written by the Count de Yebes. Each one has his own destiny, and mine, apparently, was to talk of Scipio Emiliano for the purposes of a book on hunting.

Mommsen, in his masterly book on Roman public law, defines the institution that is the *imperium*, but in spite of his being, as I said the other day and now repeat, a magnificent person and one of the few geniuses ever occupied with history, he is not, in my judgment, in his juridical work, sufficiently the historian, as we shall shortly see.

He says that "the Romans called the public power *imperium* and *potestas*. Imperium meant the supreme public power which included military command and jurisdiction." "Compared with *imperium*, the term *potestas*—'*potestad*'—represents the broader idea." The *imperium* is *potestas*, but there are instances of *potestas* which, not being supreme, are not *imperium*. There is the power of the tribune, of the *quaestor*, of the *aediles* which are not *imperium*—because they neither judge nor command— these phrases are mine, and with them I begin to condense Mommsen; for this I ask pardon of his ghost.

Later, in terms not of printed pages but of ideas, Mommsen notes that in Republican Rome there were two forms of *imperium: imperium domi* and *imperium militiae*. Undoubtedly these terms were used frequently and normally, at that time. But we do not understand how a power that is supreme, and therefore total or maximum, may be of two kinds, just as we would not understand anyone who told us that there are two or more universes. The universe does not admit of pluralizing, because it does not admit specifications. If there are several, there is not a single one, not a universe but a pluriverse. And in fact the result is that the *imperium domi* is the greatest power that existed in civil life, the power of the consul and beyond that, of the praetor.

But at that date this *imperium* was not yet maximum,

total; it was still limited. Neither the consul nor the praetor, for example, could condemn anyone to death or make decisions by himself, without the law. Even more—and we must emphasize what may seem to be a very small detail—while in this period the consul still had the power to gather an army, *in fact* this did not happen, and it is the Senate which issued a decree when armies were to be formed. Why should this be emphasized? Very simple. The coexistence of two contradictory legal states: one conventionally in force, but with a force that is unreal, ineffective; the other fully in force. In my way of thinking about history, such a fact means to me automatically that that ideal "in force" is not actually in force, because it is not a complete historic present, but a mere residue and vestige of the past, and invalid as any other ghost. If instead of a surviving vestige we wished to call it superstition, we would show that we know what historical reality is and what is superstition.

As one can see, Mommsen had no choice but to recognize the way in which the *imperium* of the magistrate—be he consul or praetor—is a lesser *imperium*, but note how *inadequate* his statement is: "The unlimited power of command," he says, "of giving order or of ordering—which is what one finally defines as *imperium*—is, in the Rome of the kings, concentrated in a single hand, and in the Rome of the Republic it belongs equally, *although weakened*, to the consuls." Let us recognize that this notion of a power at once total and at the same time weakened—that is, not total—is not a clear idea. It is adding to one side while taking away from the other. And I do not think it is too critical of Mommsen—whom I venerate—if I recall here that when I was a boy I read in the *Correspondencia de España* of a bullfight in which the *torero* was hurt, and the reporter referred to the goring by saying that the horn had given the fighter a wound "barely more than three fingers in length." Rather like this "power that is supreme but weakened."

We are, then, facing a human fact—nothing less than that of that fundamental institution, the *imperium*—which is as unintelligible to us as was the earlier verbal fact of saying, "*hígado*." The data, that is, the facts that Mommsen describes, are obviously not exact, but the facts are not the reality. The reality of a fact consists in this fact being more than just a thing that happened. If we now hear a great noise, it would at that moment be a fact, but we would not know until later what the noise was, we would be ignorant of its reality. Was it thunder? Was it a cannon?

What Mommsen said is to us an enigma, because he did not look at those facts with the oscillating glance of the historian. He congealed them, because the truth is that there never was a thing called the *imperium* that was motionless. In 190 the *imperium* was a reality that was coming out of an earlier one and moving toward another later one; therefore there remained within it a past that was inert, while a germinal future was pointing forward. In fact Mommsen himself, in a note which he did not stress, following—despite the great historian that he was —the bad historical custom of not explaining things in narrative with *historic reason*, says—and this refers to a period which must have been more or less about the year 100, "At that time" (therefore some ninety years after 190 B.C.) "one no longer said *imperium militare* and *imperium domesticum* or civil, because the custom had recently arisen of calling the *imperium militare* simply the *imperium*." Nothing more.

Well now, this shows very clearly that toward the year 100 the consciousness of the Roman people had fully matured and had consolidated the fact that there was not properly more than one *imperium*, that of the army's chief, because that was the only total one. And as that consciousness must have been late in forming, he tells us in turn that ninety years earlier, in the time of Scipio Emiliano, the *imperium* had already begun to move toward an exclusive institutional value which was subsidiary only to the head of the army. And vice versa, if, even conventionally, one went on talking about the *imperium domi*, the empire of the civil magistrate, this was for some reason that remained hidden in the past, and in being hidden, it gave to the fact the character of a reality that was living past its time. The story which must be told in order to clear up the whole question is very simple, and Mommsen himself stumbled on it, but did not succeed in giving it the effective historic meaning which Ihering gives it in his book, *The Spirit of Roman Law*, one of the gigantic works of the past century which newer generations do not know. It being an enormous work, five volumes long, not to be found in the market either in the original tongue or in translation, I took the occasion to ask a great friend of mine, Don Fernando Vela, to make a very fine summary of it, because he was eager that younger generations should have contact with a work of such profound historic science, such genuine historic meaning.[6]

At first, the head of the Roman state was the king. His power was impersonal and absolute. He was at the same time head of the army, legislator, and supreme judge. That is to say, he possessed the full *imperium* without any weakening. The revolution dislodged the monarchy, and in place of the king two special magistrates were named who were called consuls. In addition to being chiefs of state, these consuls kept, through historic iner-

6. Summary of *The Spirit of Roman Law* by R. von Ihering, made by Fernando Vela (Buenos Aires: Revista de Occidente, 1947).

tia, all the powers of the king, except that now those were divided into powers outside the city—*militiae* or military—and powers within the city—*domi* or civil. This separation, typical of the Republic, was inevitable for the precise reason that, like the king in ancient times, the consul or civil magistrate is the same one who acts as chief of the army in case of war. More than that, the consuls were very probably not the first institution to be substituted for the king, but there were those who were called *praetores* and who, along with other functionaries, were going to endure under the consuls. Well now, *praetor* means "the one who goes ahead," "the chief," "the *caudillo*"; in short, "the general."

But in 190 it did not always happen, necessarily or even normally, that the consuls became generals. Scipio Africano, the conqueror of Hannibal, had to be general of the army without being consul; moreover, it was already established that in case of war it was not the consul then in office who would direct it, but the one who had held office (also by historic inertia), the previous year and who was called "substitute for the consul," the "*pro-*consul." Thus the *imperium militare*, the only authentic *imperium*, remained ascribed to the proconsulship. See how the question has been cleared for us by merely looking at the *imperium* as a moving thing, as something in continual change from what it was in the time of the kings to what it became a century after Scipio Emiliano; therefore set up at each present moment by a residual inertia from the past and a germinating tendency to shape its immediate future form.

Now let us see what happens with the emperor, the *imperator*. In 190 this is a distinction of little importance *in itself*, although it had a good deal for the reason that it was bestowed on the military leader. In the language then current the general was called, had always been called, *imperator*, but legally, officially, *imperator* was the title that the general received and used only after he had won a battle; with it he had the right to solemn acclaim in Rome which was called a "triumph." Now—I refer to 190 B.C.—we find ourselves facing another opaque fact, and one far from lucid. There was hardly a general in Rome who had not won a battle and who therefore was not *imperator*. Practically, then, *general* and *imperator* were two concepts that covered the same reality. If you remember that a general as such then had the full *imperium*, it will surprise you that this word later appears to be added as a mere distinction. Anyone who in the face of such a fact exercises the new historical reason will at once be put on the alert, like a bird dog.

There is a trap here—something apparently irrational in the old and miserable meaning of the word—one of those historic traps in which effective historical reality *normally* consists. History is composed of traps in the sense of human ways of behavior which are apparently irrational. The obviously rational things are triangles, polyhedrons, which are not realities, not men, but abstract inventions. The trap in this case is somewhat greater in that out of it will emerge—with time—nothing less than the emperors of the Roman Empire; Emperor Charlemagne, Emperor Frederick Barbarossa, Emperor Charles V, and Emperor Napoleon. It cannot be said that this trap is not a matrix of a good breed.

In order to discover its mystery we must direct our glance to a much longer compass than the former one, although always without leaving Roman history. For this, let us imagine in the center what the *imperium* of 190 B.C. was, and let us place at the right the word *imperator*, at the time when its meaning was fully acceptable and stabilized as a formal official title of the chief of the most powerful state that has ever existed, the Roman

Empire at the time of the Spanish Emperor Trajan. This preference for Trajan is not patriotism. As a matter of fact the period of the Spanish emperors was one of the happiest seasons that humanity has ever enjoyed; thanks to them, it happened that for once, during almost a century, men felt themselves to be happy.

On the extreme left, let us designate the most primitive reality which those words *imperium* and *imperator* represented for the people before the entire Roman state existed; that is to say, for the hordes or tribes of Latins. We are going to see how, in the initial extremity at the left, we discover human realities that are suggestive and unexpected, and how at the extreme end we are surprised by a humanly tremendous, frightening reality, which affects our very selves here at this moment.

Let us begin at the beginning.

If you want to go very far back in history, you have to give up dependence on documents, because "very far back" in time people did not know how to write. There are only heaps of ruins, which are enigmatic because they are mute, and there are only words whose previous origin the linguists can reconstruct. By means of this indirect method one comes in fact to touch human situations, scenes of a truly remote existence which, where we see them, move us profoundly. What do *imperium* and *imperare* mean originally? Undoubtedly, "to command." But this word comes to mean "command," because it has previously been *im-parare*, which means "to prepare everything necessary for an enterprise," "to organize the enterprise." The *imperator* is something like "the one who begins."

What have we here? Among the most primitive peoples the state does not exist; that is, no stable organization has been created which exercises the function of the state. What we call a state, which by definition means the exercise of public power, of command, was something that within a primitive collective happened only intermittently, in definite pulsations, with a relatively periodic character, because it was produced by urgent necessity in the face of a special danger. Among primitive nomad peoples there is no authority at all, except in two intermittent cases: the first is the case of someone who, facing the threat of another people, by personal courage and his own spirited presence brings together the men of his own people, organizes them, and prepares to dispose them in a plan of battle. This is the *imperator*, the one who begins. Note that the word *im-pare* then has exactly the same two coupled meanings that the word *ordenar* has in our language. *Ordenar* ("to order") means on the one hand, "to project a series of effective acts and to impose those decisions." But the verb *ordenar*—which is the twin of *im-parare* and *imperare*—is going to uncover something that is very moving. *Ordenar* comes from *ordo* ("order"), and the oldest meaning yet found for *order* is the "lining up of threads," which must be done in order to weave. And in fact the verb *ordior* first meant "to begin to weave" and then was broadened to mean "to commence" everything. *Ordo*, "order," is simply *urdir* ("to weave," "to plot"). And so we discover here that the primitive idea of order among humans was probably a feminine invention, the ordering of threads in a loom.

But this follows an earlier movement of which we have full historic knowledge. When history begins we find that the word *order* has leaped from the peaceful loom to the other extreme and begins in history, I repeat, by having a techno-military meaning. Order, then, means the lines not of threads but of soldiers who make up tactical unity. From here onward the Roman army, and by reflection the Roman electors, would be divided into the Senatorial order, equestrian order, and order of the plebs, and all Roman history would be a struggle and an agreement swinging back and forth among those three orders; the agreement was, in fine political language, always called *concordia ordine*. *Imperator*, therefore, is the improviser for whom things usually go wrong, who leaves behind a memory that is not good. The matter has its interest for things we are going to see later.

The other authority, also intermittent, which springs forth in primitive peoples, and which still exists among certain tribes, is what they call "food tester" (*probador*.) Fearing ailments which might arise from their food supply, the people had a man whom they charged—and this gave him a certain transitory authority each week or each month, when food was parceled out—with testing their foods. And this implies that this man was able to distinguish flavors. It was he who knew how to tell good foods from bad ones. Here you have the origin of the *sabio* ("sage"), and of the word *saber* ("to know"); a primitive authority who knew savors. *Sapiens* simply means—"he who distinguishes savors." There still is, for example, a tribe in the southern Cameroons, close to the frontier, north of Angola, which has as its only authority what it calls in its language (influenced by the Hottentot tongue) "he who tests the foods." He is the sage, who will become the mage, the medicine man, the doctor, the one who knows.

When, as social existence progresses, the life of peoples becomes organized, there appears the figure of the *king*, who has at once a religious, military, and administrative origin; his appearance in the history of a people represents a stage of moral improvement, of the betterment of the whole life. One understands that before the emergence of the king—who would continue to exercise those intermittent adventurous functions which belonged to the *imperator*—there would have been a whole series of centuries in which this word *emperor* did not sound well, was being abandoned, and was never taken as the official title of a magistracy. In my judgment this explains that transitory and relative submergence of the word *imperator*, which would appear again simply as a secondary distinction given to a general after he won a war.

But let us go to the other end of the process. Trajan, who governed at the beginning of the second century after Christ, when the Roman empire was more than a century old, is the first emperor who dared, or considered it opportune (because he was not an audacious but a reflective man) to use officially, normally, and in a certain way exclusively, the title of *emperor*. None of the others succeeded in so naming themselves. Caesar, who would create the preparation for the empire, received the name of *imperator* in the Senate, but this did not mean a title which represented any power; it was a *praenomen*, a personal name for Caesar; so much so that in his inscription, from that moment on he drops his *praenomen* Caius and uses instead *imperator*. Therefore the title is something that belonged only to Caesar, and if it passed to his descendants, this was as something purely personal, not as meaning, "a magistracy." The proof of this is that of the emperors who followed him —Claudius, Nero, and on to Otho—no one went back to its use. The name *emperor* reappears with Otho, but as a *praenomen;* the curious thing is that *imperator* continues to be the authentic title given to the winner of battles; it is really amusing that in the imperial inscriptions of the time, in the titling of the emperor, the word *imperator* appears twice, with a double meaning—as a mere *praenomen* of the person, and as a normal title after a battle.

In the year 40, Augustus used the *praenomen* of *imperator* formally for the first time; this is where the inscription says *Imperator Caesar divus Julius Triumvir.*

But this is by no means the basis of Augustus's power; not for an instant did it occur to him to think that in having put down *imperator*—which meant nothing, either juridically or administratively—he had managed to find a title which belonged to him or which he wanted; at other times he used the title of *tribunicia potestate*. But the fact is that there are ten or twelve forms that the creator of the Roman Empire used in order to write his titular name of head of state. There is no point in our insisting on details, interesting as some would be, in order to get the impression of this strange fact.

I ask your pardon for having burdened your patience so excessively. Why spend time in making you note the variable and confusing titles which were given to those emperors who governed the world not for one day or two, but for two continuous centuries? Have you not noted why I did this? In watching those uncertain titles pass, changing for the same emperor, not controllable by law, have we not felt and touched beneath this a tremendous human reality? Those simple facts, those inscriptions, disclose to us that those men, heads of the most powerful state that existed, masters of the most absolute public power did not know how to name their function, did not find any legitimate legal titles with which to designate their right to the exercise of power; in short, they did not know the basis on which they ruled. The Romans did not know it, nor did the innumerable peoples who submitted to them.

They were not usurpers of power—no genuine opposition confronted them. Nevertheless they did not know why it was that they ruled and not others, nor with what right, what legitimate title, they were chiefs of state! The history of the Roman people had put foot into that zone which almost all the histories that we know have reached: the zone in which legitimacy disappeared from their world. This is not a matter of adventurers having overthrown a legitimate government in order to install themselves fraudulently and temporarily in power, but of something incomparably more serious than all that, something entirely different in substance. It is not that no one wanted to recognize legitimacy: it is that there was no such thing—that which had existed previously had evaporated. No one had a clear idea and one in which he would firmly believe about who should legitimately command. Someone had to do that, but no one, in the minds of the citizens, held the legitimate titles for it. At a certain moment the history of a civilization overflowed into the unpleasant, perhaps frightening ambit of illegitimacy.

I am attempting seriously to set forth some deep truths, and words are not to be interpreted childishly, parochially, as if they were meant to hide allusions to Spanish life. Not only are they not that sort of thing, they could not be. Because no one single people can reach what I call the unpleasant, frightening ambit of constitutive illegitimacy. The terrible phenomenon is too profound to be produced only in a single collectivity. It affects all those who live together in a civilization, and sooner or later the peoples who make up that civilization come into it publicly.

But moreover, what I am now saying—and what for half my life has been a preoccupation and an anguish which has gone with me, I wrote in 1928 and 1929 in my book *The Revolt of the Masses*. There I said, referring to all the West,[7]

The function of commanding and obeying is the decisive one in every society. As long as there is any doubt as to who commands and who obeys, all the rest will be imperfect and

7. *The Revolt of the Masses* (New York: W. W. Norton & Co., 1957), pp. 140–41.

ineffective. Even the very consciences of men, apart from special exceptions, will be disturbed and falsified. If man were a solitary being, finding himself only on occasion thrown into association with others, he might come out intact from such disturbances, brought about by the displacements and crises of the ruling Power. But as he is social in his most intimate texture, his personal character is transformed by changes which, strictly speaking, only immediately affect the collectivity. Hence it is, that if an individual be taken apart and analysed, it is possible without further data to deduce how his country's conscience is organized in the matter of command and obedience.

It would be interesting and even useful to submit to this test the individual character of the average Spaniard. However, the operation would be an unpleasant one, and though useful, depressing, so I avoid it. But it would make clear the enormous dose of personal demoralization, of degradation, which is produced in the average man of our country by the fact that Spain is a nation which has lived for centuries with a false conscience in the matter of commanding and obeying. This degradation is nothing else than the acceptance, as a normal, constituted condition, of an irregularity, of something which, though accepted, is regarded as not right. As it is impossible to change into healthy normality what is of its essence unhealthy and abnormal, the individual decides to adapt himself to the thing that is wrong, making himself a part of the crime or irregularity. It is a mechanism similar to that indicated by the popular saying, "One lie makes a hundred." All countries have passed through periods when someone who should not rule has made the attempt to rule over them, but a strong instinct forced them at once to concentrate their energies and to crush that irregular claim to exercise power. They rejected the passing irregularity and thus reconstituted their morale as a people. But the Spaniard has done just the opposite; instead of resisting a form of authority which his innermost conscience repudiated, he has preferred to falsify all the rest of his being in order to bring it into line with that initial unreality. As long as this continues in our country it is vain to hope for anything from the men of our race. There can be no elastic vigor for the difficult task of retaining a worthy position in history in a society whose State, whose authority, is of its very nature a fraud.

There is, then, nothing strange in the fact that a slight doubt, a simple hesitation as to who rules in the world, should be sufficient to bring about a commencement of demoralization in everyone, both in his public and his private life.

I ask you to accompany me in the serious study of these great, tremendous problems and—if possible—in their solution.

Next we will begin by describing in what illegitimacy consists as a form of total life. With this we have anticipated Toynbee's other great theme—what he calls "Schism in the Soul."

I hope that now it does not seem to you so senseless to affirm that it is very important for us to see clearly what imperium and *imperator* meant and were in the Roman Empire.

VI

Stages in the origin of the state.
The evolution of the Roman state.
The end of legitimacy. The symbol
of the British past.

LET US REFRESH our recollection of the milestones of our
journey so that, with these in view, we will not feel lost,
and can with perfect clarity see why we were talking in
the previous lesson, and will continue to talk insistently in
this one, of what we have discussed and are going to discuss. We were proposing to set forth Toynbee's thought.
This begins by making us see that the nations are societies
of a definite species, that they are characterized by being
essentially parts of a broader society in which various
nations live together; therefore, this is a society of a new
kind which Toynbee calls "civilization." Its attributes
will have to be determined, for these new societies or
civilizations are for Toynbee the proper subject of history.

History must be constructed as a joining together of
those great civilizations. In order to define a civilization,
the first thing to do is to determine its extension in space
and fix the chronology of its beginning and its end. We
must at the same time manage to discover what civilizations and how many of them there were, and are. At
the moment we find ourselves with our own, still living,
and with four other civilizations that accompany it in
existence. With our own, we undertook that process of
defining by sketching our geographic figure; then, in
trying to reconstruct its progress in time, we found that

while we know the past we do not know the future, because we have not yet disappeared. We can only go backward toward the beginning. In this rearward trip we find that our civilization has proceeded from another which is earlier and very different; namely, the Greco-Roman civilization. We then find, at once, that some civilizations have a relationship which can be described as that of mother and son—as has the Greco-Roman civilization with our own.

Undertaking the same process with that Greco-Roman civilization, we first outline its shape in space, comparing it with the figure that ours has; then we begin the rearward trip in order to pass its entire history before our eyes. The first thing we find is the death of that civilization, we see it trembling, collapsing, dying before our eyes. Going still farther back, we find ourselves installed in a magnificent form of civilization in the shape of the Roman Empire, perfect of its kind, and what Toynbee calls a universal state. Well, now, the idea of a universal state of which the Roman Empire is the prototype for Toynbee and everyone else is, together with the universal church, the central theme of Toynbee's work; consequently, it was natural that we should insist on this theme, out of all comparison in importance and significant size with all the others, for these three reasons:

First, because it is in fact Toynbee's central theme.

Second, because it has served me as an example in order to show how, in my judgment, the historian's glance must act—this is what we did in the previous lesson; and finally,

Third, and new to you, because what we did in the previous lesson and will do in this, barely quoting Toynbee, is to prepare as we should for the exposition of the last part of Toynbee's work, which is very much the most interesting, because in it he occupies himself with how and why a civilization gives way and goes down. Toynbee attributes this to what he calls a "schism in the soul"; I see the same reality, or a similar one, in the idea of "illegitimacy."

The other day, casting our historic glance over a very broad range, we followed the word *imperator* and the word *imperium* from oldest times up to the second century after Christ, when the Sevillian Emperor Trajan was ruling. And as the Roman people were not going to vary much in anything essential (at least in what made their state) until the hour of their downfall (when the Empire of the West was cut apart from the Empire of the East) except in tone—and what I call tone is, for example, the shift from the principality and the protectorate—we could do what can be done only in the case of Rome; namely, to retrace the complete evolution of a people from the cradle to the grave in what appertains to its supreme power, that is, its state. This gives our study the value of a paradigm, an example which may serve us as a standard and perhaps as a key for the history of every other people, and hence for the same systematic and yet not historical conception of what, absolutely, the state *is*.

Those of you who are busy with legal matters, especially with the history of institutions, will perhaps have been able to glimpse or to hear hints that, in the historical development which I traced the other day, there beat like counterpoint an entire, very precise theory. This theory of what the state was, was not formulated there, but rather represented as if by actors of historic facts. The theory will be completed today and in the next lesson. Note, then, that with some humor because I do not like to give these things great and solemn airs—we are treating of what is the deepest, most substantial and serious problem that confronts modern man.

Toynbee carries this exemplary character of Roman history to the extreme: while he pretends to construct for the first time a genuine universal history in which all the peoples of the past and the present are treated equally, what he does is exactly the opposite—he drains each people of its own peculiar history and fills the hole with the unique Greco-Roman history which he finds repeated in all the rest. Note, then, that when I say that Roman history is the example, I do not mean to say that there may be simply an identity with the other histories.

And in what does that thousand-year film that we saw earlier consist? I say "thousand-year" because, from the oldest times mentioned, up to Trajan, we can count approximately a thousand years. So in what does this millenary film consist? We saw that in primitive society, among primitive people, there is no state—that is, no constituted public power. Ordinarily no one rules with any collective authority—that is, with society's formal consent. This compliance of society, when it refers not to the momentary behavior of a single man, but to generic forms of conduct, will be what we call law. For among primitive peoples there is no stable or continued state or authority; therefore there is no law. There is nothing more than custom, which is the pure past acting mechanically on individuals.

It has been said with a certain degree of reason—although perhaps those who said it did not take account of all the intimately profound reasons which exist for this—that custom is in man what instincts are in the animal, especially among those insects that are improperly called social: the termites, the ants, and the bees. The primogenitive state, which is the original authority, comes forth in extreme situations only suddenly and with no continuity. In a moment of danger, when the neighboring tribe threatens or hunger presses, and no one has a remedy

for the problem of passivity, there comes forth spontaneously a man with more courage and warrior skill than
the others possess, a man more capable of organizing, of
formulating plots or finding resources. Such a man becomes the focal center of the male adults of the tribe,
who, drawn and caught by the contagion of his energy
and enthusiasm, filled with sudden faith in him, group
themselves around him with equal spontaneity.

When faith is directed toward a personal being, it takes
on the character of confidence and hope. So, too, does
faith in God, and it is not, as those totally remote from
theology commonly think, that believing in God is
simply believing that He exists, in that there is such a
being. Many men believe that God exists, yet they are
not religious nor have they any faith in God. Belief or
faith in God, even more—and this is no paradox—their
believing that He exists, is a matter of confiding in Him
and having hope in Him; it is the difference which St.
Augustine stamped on a die when he distinguished between believing that there is a God and believing God.
And it is very possible that the only way in which man is
able to believe truly that God exists is—before believing
this—to believe in Him, have confidence in Him, even
though He may still seem nonexistent. This strange combination is genuine faith. I do not know whether there
may be heresy in what I said, but what I am sure of is
that it is the most effective idea one can have of faith in
God.

Well, then, I was saying that in that moment of danger
a more capable man steps forward in front of the others,
the rest group themselves around him, follow him, and
are disposed to do what he tells them. All this, among
primitive peoples, happens as with an air of contagion;
I said the word, but now I am going to complete it with
a term which is not used in its technical sense, because

that would be inappropriate, but in the sense it has in current language, and this is "hysterical contagion." As you know, primitive peoples—for example, modern primitives—live in collective states of contagion which we might well call "hysterical"; this happens every day with Negroes in the United States.[1]

Well then, that man who is capable of creating a common plan or program of action, and of *preparing* what is necessary so that the enterprise will be successful, is the *imparator* or *imperator*. This is what the word properly means. And that name is undoubtedly exact, as is shown by the fact that Rome's oldest poet, Ennius, uses a term which in his time was considered highly archaic, the word *induperator*, which is the oldest form of the word; Oscan, the sister language of Latin, also has *embratur*. This sameness of words in Oscan and Latin would indicate that *possibly* the word existed before the two peoples were separated, when they were a single people who had the same language; this would take us farther back from the year 1000, behind the year 2000 B.C.; therefore, into the enormous depths of history.

There we have, though ephemeral and momentary, existing only while the battle lasts, then to dissolve or later to disappear, the first state and the first authority. There we have the momentary chieftain, the leader, and those who followed him, his partisans. Perhaps it may interest some of you to know that there are serious reasons for assuming that the word "society" comes from

1. This contagious origin of the first spontaneous and instantaneous authority which was produced among humanity is a theme that I would like to discuss at length with a neurologist like Dr. Lapora and with a psychopathologist like Señor López Ibor, because I believe it is an interesting subject and by no means fantastic; not at all fantastic for those who have lived in a period in which a phenomenon like Hitlerism was produced. It is a theme that we might call "the neurotic origin of the state."

socius ("member"), but that the word *socius* comes in turn from *sequor* (*seguir*, "to follow"); *socius* ("member") is he who follows, the partisan; hence, there would not be a society without someone who stepped out ahead, and others who followed him. I talked about the thing (not about the etymology, which I learned much later) in my book *Invertebrate Spain*,[2] which was published in 1921. I am interested to point out the date because this idea had, I think almost surely, a great influence later on a group of young Spaniards who intervened very energetically in Spanish existence.

I have called this originating chieftainship or magistrature which is discontinuous and intermittent the primogenitive state. That, concrete and precisely, is what *imperator* means: that which is born ascribed to a momentary enterprise, to something occasional—a battle or something similar. It happens, then, that there is still no law, and therefore no one has rights; that chieftain is what he is, not through a right, but simply by a fact, produced automatically by a situation. Consequently, no one originally had a right to be *imperator*, to exercise *imperium*, but anyone could be or could do that. One might prefer that this should be reversed; namely, that the chief of State should begin by being some special person because no one had a better particular right; therefore that he would begin by being somebody in any manner whatsoever, or to put it in a better way, without any legitimate title, because neither titles nor legal attributions existed, because there was no law, because as yet there was no legitimacy. The consequence of this is that the word *imperator*, in that initial step, could not mean either magistracy or any title, but was merely a popular name. Just as we call anyone who is busy making wooden objects a carpenter, so anyone who is busy directing and

2. In English (New York: W. W. Norton, 1937).

planning and leading battles was called *imperator*, neither more nor less.

Second stage: the life of the tribe advanced, became complicated. The number of its individuals increased greatly; its material techniques improved and became complicated; disputes among men arose about this or that—above all about the ownership of lands, a matter on which the Romans were hypersensitive. This brought with it formulas of compromise which, establishing themselves century after century, in obscure continuity, began to seem immemorial, began to be the institutions of private law. But there also had matured a complex and at the same time precise conception of life and the world. Whether he likes it or not, every man, in order to keep on living, has no choice but to have an idea about what his life is, about what the world is in which his life takes place. But among a people like the Romans, as among all peoples in all times, the conception of the world, of a people as such, could be no other than a religious conception. An individual or a group of individuals can live with a conception of life which is not religious—for example, scientific—but a people as such cannot have any other idea about the world than a religious one.

Unfortunately it is not now possible, for reasons of time, to give the motives and reasoning which support that statement, but if anyone tells me in passing that perhaps people in Russia now believe in Marxism, that is to say that the Russian people have a Marxist conception which is supposed to be theoretic or pseudotheoretic about the world, I will ask him to do me the favor of not talking of things from far off, which is one of the great sins of our time; I referred to this when I was emphasizing that the fact of people coming closer together had made them believe that because they were nearer they understood each other better, forgetting that he who least understands a neighbor is his neighbor in the nearby house. Well, then, if instead of talking as if one knew nearby what is seen from afar, if you looked with care and attention, you would see that the result is this: if in fact the Russian people believe in Marxism, this is because Marxism has taken on all the characteristics of a religious conception of the world.

This happened in an extreme fashion with the peoples of Latium, later to become the Roman people, who were one of the most religious peoples that ever existed. Their religion, like the Greek, compared with Christianity or any of the religions born in the near-oriental culture which includes Persia—hence with Mazdaism, the religion of Zoroaster; or with Islamism—is extremely harsh in its doctrine, but one must emphasize that it penetrated the entire life of that people much more than Christianity, even in its most triumphant moments, has ever entered into the lives of Europeans. One must recognize this without any malice, for there is overflowing evidence to support it. Nor can I say why. Perhaps one of the reasons might be the relative harshness of this religion. In Roman life there was scarcely a public or a private act which did not have to go accompanied by precise and very strict rites. Those who have not read the prodigious work of Fustel de Coulanges, *The Ancient City*, should hasten to do so. Errors of detail which have later been discovered in it are of no importance. This work, emphasizing what I have just said, presents us with the fact of how that life was impregnated with religion, while among European peoples religion has never succeeded in penetrating into and impregnating life as completely, but has remained as something which is put just above us.

Well, then, the principal rites which referred to the most important themes of public life could not be carried out by just anyone, but only by certain men belonging to specific families who had been stepping forward throughout long, dark centuries, in turn for their warrior value, for their acquisition of riches, and for their religious character. This led to the appearance of the first stable authority of the state in the person of the director of sacrifices, therefore of the religious rites—the man whose mission it was to carry out with all precision the rites of the collective religious life. This man was called *rex*, "king," which means "rector," because he ruled or directed the religious rites, the sacrifices—*rex sacrorum*. And "sacrifice" did not mean simply killing animals as an offering to a god but included the whole group of the sacred acts; everything which is "to make sacred" is sacri-fice.

Now we have the institution of royalty, which first came into being as a religious office, but, as the functions had not been differentiated, all the tasks were going to fall on that office of the supreme priest. He would be at once the general of the army, the legislator, and the highest judge. He would fully exercise the *imperium*. This shows us how the chief of the first state—which merits that name because it was the first stable, permanent state—that chief was not just anyone, but someone who had a right to the name. This man, the *rex*, the king, was not spontaneously a chief, a leader, or whatever he might be, but was king because he had the right to be, and he had the right because all his people believed that the gods wanted him to have it, they having conferred on the blood of his family that gift of making rites effective, that magic grace, or as the Greeks say, that *charisma* of being nearer the gods than were all the others. And as all the people depended on the favor of the gods, that man would, for the collectivity, be absolutely indispensable.

The king, then, was the chief of state—not spontaneously like the primitive *imperator*, but with a legitimate title. It has not been duly noted that the historian Sallust, when he reviewed the whole ancient story of Rome—a very rapid and concise review, as was customary with the writers of that period (and Sallust lived in the times of the illegitimacy, amid the full civil wars of Rome)—Sallust believed it important to point out this peculiarity of the legitimacy of the king when he talked of the *imperium legitimum*, the "legitimate empire" which is the true name of the power.

The king, then, was the chief of state with a title which comes from the grace of God, which we call a gift, or "charisma." The originating legitimacy, prototypic, the only one, compact and complete, has, among almost all known peoples, been that of "king by the grace of God." Pure, *there is* no other. The question is, What is to be understood by this "there is," for this does not imply that it may always be true perforce? The phrase implies only that this, when it is there, is the only pure legitimacy.

You will understand that in the face of this pathetic, venerable, traditional, immemorial, and mystical institution of royalty, that spontaneous, venturesome and fugitive office of the *imperator* would have to disappear. The name continues in the language, in that at the end of a certain period it rose again to become a title, and it was even possible that at one time or another that name might be attributed to or used for the king, as signifying one of his competencies. But the most probable thing was that the memory of the primitive meaning of that name might be forbidden as a symbol of that rude and primitive period in which there was no established order, no law, no legitimacy.

The fact is that the word seemed to have sunk into the depths of the language, and it did not reappear for a long time. But nevertheless, with regard to royalty, we stumble on what is perhaps the only point in which Roman history cannot serve us as a paradigm, as an example in studying the other histories. The abnormal fact, which makes it invalid, arose out of very precise circumstances. These were as follows: the Etruscans, who occupied Tuscany, a country next to that of the Latins, were a people completely different from the latter. They had come, probably by sea, at the end of the eighth century before Christ. (Personally I do not believe it was that way; this is not rare in matters of ancient or archeological history, but is simply a literary expression; personally I believe they came earlier, but according to the accepted date they arrived at the end of the eighth century.) They came by sea to the coasts of Italy, starting almost surely from Asia Minor, where there was a prodigious matrix of peoples who, from time to time, without any known rhythm, launched portions of themselves into geographic space like swarms of projectiles. And each time they spread farther. The first of these emissions were the Cretans, who created an admirable civilization on the Isle of Crete; of this, following Toynbee, we will have to talk a bit in the next lesson. The second group to go were the Etruscans. And the third, according to some authors—Schulten, for example—were the Andalusians—imagine!—who were called Tartesians.

The genuine Andalusians, let it be understood—for, completely apart from any historical studies, I will say that from my experience among the Andalusians (I am half Andalusian)—for me the true Andalusians have always been the inhabitants of the region that begins in Ecija, goes down to the Peñon, continues along the coast of Cadiz and Huelva, and returns, including the province of Seville, back to Ecija. The rest are adjuncts, people of a very different composition, of another and more recent ethnic origin, very different in character and manner. They are, let us say, "semi" or "sub" Andalusians. The true Andalusians are those old Tartesians, or Turdetanos, or people from Tarsis; if they were actually Tartesians, they would be the oldest living people not only of Spain but of Europe. When I was talking of Spaniards and saying that we were the old Chinese of the Occident, one of the ingredients of that statement was our Tartesian-Andalusian background.

This hypothesis would at least explain the surprising fact that there has been dug up in Crete a mosaic whose chronology is attributed to thirteen hundred or fourteen hundred years before Christ, in which ladies appear dressed in mantillas and long flounced skirts, seated in a box and watching, with complete verisimilitude, a bullfight. That is to say, a picture—it is almost photographic —of what could have been seen in Seville around 1890. Certainly it would be curious to find out how many of you understand precisely what "flounces" are; because if you do not understand it, we would have a very simple but significant fact which could symbolize the radical change in Spain from 1900 up to now. In fact, I would say more: I would dare to say that if the greater part of you do not know perfectly what "flounces" means, this is due, as one of the principal causes, to Marxism. You will think me foolish or extravagant. Nevertheless, if we applied the intellectual magnifying glass to the fact, we would see how the study of this most simple, humble, and trivial fact of the present wide ignorance of that word, which in 1900 all Spaniards knew, revealed to us deep secrets of what has happened in the half century of our present history. A simple example of how the study of words leads us to the discovery of historic human realities.

A small theme, but it would bring forth the whole

history of Spain. By pulling the end of the thread which is the fact of this discovery, one could deduce with almost geometric precision all that Spain was in 1900, what it is now, and why the change has come about. You will think these are exaggerations; nevertheless, it is possible that some day, I may accept the challenge of fulfilling these promises or these pretensions.

Well then, the Etruscans, from Etruria (which was also called Tuscany, because the Etruscans themselves were also called *tusci*) dominated the Latin country and forced some of its tribes to join in forming a city, to to which they gave the name Rome—which is an Etruscan and not a Latin word—replacing the kings of the tribes with an Etruscan king. Nevertheless, the Latins recognized the legitimacy of the Etruscan kings, for it was divine, and to these they owed (they never hid it) the principal institutions of their state, above all the religious ones, which they always kept. But because of the abuses inflicted by some of these kings, and their tyrannical behavior—of which memory persists in the legend of Tarquin the Proud—together with a racial, ethnic resistance which ought never to have faltered, there occurred an abnormal event which is the cause of the lack of validity on this point of Roman history as an example.

This abnormal event consisted in the fact that the Romans quickly and prematurely expelled the Etruscan kings, and out of hatred of them, as much for their alien quality as for their tyranny, felt from then on an inextinguishable repulsion for the very idea of monarchy, and set up what was called the Republic. But that Republic, that new state, began by being—except for the elimination of the kings—identical in everything with the ancient monarchy. The king had always had the Senate at his side, at least as the consultative body composed of the ancient kings of the tribes, that is, of the leaders of the most ancient, respected, and powerful families. The only innovation in this new state, the Republic, was to divide the ousted kingship—the institution of monarchy —among two men, who were the two consuls. These were charged with directing the most important religious rites of the Roman people as a people, which were the predictions. These two men were at once the consuls, the heads of the army, the highest judges, the legislators; though in order to establish laws they had to begin by counting on the Senate and later on the people.

Why this last? The expulsion of the kings could not be carried out in a moment; it cost long wars, because the Etruscans supported the dynasty of their relatives. This is why, although the rebellion was a matter of the aristocrats, there was no choice but to employ all the usable men of Rome, rich or poor, nobles or common people. This total contingent of male inhabitants, without distinction of class, acting in time of war in the formation of the army, is what is called *populus*. Strictly speaking, *populus* is the group of citizens organized for war on foot. It becomes what the French in 1790 came to call *la nation en armes*, or what the same French (not the Germans to whom this was erroneously attributed) called after 1918 "total war." *Populus*, I said, means "all the citizens confronting a common danger." From the noun *populus* the adjective *publicus* is formed. The Senators had no choice but to make concessions to the *populus* in matters of legislation, and then they had the new Roman state, which was going to get a new name—crudely clear, as we said the other day, without affectations, as the Romans called things—a very strange name, because it was two names, *Senatus populusque;* and from this all laws would issue, from the Senate and the people. That duality was the new Rome.

Nevertheless, they did not dare to break radically with

the legitimacy of royalty. They would have felt this to be sacrilege, and they had to keep the royal aspect, at least on its religious side, by creating the *rex sacrorum*—charged with that most immediate relationship of the people with the gods. But fearful, at the same time, that the hated monarchy might be reborn in this, they provided by law that the *rex sacrorum* could never occupy a political or military post, which always made it difficult to find people disposed to make such a renunciation. The *rex sacrorum* was no other than the genuine king—as always, the legitimate king—exonerated from all political powers; therefore dessicated, as it were, mummified. A melancholy figure, this man who was politically paralyzed—and remember that for Roman life political activity was everything—he was a sovereign example of the immanence of the past in the present, which I defined as being present while absent, which is being while not being, and which, in this extreme case, takes on the character of survival or superstition.

We see, then, that the legitimacy of royalty is first-born, prototypical, and exemplary; therefore, it is the only original one and the one which, in its larval form, endures under every other form.

Among our European peoples the process is more normal. The pure monarchy survived during the greater part of its chronology. It was legitimacy *par excellence*. I assume you understand what I am saying not as my political opinion, which would here be extremely impertinent, but as a description of the most normal historic reality. It is not that I believe privately and personally that the monarchy must be the only form of legitimate government. What I am saying has nothing to do with possible political opinions held by me or by anyone else. What I maintain is that when there was pure and full legitimacy among people in Greece, Italy, or Europe this was always monarchy—whether we like it or not. This firstborn legitimacy was followed prematurely in Rome by a republican legitimacy which was not pure by the grace of God, which was founded not solely on the belief that God had bestowed on one or more families the right to govern, but on the belief that the law emanates from the joint will of the Senate and the people. This second legitimacy was neither as full nor as pure as was the royal type. The proof of this lies in the fact that for a long time people went on believing that senators, consuls, the *rex sacrorum*, and the *pontifex maximum* could be chosen only from among certain families. In Europe this second and deficient legitimacy began very soon in England and between 1800 (?) and 1850 would be adopted in all the European nations. This is the constitutional monarchy; or when the king is eliminated and a republic installed, it is the chief of state, whose legitimate title consists in election emanating from popular sovereignty. This last form of legitimacy is what has been called with a word that is difficult to use today because it was maltreated in Yalta (perhaps forever) when three men put their signature beneath it who understood it in three different ways. This is the word "democracy."

So what I mean to say is clear: in the Greco-Roman civilization, as in Western civilization, there was a primary, basic, and prototypical legitimacy which was the monarchy; to this there succeeded another; a legitimacy founded in part or in whole on popular sovereignty— democratic legitimacy which is also, *or even*, effective legitimacy, but which is a deficient, rebuilt, superficial form and without deep roots in the collective soul. May I say parenthetically that I find it unpleasant to have to use this expression "collective soul" which everyone uses irresponsibly, without measuring any clarity of idea in the word; for me, it has an exceedingly precise meaning which I can make manifest only next autumn when I am going to propose a course in basic sociology to be entitled "Man and People." [3]

If any North American knows I describe democratic legitimacy as deficient, my words must seem bad to him, and I would say that for the moment he—the North American as North American—will be entirely right. But differing radically from Toynbee, you will remember that I have left present-day America outside our consideration because in my judgment it represents a historic phenomenon completely apart from our civilization and one which demands being treated by itself. I think that America, North, Center, and South, is a human fact still intellectually virgin, on which *no single basic word* with any real meaning has yet been said; or, what is the same thing, that it is an immense and most original human reality, which, precisely because it is so original, so different from the others, has not yet been either seen or made clear. Therefore, let that imaginary North American concede me a margin of hope. One must clarify things bit by bit.

Full clarity about why the monarchy was genuine legitimacy and why democratic legitimacy has a weak and feeble character will appear to us this very moment, when we pass from the second stage in the evolution of the Roman state to the third. But one cannot enter this third stage without making a superlative effort at abbreviation. I have managed to condense as follows:

The Republic grew old. It represented the focal centuries of Rome, normal and exemplary, which does not mean that they were tranquil. In spite of the lack of a king, and therefore of what I call basic legitimacy, the

3. A book of this title was published in English translation (New York: W. W. Norton, 1957) under the title *Man and People* [*Translator's note*].

form of Roman government—that division of powers, of sovereignty among the consuls, the Senate, and the *populus*—remained one of the most solid forms that has ever existed. Do not see in this an immediate contradiction of what came before. The form of the Roman state, the articulation of its contradictory institutions is, as we know, something unique in history and similar only to the English state. To the Greeks it seemed very strange and, having the heads of geometricians, they did not succeed in understanding that juxtaposition of opposed principles. Only Polybius, with his clear mind of a historian and a man of affairs, came close to comprehending it, applying to it the idea of a "mixed constitution" (to which I referred—*et pour cause*—in the first lesson), that figure of the state of which the Greeks dreamed under the pressure of a thousand years of experience in which they saw all constitutions collapse—that is, all the political structures conforming to pure principle that pretended to be rational: monarchy, aristocracy, democracy. The "mixed constitution" is a picture of the state that I called *theriaca maxima* ("the total dose"), in which, despairing of political cures, people try an absurd mixture of all political forms; all of them being apparently bad, health is obtainable only by putting them all together and hoping that their peculiar perversions would thus be reciprocally canceled and neutralized.

But if we propose—and this is history's decisive anxiety—to *repeat* the past, that is, to relive their form of government as the Romans lived it effectively in their souls, and to relive it in the most succinct way, I would say the following:

For the Roman of the Republic, the Senate was the institution which represented the most genuine and venerable legitimacy—what they called the *auctoritatis patrum*. And the reason for this is that they felt the

Senate to be the institution which, in larval form, conserved the monarchy without its inconveniences. In fact,
the king had always kept it close to him, at least as a
consultative body. Moreover, in its most famous and
respected nucleus, it was composed of the *patres* or chiefs
of the *gentes*, the leading families or clans. The Senate,
too, was and continued to be *by the grace of God*.
Hence, in constructing the origins of Rome by means of
legends, Cicero, during the full period of tragic illegitimacy, would still say that the Romans owed to Romulus
the institution or the creation of the two most important
things in the public life of Rome: its augurs and the
Senate. In the word which would stay with them to the
end, the Roman people *believed* in the transcendent, as if
superhuman, right of the Senate to exercise its authority.
I say that the Roman people *believed*—not that this or
that or the other individual believed it. This was a matter
of collected belief, of general *consensus* which possessed
full force in the social body.

Now we are going to make use of the method defined
in the previous lesson.

At the same time as they believed sincerely in the authority of the Senate, they were clearly conscious that
this was a matter of the past, and that the present, with
new problems brought in by a new life, was obliged to
invent new institutions which, on being invented, were
founding their validity not on the grace of God, not on
immemorial tradition, but simply on their effectiveness.
(Keep in mind that these Romans were not only incapable
of all theory but even inimical to it, and that therefore
the theory of popular sovereignty, the theory that the
origin of all legitimacy lies in the people, never existed in
Rome.) As it grew, Rome filled with new inhabitants,
new families who did not have the old tradition of the
patricians, who did not have any special and most direct

relation with the Gods—these were just citizens of whatever kind; they were the *plebs*. It was these citizens who represented numerically a heavy majority, who created and possessed the new wealth of commerce and industry, and who financed the state as contractors in the matter of the public debt; these were undoubtedly the effective present. Like every present, this one affirmed itself in itself, and that was all; that is to say, without seeking previous justification in the law, without any formal pretense of legitimacy, sustained at most by a vague idea— hence not a genuine belief—that in contributing a greater number of men to the wars than did the patricians, they, the plebs, should have a part in the command, the *imperium*. And this resulted in people's committees and universal suffrage.

But it never occurred to the plebs to suppress the Senate, because they went on believing in its right, its law, insofar as it was an ultimately religious law which came from the past. The Roman, even the most plebeian, was a conservative in the sense that any break with the past, any cutting apart of continuity with the past, infused him with a mystic terror—on this point exactly as the English people have been.

Here, then, is the way we must represent to ourselves the genuine public life of the Romans in the centuries from the beginning of the Republic—500 B.C.—to the time, for example, of Scipio Emiliano in 190 B.C. United, and at the same time face to face with each other, they lived together with a vulnerable past of legitimacy and a present—in itself illegitimate—which nevertheless affirmed their aspirations, their appetites, and their will to be.

This present, which belonged to the *pleb*, felt that venerable past as a thing that had in fact passed, something that came out of the mysterious and sacred depth of time; but at the same time and by the same token they felt it as a model of legitimacy. But that past, being what it was, could not by itself be the present; it had to be adapted to the present.

This adaptation took the form of an incessant struggle which would last five centuries. Because that duality between the legitimate and the oncoming illegitimacy could result only in what I have called the deficient, feeble, superficial, equivocal, weak legitimacy of the Roman Republic which followed the full, compact, and complete legitimacy of the monarchy. (I forgot to say earlier that I see the end of the monarchy, that collapse of a civilization—which Toynbee would call, thinking it the cause itself, "the schism of the soul"—this I see as a very different form, in the idea of illegitimacy.) Hence the new legitimacy must inevitably consist in a constant struggle, and this is why Roman history is for five uninterrupted centuries the history of the struggle between the plebs and the patricians. A legitimacy which consists chiefly in contention cannot be called exemplary. In those centuries the Roman people consisted really of two peoples in almost permanent (although not basic) disaccord; and this warring duality is what is crudely, and without attenuation, expressed in the official name of the Roman state—*Senatus populusque* or, in our terminology of historical reason, the Roman *past* and *present* both joined and in opposition.

What happened to us yesterday, although it is in fact a past, is still here, so to speak, at hand's reach. But as the days go on, what happened to us yesterday becomes more and more the past, it is no longer so close at hand, it goes further away from us, weakening, fading away until a day comes in which we have completely forgotten it; that is to say, it has been converted into an absolute past. The same thing happens in the life of peoples. It is useless in the present to try to yearn for a past, to want to hold onto it and keep it perennial. New presents keep arriving unceasingly, go on accumulating, and inexorably separate us one by one from what has passed.

The dividing line in Roman history is imposed on us with complete clarity. It is the victory over Carthage in 204 B.C. Until then the life of the Romans was shaped by the traditional past, and the legitimacy which I described as secondary and deficient was still healthy and completely in force. Things changed after the Punic Wars.

Until the time of the first great Scipio—the African, the conqueror of Hannibal—the idea of life, even for the better dowered of the Latins, was still a matter of fulfilling the rules, the discipline which we can call that of "the good Roman"—that is, it did not occur to that Roman to propose a profile of life which he had invented individually and for his own particular use, benefit, and exclusive realization, but, on the contrary, he followed a program which came to him as proposed and imposed by the collectivity. All the common, topical beliefs were alive in him, and, together with the collective beliefs, his appetites and aspirations were held spontaneously within the established molds. For this reason, the general who might win more battles did not feel himself a personality apart and, by virtue of this, perhaps have pretensions and rights apart, but knew that, once having won the battles, he would be submerged anew in the social body like any one among many others.

Nothing shows better how much Cato felt himself an old Roman and therefore impersonal, collectivized (though, since he lived in the time of Caesar and illegitimacy, his feeling was an anachronism) than noting that, in his history of Rome entitled *De originbus,* he cites only a single proper name, and that one the name of an elephant belonging to Pyhrrus. This means that for him it was not individuals who made history, but peoples. To such a point, old and still legitimate Rome was living, that for the individual, this meant a matter of living among everyone, for everyone, and as one among many. And this, note, not for any reason of equalitarianism and democratization—which would be a reason come from without and astonishing the soul—but because in the depths of their hearts, as a matter of course and *a navitate*, they felt the same way and were incapable of differentiating themselves one from the other.

Now you will understand what I called legitimacy. Something is juridically legitimate—the king, the Senate, the consul—when its exercise of power is founded on the compact belief which shelters all people, who are, in fact, the ones who have the right to exercise it. As we have seen, the king does not recognize this right easily; but the belief that it is the king or the Senate which has the right to govern exists only as part of a total belief in a certain concept of the world which is equally shared by the whole people, in short, the *consensus*. That conception, we said, is and must be religious. Hence, when, for this reason or that, this total common belief is beginning to crack, to weaken, or to disappear, legitimacy begins at the same time to crack, to weaken, to disappear.

And this happens irremediably throughout all history; a day arrives in which men, as we said, when they get up in the morning, find themselves with the fact that *there is no* legitimacy—it has evaporated—although there was no one who intended even to crack it. A substitute can be found by this or that group of citizens who go on believing with equal firmness in the traditional religious concepts and consequently in the legitimacy of the king. But here one is not talking about what an individual or a group of individuals believes, but of what the entire people believes; this is where legitimacy is born, nourished, and has its being. This did not disappear in Rome in that smooth way. First it was broken; then it went on being crushed to bits, day by day from the year 200 B.C. —perhaps from 225, when Rome conquered Greece, and contact with that older, much more rich and restless life and culture began the disintegration of the compact bloc that was the total common belief of the Romans. It is not possible to describe how this was produced, because even to touch on it would take a long time. Next time I will hint at something about it.

Instead, let us now turn our attention to a marvelous inverse case which we have in mind, in which the purest royal legitimacy, respected without interruption, conserved and venerated by the entire people, nevertheless no longer exists, nor is it there. Note the paradox: there it is, conserved; nevertheless, it is no longer there. This prodigious fact, a moving example to anyone who is capable of feeling the inexorable quality that lies in human destinies, is the present English monarchy. By a chance which helps to make the case more pathetic, more pitiable, the English monarchy is today personified by a sweet, very modest man,[4] fulfilling all his duties, a man of whom nobody knows a single word or gesture which are not the very measure of a king; even more, which are not the complete expression of his own person. This man, properly speaking, does not govern, does not exercise *imperium*, although he has, or had until a few days ago, the title of emperor. His function in the state has been reduced to the smallest minimum imaginable: to establish continuity in the succession of effective governments. Strictly speaking, he represents only that continuity—the continuity of the millenary English life. No

4. George V is the king to whom Ortega refers [*Translator's note*].

longer an effective chief of state, he is only (or almost exclusively) a symbol.

A symbol of what? Of the English past, and the intention that this English past shall subsist in the future; it is, then, the English past itself which is preserved in the present for the very reason that it is the past. Hence that good and sweet specter, that ghost whose appearance is offered to us when we see his most respectable figure in illustrated weeklies, a figure which seems, by its limitless modesty, to want to blot out the present and go back to his own time—to the past, where his mystical legitimacy was in force. He is a visible and concrete example of what I defined in general the other day (with the inevitable abstractions of thought)—the past which is in the present although it is absent. And the fact was made so sharply clear in this unique case that, without realizing it, this was the reason why almost all the world, when it heard recently that the king of England was ill, was surprised to feel an unaccustomed sorrow, hard to diagnose, a mixture of sadness and tenderness which differed from the natural and customary human compassion. It seemed to us as if someone so absolutely ill as he was coming to be, would, over and above this, be suffering a concrete illness.

But now we are equipped to understand what life is, all life—personal and collective—when the hour comes in which it appears to us formally constituted as illegitimacy.

VII

Bullfights. Review. Enrichment:
self-absorbed and open; the scaling
magnitude. Parenthesis: the Tibetization
of Spain in the seventeenth century
and the end of Madrid's century.

Two MOONS AGO, when the lesson ended, my friend and
namesake, the bullfighter Domingo Ortega, said to me,
"The fight was hard today."

He was absolutely right. It had been very hard. Later I
will point out why this had to be. But, before that, I
want you to note that if I quote Domingo Ortega not
only by name, but also by profession, it is because certain
journalistic insects—who strike like cuckoo clocks on the
pages of newspapers and magazines, appearing suddenly
in order to spit out some irresponsible and gratuitous bit
of insolence, which in this case goes unpunished because
they know that in Spanish papers I cannot answer them
as I have often done in my lifetime—some journalistic
insects, as I said, thought that they could discredit these
lessons by saying that bullfighters were interested. But
what kind of idea have they of what science must be,
especially the human sciences, and what kind of an idea
have those idiots of what the bullfighter always is and always has been in Spain?

The Institute of the Humanities, if it succeeds in making its existence permanent, will propose a profound reform in those sciences which study what is human, and

this reform, which begins with its scientific content, will go on to be a reform in the way in which science lives, in its way of existing within the social body. We want it to cease to be the exclusive property of the mandarins— of the academicians, the university professors (note that I am one of those)—not because we believe that their intellectual labor does not continue to represent a fertile and important function, but because their ways of acting are not enough. It is necessary, if we are not to endanger our Western culture—too mandarinesque up to now—that science be made more lively, that it enter into the whole social body, that everybody live with and collaborate in its exercise, each one, naturally, within his own grade and bias. For this purpose it would be ideal if the audience in these courses and other colloquies which I hold elsewhere represented a perfect model of all Spanish society, from the manual worker who unfortunately lacks even a secondary preparation, to the men who know more than we do, and who on hearing us can correct us and complement us. I invite the young to consider this proposal well, and once they have done it, let them judge for themselves whether the thing does not have a great meaning, and therefore whether they should not blow into the sails of this project the magnificent tropic breezes of their youth.

It is clear that such a purpose carries with it the danger that sometimes the going may be hard. But one must be capable of being obscure when duty recommends it. This allowed me to set forth with sufficient strictness the detailed fundamentals for a new and important doctrine which will seem more or less decisive to men of science, but will be taken into account very seriously by them, commented on, discussed, and treated as it now is, I suppose, by philologists, historians, and jurists.

You ought to see how the journalistic insects that I

mentioned earlier reacted to the presence of *toreros* at one of my lectures. Those reporters not only do not know what a bullfighter is, but they are incapable of sensing this, or of having a feeling about one as many Spaniards do. I am sorry to say, with strictly scientific sorrow, that neither do any of them even know what a *torero* is, for there is no one in Spain, or in the world, who knows what a *torero* is, in the real sense of knowing, except me. You see to what lengths a man's pride takes him! And I dare take the risk of saying this, moved by the fact that my great friend José María Cossío—that fine writer, that man of science, the one best acquainted with how many documents there are that refer to bullfighting—would recognize that if there is anyone in the world who truly knows what a bullfighter—that two-hundred-year-old Spanish reality—is, that someone is I. To confirm this, it is enough that you read certain excessively modest phrases in the prologue that Cossío placed at the beginning of his monumental work *The Bulls;* I confess to having been the progenitor of the initial idea.

The amusing legend that I am very devoted to bullfights, which is not exact, has nothing to do with this. If one understands by *aficionado* ("fan") that familiar Spanish phrase "to go to the bulls," the truth is that for the past forty years I have scarcely ever been present at a bullfight. But if I have not gone to bullfights, I have done my duty as an intellectual Spaniard, and this is what the others have not done—I have thought seriously above those fights, which is what no one did earlier. And note that this lack of care or attention is a bad practice. Because, think what you like about that spectacle, it is a fact with well-developed evidence, that for generations and generations that entertainment was perhaps the thing that made the greatest number of Spaniards happiest; it has fed their conversation in speeches and private discus-

sion, gaily and passionately; it has engendered an economic movement which some years ago—I have not the
exact date in my head—I calculated, in money of that
period, to be some twenty million dollars; also it inspired
the pictorial art of Goya, no less, and poetry and music.
Nevertheless, no Spaniard has said anything serious about
it, no one has made a question of it—that is the mission
of the intellectual, to make a question out of what seems
not to be a question, but the most natural thing in the
world, yet no one has asked, What in its substantial
reality is that business of the bullfight? Why are there
bullfights in Spain in place of their not being there?
When did this strange event begin?—no one has even
asked this—Why did bullfights begin to occur at a date
which, according to my calculations, was about 1728?
Such behavior—and you will judge whether this is sufficient—I call stupidity and impiety; lack of gratitude and
lack of a genuinely scientific appetite.

As a matter of fact, the bullfights not only are a reality
of the first order in Spanish history after 1740, when
the ministers of Ferdinand VI—for example, the admirable Governor Campillo—published worried statements
because men in Zaragoza pawned their shirts in order to
go to the bullfight—not only do I say that the bullfight
is a Spanish reality of the first order, but that when one
pays attention to it and brings historic reason to bear on
it, one finds that it leads, as it led me, to discover a fact,
unknown up to now, of such importance that *without
having it clearly in mind* one cannot, I insist very formally, write the history of Spain from 1650 up to the
present time. Here you have the reason why in order to
know what a bullfighter is one must know many other
things; and vice versa, that only one who knows what
a bullfight is can find out certain *fundamental* secrets
of our modern history.

That fact, which I am not going to develop because

it would take us a long time merely to touch on it, began, clearly, at the end of the seventeenth century, when Don Carlos II, the Bewitched, was ruling, and its effect was no less than a profound change in the social structure of Spain even to the point of turning it upside down. This inversion lasted more than two centuries, giving the Spanish collective body characteristics contrary to those which the other European nations had, at least those on the other side of the Pyrenees. But in order to discover so important a thing, one must weary oneself in constructing with a strict historical method the history of bullfights. And then we find another gain, of the purest scientific order: namely, that once constructed, the history of bullfights, in its simplicity and transparences, becomes an ideal scientific model, applicable to the evolution of every other art—architecture, painting, or poetry.

And these two things—that the history of bullfights leads one to discover a fact of the first order about the history of Spain, a fact hitherto arcane; and that the history of bullfights is a scientific model for the historic evolution of all the arts—these I am disposed to demonstrate if I am challenged.

The cause of all this is the sad provincialism into which a good part of Spanish intellectual life has fallen. With this, all the well-known repertoire of that characteristic has reappeared; the explosion of envy, the childish hurling of insolence, and a vain agitation in the bony top of the head. In some of the villages there still endures a fear of ghosts, of those believed to be dead, of those thought to have gone, and it should not surprise you that there are people who are irritated by finding that they might come back. Therefore let us get together, especially with the young, to help banish this provincialism from Spanish intellectual life, for provincialism, which in the village itself may be grace and perfection, is outside of it no more than a circus number.

After this skirmish with the insects—which we will continue as long as it is necessary—let us go quietly back to our principal task; I call it "principal," although I find what I just said to be also, in its own way, a marginally obligatory labor.

But first I want to pick up a few things, big and little, which I forgot to state or had to throw overboard, for each one of these lessons in which I have so much to say is a desperate maneuver in the storm of minutes and a constant shipwreck in time.

Thus in the earlier lesson I would have preferred not to present the expulsion of the Etruscan kings by the Romans as due solely to the hatred which their tyranny and their character as foreigners stirred up, but to have shown certain other causes, general and common to all the Mediterranean peoples of that time, which contributed to it, especially the movement of the Greek cities. But for the schematic effects which we were attempting, the most significant and important factors were, in fact, that double hatred, an elemental fact known to everyone. In the same way I simplified the process in the stage that corresponds to the shift from the monarchy to the Republic. It is most probable—and this is by no means elemental—that between the expulsion of the kings and the full and formal constitution of the new shape of government, a whole series of attempts was made with temporary magistracies, one of these being perhaps that one which the Romans, defining it with certain requirements, were going to call "dictatorship." Another, as I indicated earlier, must have been the *praetores*.

Let us remember from the previous lesson that the state and its chieftain passed in Rome through three different stages. In the first, the state—that is to say the exercise of collective public power with the consent of society—did not exist in any permanent way but only intermittently, in periods of difficulty and danger in which a chief or leader came forth spontaneously, to disappear once the crisis was over; he was the *imperator*, or "starter" for the occasion. This man was not chief by any right, because there were no rights. He was not chief by any legitimate title, because there was no legitimacy. *The chief of state, then, might be anyone at all.* I ask you to remember this because you are going to see it again at the end of this lesson. In the second stage, the state's function was made stable, and hence it merited being called a state. Its chief is the king, the *rex*, who is this because he has been granted the magic *grace* of making rites effective; without these the people could not live, because those rites ward off the wrath of the gods or assure their favor. And the gods, all the gods, including the god of Christianity, always have two aspects: one is terrible because of his power and his wrath; in the strict sense of the word he is tremendous, he is the *mysterium tremendum;* the other, inversely, is infinitely seductive, benevolent, enchanting, fascinating; he is the *mysterium fascinans.* So that the idea of divinity itself, of God, has the dual character of being at once hostile and favorable, against us and for us. In his energetic and twisted way of speaking, Saint Augustine, feeling himself in God's presence, cried out, "*Et inhorresco et inardesco,*" "You frighten me and fire me; you horrify me and bewitch me." The Roman people believed with a complete common and collective belief in a picture of life and the world according to which the magic grace resided and was perpetuated in the blood of certain families, that magic grace which made rites effective, and hence the king who is above all the greatest priest; the *rex sacrorum*, rector of sacrifices, is chief of state with a specific right and a legitimate title. This legitimate title comes from the grace of God; he is king by the grace of God. This primary, basic legitimacy is the only one which is pure, solid, impregnated, and exemplary. Founded on this, the king exercises the *imperium*, having always at his side, as an integrating part of that power, the Senate; this is the consultative assembly formed by the ancient *reges* of the tribes, that is, by the chiefs of the people, the *patres* or kinfolk or clans that were oldest, most respected, most powerful. In the third stage, thanks to very concrete and unfortunate circumstances, the Romans had no remedy but to suppress the monarchy, but they did not therefore suppress that primary and purest legitimacy. On the contrary, they managed to keep, to preserve all they could of it. Royal authority lived on in the *auctoritas patrum*, the authority of the Senate, which continued to be the genuine Roman state. But the times created a new Rome alongside the Senate's traditional Rome; this new Rome lived on during the first centuries of the Republic with a greater vigor than ever.

That ancient Rome was made up of men who, in reality or in pretense, came from a progenitor who was actually the chief of those *people*. They were groups of blood relatives; they were the Rome that came from a past that was, so to speak, immemorial and divine. The new Rome was something else, and very different: the greater part of its citizens were new men; they had no connections, no blood relationship with any of those old families, but simply were there, each one by himself.

Listen to Fustel de Coulanges: "Rome" (he was referring to this new Rome) "was the gathering together of men of two or three hundred families, around each of which were grouped thousands of men" (If any one of you seeks this quotation in Fustel, note that it is not in *La cité antique*, but in his *Histoire des institutions politiques de l'ancienne France*, first volume—I think the only one published—on *Les origines du système féodal*, page 2). Again and again in history one finds a desperately monotonous mention, for or against, of those "two hundred families."

The old families continued to be the genuine state, and hence certain men grouped themselves around them, seeking social and legal aid: these are clients, dependents. The client owes his patron the duty of *obsequium*, which means to accompany him in the street, follow him wherever he goes, act as his aid and attendant for whatever is needed; that is to say, the client's *obsequium* means only attendance. And here there reappears once again that meaning which we found in *societas*, through *socius*, which in turn comes from *sequens*, the follower or attendant. A bit of the Latin meaning remains in French, for *obsèques* means the gathering around a dead man, the following of him to the cemetery—what we say in Spanish, is *exequias*.

The bad habits of Spanish intellectual life oblige me to make the inelegant observation that this connection of *obsequium* with *societas*, like that meaning of *societas*, and in the same way all the schematic history of the evolution of the public institutions of Rome set forth in earlier lessons (except for topical facts), are completely new in historical science. And this deserves emphasis, so that it may serve as a stimulus to the studious; thus they may see how, even when one is treating of one of the most overworked subjects in history—the evolution of the Roman state—there is always room for interpretations that are totally new and enlightening.

In order to compensate for such inelegance, I will now

tell you a tale of bullfighters in which there appears—amusingly underlined—this marked contrast between what [Spanish] *obsequios* meant for the Latins (it was one of the most important things in Rome's history) and what it means to us. The incident happened in Sevilla, where there was a bullfighter named "Lentejica," so bad a fighter that no one gave him a contract, and consequently he suffered the cruelest hunger. One day certain young Sevillians who were sorry for him decided to invite him to dinner so that for once in his life he could do as he liked and satisfy his hunger. This he did —so well, in fact, that he was overcome with indigestion and died of it. Once buried, someone put on his tombstone this inscription: "Here lies Lentejica—he died of an obsequio." [1]

The *obsequio* is very different from the *obsequium* or attendance, which, in grouping thousands of men around a few people, made of the latter what in Rome became true and permanent citizen armies. Because republican Rome never was—as our modern nations have been for more than two centuries—a homogeneous mass of individuals having an equally direct relationship with the state; those thousands of men in Rome were incorporated spontaneously and almost extralegally into those groups of clients, forming something like multiple heterogeneous cities within the city, where they were in perpetual and continuous tension among themselves.

The unity of Roman life, which was the most solid ever known, was in no way an inert and subsidized unity, but one that was won and achieved by the constant intershock of the formidable dynamism and quarrelsome spirit of those social groups; it was a unity of the equilibrium

1. This pun pulls together the ancient funereal meaning of *obsequio* (English, "obsequy") with the present Spanish meaning of a courtesy offered, as in the dinner [*Translator's note*].

of forces—therefore a unity of compromise. It is clear that what gave the most solidity to this unity of rivals was the *consensus*, that total common belief in a certain conception of life and of the world; and in addition, the resolution agreed to by all of them that whatever happened in their own quarrels and discussions, Rome would always exist, Rome would always win, and they would always go on being Romans. Unless one recognizes these assumptions, which appear to be contradictory, one cannot understand Roman history very well.

In Rome, especially primitive Rome, everything smells of contest and struggle. Life is rough, crude. Remember that those who came before the judge as witnesses in a case were primarily those who accompanied the complainant to lend him their support; and as nothing in Rome becomes a joke (because Latins lack a sense of humor), "to lend support" meant, at least primitively, to go to blows with the witnesses for the other side. Hence, between the litigants, those witnesses represented a third factor in the dispute. And this meaning, more or less crude, endures in our own tongue; for example, in *contestar* ("answer"), which meant to them "to bring the two groups of witnesses face to face"; even clearer is the violent meaning which still resides in our word *detestar* ("to detest"), which meant to the Latins simply "to dismiss one of the witnesses," which was not the same thing as doing it with a formal bow.

This new Rome of the crowding plebs, no longer the old Rome of the Senate, corresponded to the new needs which were being imposed by collective evolution through growth in population; victories of the army; increase in agricultural, commercial, and industrial traffic. In this first enrichment—and I call it first, because others would follow, not only in the economic sense, but including the whole of life, and how much men may make and have—in this first enrichment, then, we find the force which is going to transform Rome.

I call "enrichment" the fact that man may find himself possessed of possibilities of life which, in comparison with those that he had earlier, are extremely abundant. I give it this name, which history may some day adopt in explaining the fact that the primary meaning of "riches" is not to be considered as referring to economic abundance alone, but basically to the riches of life as a whole. The economic meaning of the word is secondary and derivative.

Through this enrichment of the present, this period begins to shape itself as something new in comparison with the traditional past. The result is an enlargement or enrichment of the possibilities of life, of ways of conduct, of things to have, which naturally pushes aside all the vital repertory of the past as something greatly inferior. This more abundant form of life (as compared with the past) has the enormous advantage that it lacks consecration. The ideas, the things, the ways of behavior, the usages which have come surging forth are of one kind today, of another tomorrow, but these are mere crude and naked facts; at the same time we would say that they are materially and technically more abundant, satisfactory, and effective than the old ones they replace. Hence they make up a program of existence which is enormously more nourishing than the earlier ones. Just as you—perhaps not now, but certainly a few years ago —could have and could do any number of things more than the residents of Madrid could have and could do during my adolescence.

These, in short, are new ways of life which are different from and in part opposed to the old and traditional ones. The Romans were clearly aware of this. I mean to say that they perceived they had entered into a way, a form of existence, which had new modes, and was thereby modern. By an accident which may have an explanation and should be looked into by Latinists, the Latins did not describe the matter with that adjective. So far as I know, *modernus* does not appear until the period of Low Latin, in the work of a man named Casiodorus, the last writer who was properly a Latin. But what seems beyond doubt to be true is that a moment arrived in which the whole people discovered the *invading modernity* of their lives as compared with the *legitimate traditionality* of the old. All modernity is the beginning of illegitimacy, of deconsecration. Because, as I said before, it is the mere enlargement of the present which, being made more nourishing, leaves the past behind as a small thing, compresses it, threatens to dislodge it, even in the case of the Romans, who were a superlatively conservative people.

Many of us may not like the idea that modernity in itself may be a germinating illegitimacy and a form of deconsecration, but we have not come here to set forth our own private taste. We are trying to find out what things *are*, whether or not we like them. It does not seem possible that the historians—and I am not referring to Spaniards, but to those of other countries—have not noticed the profound effects which the thing that I have called "enrichment" produces in human life, and therefore in historical reality. Apparently they have rested content—as they could do no less—with noting its superficial effects. But it is this theme, highly important and deeply passionate, from which I must flee as soon as I can.

The fact is that enrichment means modernity, and modernity is a stage of germinating illegitimacy, a life without sacraments that are recognized and meaningful. But if modernity means a life without sacraments, it obviously has other advantages over the legitimate life, in that it occurs in an inexorable manner which triumphs very quickly over legitimate tradition. These advantages of modernity are, in turn, limited by new disadvantages. Of everything that is human one can say that it is at once natal, because something is born and created in it; and mortal, or fatal, because it carries within itself its own congenital poison and the cause of its own extermination. If any one of you prefers not to accept this inescapable destiny joyfully, let him prove himself to be a mineral, or—if he can—an angel.

The disadvantage, the distemper which the enrichment of a people carries within itself is one and the same things as the causes which brought it about, the causes which originated modernity. The life of a people is broadened, made complicated, and enriched as it enters one by one into contact with other peoples who are different from it, peoples with other ways of living that diverge from its own. It begins to recognize intensively that there are other ways of being a man which are different from the only one it has known and practiced, different from its own way, the traditional and immemorial way. Every man, like every people, begins by behaving ingenuously in his primitive isolation—which need not be total; it is enough that it be normal. He begins by believing that he is humanity itself, that he is that which is human. Hence that instant criticism, through which every life goes, in which the "I" that each of us is, discovers suddenly the "you." That is, we find that someone we have believed to be completely identical with the "I" that we are, suddenly reveals himself also to be a human being, but in his own way, in a human way completely different from our own; someone who has the audacity not to be "I," and who persists in being "he"—that one is the "you." This causes us a profound injury, and through the wound which this injury leaves in us we are always open to the infinite diversity of the human being, which D'Annunzio praised: *"Laudate sii, Diversita delle creature, sirena del mondo."*

But this is not a matter of vague poetic suggestions, but a strict concept in the system of historical thought. The life of a people in each of its stages can be characterized by one of these two attitudes: first, being open to other ways of being a man which are different from their own; second, to be—I will not say "closed," because this would be improper, but to be submerged in their own way of being, heedful only of themselves, in short, absorbed in themselves. This affords us a dual historical category whose two concepts stand opposed to one another—that of the open versus that of the self-absorbed. For abstruse reasons which are inopportune here, every category or concept about human reality must be of a scaling magnitude. Do not be surprised—I am not saying anything that cannot be understood. Otherwise I would be failing in that project which I stated at the start. The thing is utterly simple, to the point of being a cliché.

I mean to say that the reality to which that concept refers, although being effectively the reality which it is, has in itself, from time to time, a greater fullness. This explains why, if we review the thing that each period has said about itself, we find ourselves surprised that many of them are always the same. For example, it is probable that there never has been, and never will be a human generation, since civilizations have existed and money was invented, in which its long-lived individuals have not gone through the experience that in the space of their fifty or seventy years, "money has changed hands." Probably this was true each time it was said, but each time it was true with a different intensity, and a different degree of completeness; in some cases it happened in maximum doses, and then that phrase about money changing hands took on a full, exemplary, complete, and prototypical meaning. This must be applied to all the general concepts of history, and it allows us to form in the history of each people a scale of the phenomenon of "money changing hands." And we could do the same thing with any other order of historical reality, a scale in which each period has a greater or lesser coefficient.

Thus, in their dual category—at once open and self-absorbed—those periods have a meaning that is full and complete, but they have other meanings which are weaker and more fragile. One example will show this with greater clarity:

Up to the First Punic War, which ended in 241 B.C., Rome lived completely absorbed in itself, submerged in its own traditions, in its own immemorial customs, and therefore with an intact and solid faith in its conception of every single thing in the world. In this first case we have an example of what values "absorption" has in its greatest sense. After the First Punic War, Rome opened itself to that which was foreign, divergent, and other than itself, but at first this openness was very moderate and relative. Only during the Second Punic War, which ended in 202 B.C., and more particularly a few years later, after the Romans had decided to declare war on Perseus, King of Macedonia—a war which brought with it the conquest of Greece, drenched in an old and most refined culture—at this time Rome opened itself completely to the foreign and the different. The general who conquered Perseus was Paulus Emilio, father of Scipio Emilio, who was then an adolescent, only eighteen. Nevertheless his father made him take part in the battles, and there he forged an imperishable friendship with the great historian

Polybius, a friendship which the latter describes for us so minutely in his book.

Although this may seem a bit of a parenthesis, it is worth noting as a consequence of what I have just said, not only that is a people self-absorbed during the early days of its history, when it is living or practically vegetating in an almost basic isolation, but also that it may return to being so at any time throughout its history, although in a more limited and reduced sense. Spain, for example, which in the sixteenth century was open to all the winds that blew and was even to be found bodily all over the planet, in almost the entire world, began in the first half of the seventeenth century during the reign of Philip IV to withdraw within itself in a very strange manner. In part, this fact is perfectly normal; although the historians have not noted it, all the nations of Europe, for constitutive and physiological reasons in the evolution of peoples, did similar things. But in Spain the phenomenon was much more surprising, for the very reason that she was all over the world, and continued to be so officially, throughout the immense orb of her empire; at the time, that phenomenon consisted in a strange retirement to or withdrawing from the immense imperial periphery into the center of the Spanish world, the newly established court of Madrid.

I cannot tell you quickly the cause of this strange phenomenon, apart from those general ones which in some normal way make up the normal part of things. I cannot even describe in a few words the appearance of that phenomenon. All I can remember are the words of Philip IV to the magistrates of Madrid when he said, "Beat the nobles with the staves of the court to make them help the army of Estremoz." That is to say, the army which, on the Portuguese border, was losing the battle for the crown of Castile. It is clear that Philip IV was the first one to live absorbed within himself in his Madrid, along with his nobles. Nor must one say that that sudden desertion from army life arose out of any lack of courage on the part of his nobles, because those same nobles who in those days were avoiding giving any help to the Army of Estremoz were thrusting swords at each other for the smile of a comedy queen. Another bit of blindness on the part of the historian—now I mean the Spanish historian—in not having noticed the enormous importance that the charms of our comedy queens have had at two moments in Spain's history.

Then came a decisive event, different from the one I alluded to when I was talking of bulls, but connected with it; this would be decisive for the history of Spain even to our own days. The fact is that Spain was not content with remaining absorbed within itself in the way that other nations did in those days, for we are talking of something natural, physiological, which is produced in every people at a certain age, without this absorption-in-self being exaggerated until it becomes a kind of hermetic life. Spain, for the first time, rendered herself hermetic toward the rest of the world, including her own Hispanic world. This is what I call the "Tibetization" of Spain that happened at that time, a concept which should be understood in terms of magnitude of scale: the full meaning of that term is apparent only in Tibet, but the fact is that within the Western world no other people has demonstrated as has Spain that tendency to withdraw and become absorbed in itself, to which, for one reason or another, it always falls back.

Let us look at another example which will serve to employ these very brief minutes that remain, an example in which absorption is very much nearer us, but somewhat less intense than the earlier one. It is the self-absorption which Spain suffered at the time of our own adolescence.

In that Spain of 1880–85, Madrid was not at all interested
in the rest of the world. People lived intent only on
themselves. Not even physically did the good citizen of
Madrid go farther afield than Carabanchal de las Ventas,
or Puerta de Hierro. On this I could give you some truly
curious data. Madrid was absorbed in itself, lived on its
own juice, was nourished on its own existence, enjoyed
itself; and it must be said that it did relish itself. It is this
self-absorbed Madrid which is preserved in that admirable
work, a fine esthetic achievement, which is called *La
verbena de la paloma*. If anyone asks how it is possible
that such a work could have been produced, one must
assume a city that is exclusively attentive to the daily
common quality of its own existence, and therefore nothing that happened in it and affected it passed unper-
ceived; hence it was not content that that reality should
be the reality that it was, but it must be made heroic,
magnified, idealized, that is, converted into myth and
legend.

Hence that Madrid of my adolescence, which was
miserable and poor in comparison to later years, was in
another sense delicious, for it was full of phantasmagoric
figures, legendary and mythological figures that walked
through the streets. If I now pronounce the name of Dr.
Garrido, a most popular apothecary who, with the figure
of another apothecary of the neighborhood, contributed
to creating the personage in *La verbena de la paloma* who
tried to be amusing with puns—and note the fact that a
city could be capable of converting a poor neighborhood
druggist into a mythological personage—this must be
explained—if I pronounce the name of Dr. Garrido and
the dog Paco (which every Madrileño knew) running
masterless through the streets, a dog that had the very
strange gift of discovering day after day in which Madrid
restaurant a banquet was being given, and getting there

punctually on the dot, you will understand that Madrid was full of myths and legends. This means that the Madrid which was absorbed in itself, for the very reason that it was absorbed, had a collective soul. Only when a country or a city is absorbed in itself does it have a soul, can it be understood collectively. And on the other hand the later Madrid, infinitely richer and more varied, is more or less a soulless Madrid, no longer capable of creating myths or legends. The earlier Madrid could not give anyone leave to be mere reality, but he must also always be in addition myth, legend, fable, and chimera.

I think that this makes us see with a certain evidence the meaning of this contraposition of concepts which I consider most important in history: life as absorbed in itself, and life as open to whatever is foreign. We will save many words when I can set before you all the final stages of the evolution of the Roman state, which proceeds in sudden enrichment, from an amplification, a modernization, and an illegitimacy of the collective life.

VIII

Riches and the origin of reason. Modernity and illegitimacy: Spanish examples. Rome's passage from the self-absorbed life to the open life. The Right; the intellectual, the prophet Amos. "Intoxication" through victory. Stoicism and the sun god. The civil wars. The imperial state. The first help for "illegitimacy."

THE OTHER DAY I was left with half a lesson inside myself, which for a professor, is as embarrassing as—to use a baroque phrase—it would be to have achieved only a half-birth because one could not rid oneself of the whole baby. This was lamentable, because it made it impossible for you to see in a single glance the evolution of the state's power (the supreme power in Rome) from start to finish; that contemplation was the more indispensable in that only on arriving at the surprising end is everything that preceded it suddenly filled with meaning.

In attacking the provincialism prevailing in a good part of Spanish intellectual life, we needed to elaborate on certain historic categories without which, one could not understand either the advent of the Roman Empire, or the times in which we live. We came, I think, close to clarification in a series or tryptich of concepts—enrichment, modernity, germinating illegitimacy. I defined *enrichment*, or *richness*, formally as that characteristic situation in which man finds himself facing possibilities of superabundant living, possibilities that are excessive in comparison with those he had earlier. I scarcely developed the content which lies within this definition; I limited myself to making you note that this enrichment, this richness, does not refer here exclusively, or even principally, to the economic field, but that in going back to the oldest meaning of the word (which was discovered first by the great Leibnitz, despite the fact that in his day hardly any one was occupied with semantics or etymology), the word *riches*, I say, refers to an abundance of possibilities in all spheres of life. Chiefly, it includes the radical change which comes to a man when he passes from knowing no other way of thinking than his own traditional one to which he is tied with unquestioned faith, to discovering other and very different ways of thinking; in the face of these he finds himself as before a keyboard of possibilities, of possible ways of thinking or of ideas among which he can and must choose for himself.

While living amid the traditional, man does not choose for himself his way of thinking and behaving but receives it automatically from the past and lives pushed by a force from the rear; when his life is being enriched, he has no recourse but to choose according to his own individual criteria which one of the possibilities now offered him he will adopt and make his own.

Here, succinctly stated, is the origin of what is vaguely called reason and rationalism. Reason is born when man sees himself obliged to choose, on his own personal account and risk, among those multiple possibilities of thinking, doing, being, for the purpose of converting one of them into his own; on this choice he is going to embark with his life, for the moment or forever. As a believer, man does not choose his way of believing or of thinking, but on the contrary he is submerged in his faith, without knowing where he entered into it or wanting to emerge from it. To him his belief does not even seem belief, but reality itself. This is why faith is so firm; it is firmness itself, it is the firmament.

On the other hand, reason, facing this keyboard of multiple possibilities of thought, is constitutionally wavering, vacillating, doubting; hence it is unquestionably less firm than faith. But nonetheless—and note this well—this does not mean that reason does not possess its own peculiar advantages; nor does it mean that whether it is advantageous or not, venturesome or deplorable, reason may not perhaps constitute (I am not now affirming anything) man's inevitable destiny. I mean that perhaps man is condemned to reason; therefore to a task which is always incomplete, always fragile, always having to be commenced anew, as Sisyphus had always to go back to pushing to the top of the mountain the rock that was eternally bent on rolling down to the valley. At this point it is worth noting, as Nietzsche pointed out, that *Sisyphus* is the oldest Greek word that means "the authentic wise man," or as we would say, "the genuine intellectual." In fact *Sisphyus* is *sí-siphos,* is *só-sophos,* and therefore is almost *philosopher*.

And here you have how, without giving ourselves great airs, we have for the first time explained a little of the historic origin of human reason; this consists in the fact that whether he likes it or not, man, at a certain period of history, finds himself disjointed, set aside from the whole ruling knowledge of his people and obliged to choose his own way of thinking for himself, on his own personal account and risk; and in order to choose it, he has no recourse but to decide for himself, and in order to decide for himself he needs to have motives which decide him, and those motives are what we are accustomed to call reasons.

The disadvantage, the infirmity which enrichment carried within itself, I said, is one and the same thing as the causes that originated it. On broadening its life a people has no remedy but to put itself into contact with others. It finds before it ways which are different from its own, and this forces it to a complete change of attitude.

Up to the Second Punic War we see how Rome was tied to its traditional way of thinking and being, and how, during that war, it began to change. And that meeting with other ways of being, different from the traditional, together with the necessities which growth itself provides, brought with it the fact that the people entered into a form of life which had different modes, and was therefore "modern." Modernity is, then, enrichment, and vice versa; but that modern life which is materially and technically more effective than the old one has been created outside and apart from the firm, compact, and consecrated belief on which the pure legitimacy of the immemorial past was founded; it is therefore a form of living without a firm sacrament. Modernity is enrichment, but it is also, on its own account, the germ of illegitimacy.

With all modernity there always begins—this is very clear to us—the struggle between the effective and the legitimate.

Together with this series of concepts, each one of which carries the other—enrichment, modernity, illegitimacy—I set forth another pair of notions—that of self-absorption and openness—descriptive of other attitudes which are adopted into the life of a people or are present in it and which are—I said—magnitudes in terms of scale; that is to say, every general concept about human realities has either a full, exemplary, and prototypical meaning, or a set of various meanings which are more tenuous and relative.

Thus Rome lived absorbed in itself until the Second

Punic War; on the other hand, in the year 168 B.C., on defeating Perseus, King of Macedonia, and conquering Greece, she had no recourse but to enter into an open life—open to that which was different from herself. In that war there took part an adolescent, Scipio Emiliano, seventeen years old; he was born in the year 185 B.C. And here you have the reason why, on constructing the sketch of the public evolution of Rome, I chose the date 190 B.C. as the central or dividing point in the times and the vicissitudes of Rome. My intention—and this is what I am now going to attempt—was to show how Rome moved from that self-absorbed life to the new form of open life which began at that time, around the year 200 B.C. Toward this end I suggested that we should see clearly the self-absorbed life, and this led me to present two examples of that life, though in a relative sense—one at the beginning of this modernity and the other at the end, that is, the end of the nineteenth century. With this I said two things: one, that although a people could not live with a fully self-absorbed life except in its archaic period, in which it is practically isolated, it can, nonetheless, go back in a less intensive sense to being self-absorbed once and again throughout the length of history; and the other, that for the peoples of the West modernity has apparently ended, and we are now in another age to which I am now not going even to give a baptismal name.

The first example consisted in looking at the change suffered by Spain when, from being in the sixteenth century open to all winds and all the worlds, it moved in the first half of the seventeenth century to becoming unexpectedly absorbed in itself; Philip IV was then reigning. In fact, I noted, about that same time this phenomenon was normal for all the nations of the continent, and this means that in the evolution of those nations it is a natural physiological phase, healthy and inevitable. Each of these European nations underwent this shift more or less intensely and in a different way, which we could very easily define and diagnose through a series of differing attributes which would make us see the peculiar figure that self-absorption took in each of them during that seventeenth century.

At that moment the internal life of each nation reached a sufficient fullness so that its own figure and profile would become clear; this led to a situation in which each nation would discover itself and take account of its own peculiar character as compared with the others. This made it draw its attention back within itself, become pleased with its own ways, become proud of them. For the first time, I believe, one began to say, "our poet," "our wise men," "our captains," "our armies." Each nation felt pride in itself. To be nation lifted it to a new potency, and "nationalism" began, which does not mean "political nationalism." (We shall see how very useful all this is in confronting the idea of nation that Toynbee holds.)

I do not know whether, in the histories of literature, this paradoxical fact has been duly emphasized—that the precise beginning of the seventeenth century, around 1600, therefore when Humanism (created in the fifteenth century, developed in the sixteenth) had fallen upon all the elegant cloaks of the social body of each nation, was the moment in which a series of national literatures began—exclusive, different, and particularist. These came just as Humanism was advocating a universal literature based on universal Latin.

This does not mean that the national literatures, once begun, did not influence each other reciprocally. Here is a paradox of great interest on which historians ought to insist.

But the fact is that the phenomenon as produced in Spain—though the dosage was normal—had a surprising character. For two reasons: first, because Spain had been, and still was officially, all over the world; she continued ruling in the world, and—*velis nolis*—had to keep seven or eight armies at the same time in the danger spots of the empire. And second, because this self-absorption came about in a manner which was extreme, we would even call it extremist.

It stuns us and grieves us to behold this sudden retirement or withdrawal of spirits, minds, attention, effort, from the immense periphery of the Empire to its national center, to its new Court, to Madrid. We seem to see the claws of the imperial eagle weaken, as if eager to loose their prey. The Spanish form, the Spanish manner of becoming absorbed in its own people was, then, no simple self-absorption, but one of an extraordinarily pronounced type; it was a kind of retreat into a hermit's life, and this is what I called the other day the "Tibetization" of Spain; a term which for some reason began to attract attention and to be discussed in the newspapers, whereas I believed that the idea which it expressed was more or less conscious in the minds of those who had read a little of the history of Spain.

The other example refers to another and lesser degree of self-absorption, but one which is clearer because we find it nearer; this is the life of Madrid immediately before 1898. I tried to make you see how, except for very small groups of people who read French writers, and of course certain individuals like Valera and others who knew German science well and for this exact reason were exceptional, nothing in the world existed for that Madrid except the city. Madrid lived submerged in itself, delighting in itself, an intimacy which was almost always ordinary and a matter of daily life, because Madrid was at that time, in every sense of the word, very poor. Nevertheless, in attending to those miserable daily realities of common life, the city managed to make out of them legends and myths about itself.

Hence the new paradox—that, although the city was incomparably more poor and miserable than is the Madrid of today, its life was fuller. In that ultimate balance which life always makes automatically and which is, for it, the decisive one, the gain was greater than it is now, for although there are many more inhabitants in the Madrid of today, and each one of them enjoys a greater repertory of possible things to do and have, on the other hand Madrid in those days as a collective entity had, we would say *más gente* ("more people"), using the word in the sense in which we use it when we say of someone that that man is a "person." That *gente* which made the life of Madrid so full was composed of the persons and situations of legend, outside the usual orbit, magnified, stylized. That is to say, life was full of myths. And what is usually called the "collective soul," without the least dependable idea of what that phrase means—as I hope to make clear to you in a future course—consisted of a treasury of myths that everybody knew and together lived them.

Only the self-absorbed peoples, those who lead a confined life and are turned in toward themselves, have enough interior warmth and interior temperature to heat and render incandescent the naked, sordid reality which things in themselves always are, transfiguring them into the brilliance of the mythological. Hence, when I cited the names of Dr. Garrido and the dog Paco I am sure that eyes lit up. And it would be a trivial error to attribute this simply to the chance that I touched sleeping memories of their adolescence.

No. It is not only reality which wakens that fire in

the eyes, but something that is also legend, myth, fable, and chimera. Therefore the same effect, except for degree and dignity, was produced among the Greeks and Romans of their self-absorbed period when they heard the names of Aesculapius and the dog Cerberus as was produced in our own city of myths by the name of our humble proletarian neighbor the dog Paco. Yes, the myths of Madrid in that period were mostly comic, burlesque, and even with a light touch of the lower classes. Remember the incredible amusement—unexpected and well aimed—of the impression which Nietzsche received when by chance, in an Italian theater, he attended a presentation of *La gran vía* by Maestro Chueca; this I am not going to repeat. Well then, if myths are of that type, this does not interest us now, because it belongs to the "content" of that life, and now we are concerned only with the "form" of that life insofar as it is self-absorbed.

In that part of life which remains to me—it cannot be much—I may not again have occasion to present in its true ideological place (which is the definition of the life of a people in its form of the self-absorbed life) an anecdote which would be included in my memoirs if I could wander off to write them. As this is not probable, I want it to be preserved in the memories of the young, for it seems to me stupendous; some day it will be useful for future historians of Spain, who will be much better historians than are those of today.

The anecdote is completely genuine, and a personal recollection of my own. The date was 1892 or 1893. The protagonist was that great Don Francisco Alcántara of whom I talked in my first lesson and who for the first time made me aware of the *Triaca magna* in Morterero's pharmacy in the then little known Segovian town of Campisábalos.

Alcántara was one of those men in the finest physical health that I have ever known. A tall man, with the dark-brown beard of a musketeer, with magnificent black hair on which he used to wear a great broad-brimmed hat, with an artist's shawl, and long feet always shod with boots of the genuine seven-league kind, for it would be hard to find a man who was more of a walker. He was a painter, an editor, and a critic of art for my family's newspaper *El imparcial,* in which my father then spent nights as editor-in-chief and director of the famous Monday editions. As those were surely the peak years of the triumph of *chulería*[1] and the chulos, who were typographers *par excellence* (they were then called "box men"), it is not chance that the protagonist of *La verbena de la paloma* should be a *cajista*—one of the typographers of *El imparcial,* men who set up Alcántara's articles about art, who, always witty, called the artist *"santi, boniti, barati,"* which was the cry with which the then-poor Italians sold their small polychrome statues of saints in Madrid's streets.

Alcántara was the intimate friend of my father from early youth, and the first to range across all Spain to its farthest corners, frequently on foot. Whenever he had a few pesetas—he was a man of most modest means—he escaped from Madrid to unknown towns, to the lost sierras—this out of a delirious love for Spain, an artistic appetite, an eagerness for sport. One night he returned to Madrid after fifteen days of adventures in the wildest and most unlikely corners of Spain. From the station he went direct to the newspaper. Scarcely had he arrived when my father said to him, "You have come just in

1. *Chulos* were young workmen, gaily dressed on Sundays, much painted by Goya, who made them famous. Their days of dominating the popular scene in Madrid were called the *chulería.* The word has no English equivalent [*Translator's note*].

time, Paco, for two of our editors are sick and you must go this minute to the opening of the Teatro Español in order to review the play."

"But how can I go like this, without washing or combing, with this greasy suit, full of stiff thistles, that I wore on my trip?"

My father, who in these matters was peremptory, insisted, nonetheless, that Alcántara go immediately.

At any opening of the Teatro Español "all Madrid" attended; the expression was not mere language, because Madrid was in fact an organic whole; the nobility was there, the writers, the artists, the politicians, the upper bourgeois, and in the gallery sat the most characteristic and savory of the people.

Alcántara arrived just as the curtain went up and sat down in his seat. A few moments later the person next to him, whom Alcántara knew—began to sniff, as if discerning an unexpected odor. Alcántara noted this, and was terrified. He assumed that he smelled like an old shepherd of Gredos who had never bathed. But no: his neighbor said, "Don't you notice a delicious odor in the theater?" Then Alcántara realized the aromatic cause. His pockets were filled with thyme, lavender, marjoram, which he had picked in the heart of the highest Castilian mountains. He had to give a fragment to his neighbor, but then the man on the other side begged a piece, and then another, and bit by bit he was spreading throughout the theater his entire collection of fragrant plants that were born in our mountains. And the Teatro Español, filled with "all Madrid," people who had never gone farther afield than the suburbs, was filled with the fine and wild aromas from those thickets that grow and endure in our countryside; that is to say, the hermetic Madrid which, except for a few hunters, was ignorant even of the nearby Guadarrama Mountains, saw itself invaded by the farthest heights and depths of Spain, the harsh and stubborn ranges, the solitary steppes, the harsh deserts, the smiling hills, the delightful fields of night-shade where the Spanish vineyards now flourish.

With these concrete examples I think we are ready to understand the very rapid glance which we are going to give the passage of Rome from its firmly consecrated and self-satisfied life to its open life, whose end and re-sult is the Roman Empire.

If I were a historian, which I am not nor have ever pretended to be, I would begin the exploration of this shift with a quote from Livy which he, customarily a mere analyst, wrote at the end of the year 212 B.C., therefore in the midst of the Second Punic War; he mixed it, as usual with all the things that had happened in that year. "In the year 212," says the quotation, the very year in which Scipio the African, father of Scipio the Great, died in a battle fought in Spain,

the war was then prolonged more and more, and with it, de-pending on whether things went well or badly, not only did the situations of men change, but so also did their state of mind. Then a mass of forms of religion, chiefly foreign, in-vaded the city, so that it seemed that suddenly either men or gods had been turned into other ones. And this to such a point that the Roman cult was abandoned not only in secret and within four walls, but also in public. The Forum and the Capitol were filled with crowds of women who neither offered sacrifices nor prayed according to the customs of the country. Mystical impostors—*sacrificuli*—and diviners took possession of the minds of the Roman people, whose number had greatly increased with the rustic plebeians, obliged to come together in the city from their uncultivated and devas-tated fields, victims of misery and terror. With all of this it was easy for the impostors, taking advantage of the ignorance of people, to carry on their business, which they exercised as if it were an authorized office. (Titus Livy, XXV, 1.)

In view of this the Roman state had to intervene, and ordered that all the books of prophecies which were found in Rome be burned. Livy, who wrote one of the most delicious books of history, had, as is well known, very little of the historian about him; better explanations could not be asked for, nor a more perspicacious comprehension of the enormity of the facts that he narrates without altering in the least the marvelous tranquillity of his style, a deliberate style with a constant rhythm in the great fluvial vein. And yet that information shows us like an official historic declaration that Rome, wounded to the heart by Hannibal, obliged by him to fight at the same time in distant countries—in Spain, in Sicily, in Africa, in Macedonia—had, through that wound, stayed open to the world of diversity, and that this penetrated Rome, boiling in like a torrent, sweeping out the traditional ways.

Note how Livy, taking it undoubtedly from old official proceedings, diagnoses the radical change in the city's way of living. "It seemed that . . . either men or gods" —the total common belief—"had been turned into other ones." Those strange religions which Livy treats as inferior superstitions are religions which were at base superior to the Roman ones and were going to triumph in the Latin world; they were the religions of Thrace, with their gods Bacchus and Zagreus; the mother-god and her daughter who, for three thousand years, since the first Mesopotamian civilization, were adored in all the Orient (the mother-god is the same as Demeter), that is, Cybele and Kore, the virgin who was adored in the Eleusinian Mysteries; these are the mystics of Orphism and Pythagoreanism.

Farewell to the consensus on which the effective unity of the state was based! Farewell to the total common belief from which this sprang and on which all legitimacy in the exercise of public power was founded! Law was not founded in the last analysis on anything juridical, as the extravagance of Kelsen pretended, an extravagance derived from having misunderstood my Marburg professor, the great Hermann Cohen, just as Stammler had misunderstood him. Stammler was a Jew who had been converted, and Cohen, talking with me, called him *Ab-Stammler*, that is, a deserter or one who has degenerated. Kelsen's theory of law—idolized by jurists and philosophers of law all over the world—could end only with a recantation. Law, I say, cannot be founded on something which in turn is juridical, just as science cannot be founded ultimately on something scientific; but both, when they exist, are founded on a certain total situation of collective human life. Therefore, when common belief is broken, legitimacy is cracked apart.

I have already said that to try to define legitimacy by means of juridical formulas is only the desire of someone who does not understand its reality. Because neither it nor the whole body of rights and laws taken by themselves is more than an abstraction, and therefore they are not truly effective legitimacy or effective law. Law is a function of the whole life of a people, and must be understood from that point of view, in its entirety as in each of its institutions. But note that it was not the intellectuals—nor the outsiders (because there was almost no contact with them) nor the insiders (for there were none)—who opened the breach and started the disintegration of the traditional faith. It was first the discovery that there were other religions different from those of the fatherland. Nothing can crack, break, and pulverize a religion except other religions.

The well-known torpor of historians—and, as usual, when I do not specify any one especially, I refer to foreigners—has never invited them to recount to us well, transparently, lucidly, the most important event that ever can happen in the life of an entire people, namely: how is it that they lose the traditional faith which they held in common? How is it that from being believers they become unbelievers? This, I repeat, is the most serious thing that can happen, but every people, insofar as they are a people, comes inevitably to that day. If they have already done this, one would see how stupid is the idea of believing that intellectuals are capable of that action even if they wanted to be. It is true that the historians, including historians of thought, have never asked peremptorily why and how it is that that being called the intellectual exists in the Universe, how it is that these intellectuals appear at certain specific dates, and I allude exclusively to those who are in every sense genuine.

I do not refer to the poet or the technician, types of mankind that have existed throughout humanity since earliest times, and who have a very definite profile. Nor do I refer to the men in special sciences, above all the natural sciences: biology, physics, chemistry; these are, as historic apparitions, much more recent than the poet and the technician, but they coincide with those in that people have always—some less, some more—had the conviction that they were needed to make things pleasant for them or to ease their sorrows, to invent for them a comedy or a novel, and to invent for them aspirin, the radio, the automobile, and the elevator.

I refer now to certain strange men whose condition has never been defined, equivocal men, without office or post, but never to be suborned, never submissive, who for the very reason of their own incomprehensive condition have not found an adequate name in *any language*. They are given only names whose content is diffuse and imprecise, ridiculous names which it is terrifying to apply to them, like "intellectual," which I chose deliberately because in our present languages it produces almost exactly the same equivocal tone, the same imprecision, the same petulance, and the same sense of the ridiculous as words that came to be applied to such men among the Greeks, such words as *phrontistés*, "thinker"; *sophós*, that is, "wise man"; *sophistés*, "know-it-all"; *philó-sofos*, "friends of wisdom"—which is pretentious —and finally, *prophet*. And I say "prophet" because the first Hebrew intellectuals, who appeared in an astonishing coincidence of dates with the first Greek intellectuals, were actually prophets, but even to them the name was disagreeable, exactly as it irritates us to be called "intellectuals" or "thinkers."

In order to explain the genuine reality of all basically peculiar human activity—whatever it be—one must surprise it in the original hour of its birth, when it is what it is in all its purity, when it still consists only in what it has of naked invention and creation, and has not yet been functionalized, officialized, socialized, and more or less bureaucratized. Hence let us take a moment to glance at the birth of that intellectual who is the prophet.

Thus Amos, first of the poets, a contemporary of Hesiod, first of the Greek intellectuals—there was very little of the poet in him—Amos, when Amaziah says to him, "Do not prophesy any more in Beth'el, which is the sanctuary of the king and the capital of the kingdom," answered, "I was not a prophet, neither was I the son of a prophet, but I was a herdsman and a gatherer of the fruit of the sycamore."

So he refuses the name of prophet because for many previous centuries there multiplied among the Hebrew people men who, in pretense or by using stupefying drugs, presented themselves as possessed, exalted men who fell into frenzies, from which they divined the collective and personal future, charging good fees for it. Professionals of delirium, they made it their business, organized themselves into societies like trade unions, in which their sons customarily inherited their posts. They were frequently a roguish and bribeable people, but extremely popular; they were called *nebihim*—singular, *nabi*. Balaam, with his prophesying ass, is a good example of this—a semi-burlesque figure of Hebrew folklore. Therefore Amos said, "I was no prophet, neither was I the son of a prophet," and made clear the source of his income. But in the verse that follows, Amos declares his genuine vocation, and he has no choice but to use the same word which he just refused—he declares it in a precise formula which affirms the most essential, solemn, and dramatic aspect of the prophet's genuine, pure vocation, and at the same time perhaps—I will not go into this—defines the constitutive and perpetual mission of the intellectual.

Amos says, "And the Lord took me as I followed the flock and the Lord said unto me, go, prophesy *against* my people Israel." But Israel, Jehovah's people, are also the people of Amos. Gentlemen, must every genuine prophet be a prophet *against?* Against what? Against whom? The Biblical word is precise. Against his people, but what does this paradox mean? In this enormous question, let us leave the matter with the prisoner's neck in the *gaucho*'s noose of this enormous interrogation, and let no one come to reduce it to triviality with momentary political interpretations when it is treating of the perennial and desperate mission of the intellectual in this world, a mission almost three times millenary. Some day, in some future course, we will go to the bottom of this theme.

In the previous lesson I said that erudition, which is paperwork in the archives, publication of documents, the editing of ancient texts scrupulously restored, is essential for history, but that even so, it is still not history, for this consists precisely in understanding the human realities to which those documents allude and what those documents are. I take advantage of the opportunity which this occasion offers to present to you a very precise and simple example, by the same token illuminating, of how what I said is true. I refer to the translation of the very short phrase in which Jehovah launched Amos on his career as a prophet. For many years in public lectures I translated those words, as I did here, "go and prophesy *against* my people." The last time was four years ago in lectures given at the University of Lisbon on "Intelligence and the Intellectual." I had learned this in an observation which Rudolf Kittel, one of the greatest contemporary Hebrew sages, made in passing.

Of course I am not a Hebraist, as—strictly speaking— I am almost no more than a man who *almost* says things to you that *almost* make sense. That is enough, enough! Well, then, none of the translators of the Old Testament have customarily translated the phrase that way, in spite of the fact that they know the Hebrew language admirably, as well as the one into which they translate. To what is this error in their versions due? Very simple: to the fact that they do not understand the human reality to which the words refer—what it is to be a prophet, to be an intellectual. As I knew this, I barely stumbled over a short linguistic allusion which permitted me, despite my erudite ignorance, to translate it well. The Seventy translated it badly—they did not understand what that matter of prophesying might be insofar as it was essentially prophesying *against*, and they used a vague preposition *epi*, which may mean "to" or "on," but never "against." The Latin Vulgate translation follows the Seventy and translates that verse as "prophesy *to* Israel" and the next one, "prophesy *about* Israel." The most popular Spanish version, that of Father Scio, follows this. The Protestant version of Cipriano de Valera does not understand the first verse in which Jehovah speaks, but at least the next one, containing words of Amaziah, he translates thus: "Do not prophesy against Israel." [2]

The recent Spanish translations by Nácar-Colunga coincides with this. But note that at last, forced like Kittel by the strictly linguistic fact and clinging to it, the most recent Castilian version (published a few months ago) by the Jesuit Father Bover and Señor Contera translates correctly, "Go and prophesy *against* my people."

Let this very clear example suffice, both for its own simplicity and as an example of how history cannot be written if one does not possess the superior technique which is a general theory of human realities, what I call *historiology*. But I have now left for the future the explanation of why the prophet is, in essence, a prophet *against* his people.

Now it is important for me to state, on account of those precise future explanations, how stupid it seems to suppose that the intellectual is he who destroys the compact and common traditional faith of a people, by the simple admonition that intellectuality itself, that is, intelligence in the strict sense of reason and rationalism, is born within a people precisely because that people has *previously* lost faith, and some of them, having no better means, seek to repair the damage with the only thing left to them, the only thing they have and on which they can count—their poor reason. Thus philosophy was born in Greece about the year 500 B.C. A long time ago I wrote, "that from this point of view, reason, and especially philosophy, is the splint which is applied to a broken faith."

To that invasion of new religions which Livy describes

2. The King James, RSV, and New English Bible all adopt essentially this reading (Amos 7:15–16) [*Translator's note*].

to us and which is going to upset definitely the unity of Roman belief, the partisans of tradition responded as they always have done, trying artificial resuscitation on the most ancient Italian rites like the *ver sacrum* and others. It is the eternal attempt, eternally failing, to return to the *mos maiorum*, the usages of one's ancestors. The result is that religion ceases to be the unitary and common base and is converted into a battleground, and concretely into an electoral battle between reactionaries and revolutionaries. But one quickly understands that as soon as religion is made, really or tacitly, a question of votes, it ceases to be the connecting substance which firmly and solidly unifies the life of a people.

The Roman mind, through its own military victories, had opened and become filled with many possible conceptions of the world. Undoubtedly it had been mentally enriched by this, but then the individual saw himself obliged to choose among that great diversity, to select according to his own personal criteria and decision. In becoming enriched, modernized, the Roman was individualized and personalized. And as the power of Rome in the world was enormous, think what absolute, unlimited authority was represented by the virtual dominion of a proconsul to whom was entrusted all Spain or all Greece or all Asia Minor. As the bloc of traditional civil life disintegrated, those huge, enormous personalities emerged, not oppressed in their development by customs or laws which continue to lose their effective force.

In the European nations personalities of this caliber and format have been impossible. Napoleon himself, as far as personality is concerned—I am not comparing gifts or talents—was an Ursuline nun when compared to Roman figures of the second class from the first century B.C. onward. This is so because all this disintegration of legitimacy, and so on, that we have just been mentioning came about—do not forget it—while Rome was enjoying an absolute predominance in the world. After the Second Macedonian War she remained without any external pressure, without any enemy worth attention which would give a compact character to her life and limit the extravagances and exorbitancies of those men. Add the fact that up to the time of Augustus the Romans kept their effective "heroic" character—a character which in itself was indifferent to good or to bad. It is in Rome that one has to learn what the perverse "hero" is.

This circumstance that Roman dominion did not, in the entire horizon known to them, come up against any competing rival or possible menace gave to their life a certain character of madness. This is the price they paid for their own triumph—what Toynbee calls acutely "the intoxication of victory." But at the same time that invulnerability, perhaps without any other example throughout history, makes Roman history radically different from all the others—for example, from our own —whatever may be its value as an example, from other points of view. And this is what Toynbee does not see.

To the collision with religions which Livy describes was added the discovery and testing of other groups of customs. Polybius, in the thirty-second book of his history, with that genuine historic genius which Livy lacks, undertakes to show us the extreme depravity in habits which the war and the intensive contact with Greece produced in Rome. It was then, for example, that Rome discovered homosexuality. "Love for both sexes," he said, "produced shameful excesses in the young; dedicated to festivals and spectacles, to luxury and to all those disorders which they *learned avidly from the Greeks during the war against Perseus.*"

Three generations later it was not only that. The shamelessness of men like Caesar, Claudius, Mark Antony is explained only if one notices that the world around them is deliberately and by proclamation *against* the old customs; these it scorned and ridiculed, seeking frivolously in contrast those *res novae*—that is, innovation for the sake of innovation, reform for the sake of reform. This prurience, this mania for the new, simply because it is new, this new-ism, is an infallible symptom that a modernity has reached its own summit and will soon consume itself in order to leave room for that other thing which is yet not modernity and into which I did not want to go. In the *Philippics* of Cicero, directed, as everyone knows, against that magnificent soldier, that heroic but infinitely shameless character Mark Antony, I find these words, which could not be better documentation for the general atmosphere. When one wants to turn back to laws, institutions, rights, we hear it said on all sides, "*Negligimus ista, et nimis antiqua et stulta ducimus.*" (Those things, which seem to us old and stupid, are not important to us.) These *Philippics*, from whose title comes our common word *filípica* ("invective") clearly cost Cicero his life. But Caesar would sum all this up in a phrase: "The Republic"—that is, the state with its legitimate constitution—"The Republic now is nothing but a word."

It would seem natural that I should not now hesitate in the least in saying that, in the third place, to the disintegration of common moral norms or norms of conduct, one would have to add the disintegrating effect of Greek philosophy. In fact this is said in almost all the books about Roman history. But it is not right for me to make such a statement, although I might well be expected to do so in order to give authority to all the rest of my doctrine by showing myself impartial, so that the peril of my profession would not be suspected.

But what am I going to do? That disintegrating effect

of Greek philosophy on the Roman people is something I do not find. In the first place, that influence, good or bad, does not appear until the first century after Christ —therefore, within the imperial era. Up to then, only a few very rare individuals or limited groups had had contact with it. It is completely certain that Rome's first revolutionary or demagogue, Gaius Sempronius Gracchus, was clearly influenced by a Greek Utopian philosopher and was therefore mad about reformism. But the same thing did not happen with the series of revolutionary demagogues who would follow, and who were what they were on their own account and not because of any philosophy.

The Romans never had philosophic heads; even worse, they considered all philosophy despicable and improper for a Roman. This is why Cicero, composing his philosophic books in two periods of temporary retirement, felt obliged on the one hand to furnish an excuse for spending his time in such an occupation. On the other hand, even at that late date—with the Roman state already in pieces—he considered it interesting to set forth clearly the doctrine of Greek philosophy for the best cultivated minorities in Rome.

The truth is—and we take advantage of the occasion to say a very quick word about various aspects of several matters, all of them decisive—that it is during the empire of the Juliuses and the Claudiuses (that is, the first century and a half of the Empire) that the Romanization of the provinces took place intensively and rapidly. Well-administered in spite of individual abuses, the provinces increased their economic riches and created for themselves a rich bourgeoisie, while in Italy the same class grew poor and degenerate. That provincial middle class, recently created and recently educated in a philosophy which we might call an intellectual "quasi-religion," in a "culture" which was, in short, Stoicism, is what was going to dominate the following period, the age of the Flaviuses and the Antonys.

One must note—and do not see, in this, specific praise for my specialty—that the only philosophy of truth influential in Rome was Stoicism, and this was not produced until four centuries after the common Roman belief began to disintegrate, precisely in the period of what we call the "Spanish emperors"—Trajan, Adrian, and, following them, Marcus Aurelius—who were themselves Stoics. Stoicism, extended throughout all the nobility and the bourgeoisie of the Empire, gave the world one of its periods of best government and sweetest happiness. It is an incontrovertible fact that when philosophy is effectively influential it is not isolated in this or that individual but prevails in broad and profound social groups—therefore, in the collective soul of Rome; there it achieves, even if temporarily, what seemed impossible; namely, that a people which had lost all vigorous common belief would recover, thanks to Stoicism, *something like* a collective faith which held them together for some time; and as it could do no less, it would promote the only period of *something like* legitimacy which the Roman Empire enjoyed in its five centuries of slow and dragging life. Without judging this fact to be decisive in any sense or for any thing, I do recommend it to the attention of those who would like seriously to follow me in the analysis of life constituted in illegitimacy which we are making, and of which the declining times of the Roman Empire and the times in which we ourselves are living are two gigantic examples.

But the army, which Marius, about the year 100 B.C., had opened to both Latin and Italian proletariats, had to be, after the Antonys, toward the year A.D. 200, opened to the proletariat of the rudest provinces—first to the

Africans with the Severos, then to those of Dalmatia with Diocletian; therefore to those whom we might call super-proletariats. These are the ones who rebelled against the governing middle class, against the bourgeoisie belonging to the Stoic quasi-religion; and then the Empire again loses all unity of belief and is scattered in innumerable mystic local religions.

One day, under Aurelius, an attempt was made to create for the Empire artificially a unique religion, a religious syncretism under the sun god, which would last as a bureaucratic phantom until the times of Constantine. On the coins of Constantine one reads, "The Sun, lord of the Roman Empire." Pharaoh Amenhotep IV had tried the same thing almost two thousand years earlier in order to prop up the Egyptian state, which was then in ruins. Apparently these empires or universal states had by their very essence always suffered from growing stiff with cold, a lack of moral and collective temperature, and terrified, had tried to warm themselves with the sun.

In one century—from the year 190 B.C. to the year 90 —and I give this last date because two years afterward the first civil war would break out between Marius and Sulla—the whole compact bloc which was Roman life had disintegrated. To the disintegration of beliefs and the system of customs that established norms of behavior, there followed immediately the disintegration of the legality of public power, as I showed a moment ago in citing phrases from Cicero and Caesar. No one believed in the Senate or respected it, among other things because the senatorial families had been the first to degenerate; the first men who rebelled, who turned against their venerable authority, were outstanding members of those families.

A series of insubordinations followed: that of the

cavalry, or *equites;* that of the plebeians; then that of the slaves with Spartacus; then that of the allies. But of course, under all of these, there beat the growing conviction that an enormous well-being—the result of the victory that seemed definitive—was possible, and that everyone would have a part of this. In that civilization of insufficient technique this rebellion and this hope corresponded to the ruling consciousness of our present times that man possesses unlimited riches, that there are riches for all, that these riches must be demanded with insolence and violence, because if all of us do not obtain them, this is only because some of us are cheated.

After the first civil war Sulla retired from the dictatorship, restoring, although with a secondary legitimacy, the traditional and legitimate state. But the necessities of the wars with Lepidus, Sertorius, and Spartacus obliged the Senate to annul Sulla's restorative laws and to entrust themselves to the generals, conceding to them powers that were illegal. And as the state had lost all prestige, the masses paid no heed to it; emphasizing the meaning of the ancient clan groups, they joined not institutions but individual men. After Marius, the army was no longer Rome's army, but the personal army of Marius or Sulla or Caesar or Pompey.

That is to say, the public power itself was disintegrating and breaking into a series of highly personal powers in an inevitable struggle of some with the others. From here on, one after another, came seven terrible civil wars. There was no principle that continued in force and to which one might recur. After the Gracchi there began the criminal period, which apparently comes at a certain stage in the life of every people. In legitimate Rome, people had been hypersensitive about everything that was personal violence in civil life. But now assassination was the order of the day, and assemblies could not be held because armed bands burst into the Forum and the Assembly. Criminality and delinquency showed themselves not only in the ease with which assassinations were carried out, but in the whole spirit of the people, and especially in the frivolousness of thinking about persons and affairs on the part of those who understood nothing of this, especially the women. A little later the wife of Claudius, to whom the severed head of Cicero had been brought, entertained herself by pricking the dead eyes with her hairpins.

It is true, then, that these Roman people, on reaching the hour of their greatest civilization, their most adult development, their greatest victory, reverted to the primitive situation of illegitimacy. There was no legal state because there was no state of common spirit in the collectivity. No one had the right to command, and hence some of them struggled with others in efforts to take over the command. The situation had no outlet; it carried within itself no organic and serious solution. Not enough attention has been paid to the fact that a few days after Julius Caesar was assassinated Cicero referred in one of his letters to the fact that he had gone to see Matius, an intimate friend of Caesar, and revealed to him that Caesar himself did not know how to put an end to the situation—literally *exitum non reperiebat*—he saw no way out. The condition which Rome reached after seven atrocious civil wars was expressed by Tacitus, as was his custom, in a verbal commitment which, by the same token, has passed unnoticed by a majority of his readers. When he wanted to explain why everybody entrusted the power definitively to Augustus and the Empire was founded, he said only these two words: *cuncta fessa*—that is, the whole world of people and things was tired, worn out, capable of doing nothing more. For years and years no one was sure of not dying any day by assassination. Horace, thanking Augustus for the order that he had established, declares it,

> Hic dies, vere mihi festus, atras
> Eximet curas; ego nec tumultum
> Nec mori per vim metuam, tenente
> Caesare terras.[3]

This was the title on which Emperor Augustus founded his power—fatigue. His was not a legitimate title, it was an effective title. It was an urgency. It was necessary that someone, whoever he might be, should exercise the public power, take command, and put an end to anarchy. About the year 30 B.C. in Rome there was a strong tide of satiety and disgust toward all politics stemming from the excessive, obsessive dedication to politics which had preceded this—the anxiety to jump over anyone, whoever he might be, in order not to have to bother with politics. And here, gentlemen, is the surprising thing: at the end of the whole thousand-year process which is Rome's history, its chief of state went back to being— just *anybody*. Hence the Empire never had any genuine juridical form, authentic legality, or legitimacy. The Empire was essentially a shapeless form of government, a form of state without authentic institutions.

Everybody—*cuncta fessa*—needed it, but as it was not and could not be a normal state because it could not enjoy legitimacy, they needed it but nobody wanted it, *not even Augustus*. Because this is the incredible but extremely revealing fact of this whole reality. Things went so badly that in the year 22 the Senate resolved to name Augustus *dictador*, "dictator" or "censor"; that is to say, with another name, Emperor. But Augustus, who was rather timid and lacking in confidence, felt terrified at the possibility of being charged with exer-

3. Horace, Ode 14, Book 3 [*Translator's note*].

cising the supreme power, and for this reason he *fled* to Sicily, that is, fled from the dictatorship, fled from the Empire itself. Then part of the Senate went out in pursuit to oblige him to return to Rome and be made *dictator, prince, emperor.* As Ferrero says very well, "the dictatorship pursued the dictator."

This imperial state which began with Augustus was going to exercise its empireship in a superlative form, never experienced until then. It was the pure compression of public power, naked of any consecration. *Apparently the state increased its pressure* on individuals strictly as and in the degree that belief diminished. Belief was an internal discipline, and as it faltered, external discipline was automatically intensified.

We have reviewed—in sketch form but completely— the evolution of public power from its beginning to its end in the only history of a people—that of Rome— which is known to us from its cradle to its grave. And we have discovered something astonishing which at the same time gives us a most penetrating light, which I have not seen noted up to now by either the historians or the jurists and philosophers of law, in spite of the fact that it is a phenomenon of such obvious importance. It is this: that the state, the exercise of public power, begins by being illegitimate and ends by being illegitimate; that as a people reaches its extreme maturity the most unexpected thing happens: the reappearance of all the characteristics which the statal function manifests when it is primitive. Of this function there remains only what it has of urgent surgery, of social reaction in the hour of peril; the agent of this function is not the Chief by any right, but anyone at all can hold this post; everybody needs it and nobody wants it.

Does this not illumine (with a cruel and impious glare) what truly constitutes the state in the very nucleus of its essence? I am not going to answer this question now. I will only do it if I can offer you next autumn a course on the basic phenomena of society with the title *Man and People*.

But what seems evident is that the State *does not consist* in legitimacy; this is a happy addition, a fortunate virtue which people in its best centuries managed to give it, thanks to their purity of spirit, the integrity of their beliefs, their loyalty and their generosity, all of them qualities which go on evaporating as illegitimacy advances.

But a new question, less theoretic than the former, more serious, more urgent, arises in us; it was sparked when I said, "What should we do when the life of a whole civilization enters the stage of constitutive illegitimacy?"

I am not going to answer this question immediately. It is possible that in subsequent lessons this answer may come in the form of delicate hints. But I can say now what is the first thing to be done if one wants to confront and correct the tremendous historic opportunity which is illegitimacy. The first thing to do is simply to recognize it, to take account of the fact that this is the deep reality which constitutes the period, rather than trying to elude it and attribute it to the insubordinations and disobediences of this man or that, this group or that class. A problem cannot be solved unless its existence and its consistence are clearly seen. Therefore the very first thing that has to be done with illegitimacy is—to swallow it. Then we will see.

IX

Revision of the itinerary. The Right and
the Just. Crete. The "universal influence."
Civilization and "primitive society."
The spontaneous civilizations.
Challenge-and-response.

IT HAS SEEMED for some time as if we had forgotten
Toynbee; nevertheless we are going to see how, with
all this we have been gaining speed in setting forth the
rest of his doctrine. We abandoned it when, led by him,
we were trying to define Greco-Roman civilization,
which is our mother civilization, by taking note of its
chronological destiny—when and where it began, when
and where it ended.

We were present at its destruction, caused, according
to Toynbee, who accepts common opinion in this, by
an invasion or immigration of barbarous peoples who,
until then, had been contained beyond the frontier; a
Völkwanderung of what he calls the "external proletariat" of that civilization. This eruption of the barbarians
brought with it centuries of chaos which he calls an
"interregnum" because these were centuries without order or agreement, in which nobody held command.
Then, going backward, we saw that the Greco-Roman
civilization enjoyed its final stage of structured existence
in the form of a universal state, which was, we might
say, invaded from bottom to top by a universal religion
born among the "internal proletariat" and lodged in the

almost subterranean depths of that society. This universal state was the Roman Empire, and in it we stopped, like a tourist or a guide, to complete the external picture which Toynbee presented to us with an image of that same reality as seen from within. But we could not do this—that is, could not understand that historical reality which was the Roman Empire, without submitting our historic glance, as the eye of the historian requires, to a great swing of the pendulum, backward and forward. This led us inevitably to uncover the entire Roman past.

All human reality, as I said, comes from a past and goes toward a future; this in no way implies any addition to its substance, but consists in essence of a "coming from" and a "going to," in getting hold of the past and the future. Hence we had to look through the Roman Empire as though it were translucent in order to discover in its present (as though in a fluoroscope), the past *whence* it came. And this is why we had to retrace the whole of Roman history from the inside, from its intimate self; we did this in an ultraschematic manner, and paying attention to what Mommsen taught us to consider as the very substance of Rome's history: namely, the evolution of its public laws, of its state.

So in previous lessons I tried, then, to construct a sketch of Roman history on the thread of the evolution followed by one of its components that is most important in the life of every people: namely, its supreme power, the function of command insofar as it is a collective command—because clearly there are constantly, along with this one, other forms of command, some of them arbitrary, some satisfactory or some vexatious; for instance, the command of the strong over the weak, of the rich over the poor, the beloved over the one who loves. Doing great violence to myself, I had to leave out of consideration the thing that most interests me in the human reality which was the Romans, the very peculiar Roman attitude toward law as such, whether public or private. This interests me because I believe that it is even more fundamental than paying exclusive attention to its supreme power, and even to its public laws. But I could not go into this because I would dare to hint that no one has properly examined what the Roman understood and lived with under the name *derecho*,[1] which for the Roman was law as such, not this institution or that.

In my judgment, it was to that peculiar manner of feeling their law that the Roman people owed its incomparable vigor—unique as a historic force. But this is, I suspect, what has not been well seen; what has been known to be admired in Roman law is the perfection of its juridical technique, and within this the almost mathematical precision which its concepts acquired; but this must inevitably lead one to ask why it was that in Rome itself the juridical technique achieved such perfection, in place of attributing it to a kind of magic gift or casual talent which the Roman people possessed.

Evidently there is something peculiar in the primary relationship (earlier than all technical perfection) of the Roman with his law which other peoples do not have in the same measure. It led the Roman naturally to lend to the exercise of his laws an unusual attention, at once energetic and continual; thanks to it, for century after century the marvel of its jurisprudence went on being shaped and woven.

If this has not been evident, I fear it is because of an erroneous and very vague idea of what law is, not only

---

1. The Spanish word *derecho*, like the French word *droit*, may mean either "law" or "right." Spanish usage is doubly complicated in translation because the English word *law* may be represented by *derecho* but also by *ley*. Ortega's distinctions are not always clear in either language [*Translator's note*].

in Rome, but absolutely, and I could not give recognized notions about this which seemed to me to accord with reality. Hence I would have been obliged to begin by developing an entire general theory which is usually called wrongly a "philosophy of law"; this is certainly not called for at the moment. The only thing I can do now, and with due attention to those who feel a genuine curiosity about this subject, is to say that for the Roman, law is not law because it is just, but on the contrary, the just is just because it is law. Therefore Law for the Roman, in its nucleus and its primary substance—and perhaps this is true in the absolute—has nothing to do with what is called these days, in the newspapers and elsewhere, justice. Justice will come as an addition or perfection of that primary reality which is the law. So the Roman idea of rights and law was completely opposed to the one predominating in European minds, at least in the last two centuries.

In that statement, I refer strictly to what Law was as a reality which the Romans lived effectively, *not* to what Cicero first, and then the "Institute," the "Digests," and the "Pandects" defined in general terms as law, these had nothing to do with the real Roman law, but were ideas received from the Greek philosophers by the Roman jurisconsuls at much later time.[2]

2. Note: This formula is deliberately made extreme in order that my idea may be seen clearly. It is beyond question that the concrete figure of the Roman juridical institutions not only permits but obliges one to sketch a general profile of Roman law concerning rights which, compared with a similar sketch of other laws, would show certain very important and partly exclusive peculiarities. There is nothing more natural than to consider those differentiating characteristics as "the Roman aspect" of Roman law, and this is what has always been done when one wanted to define or to diagnose that institution. But without denying any part of that, which is obvious, my idea would be to rework against

They are, then, the philosophic pieties surrounding right and law and for a Roman Law was the exact opposite of a piety; it was a tremendous and crude reality.

Toynbee looks from the outside at that Roman past which we have seen from within, and of it he is interested only in telling us a little more or less of the following: before the Greco-Roman civilization was established in the Roman Empire, in what was called a universal state, it passed through several centuries of wars between the nations which made it up. These wars he calls, generalizing the name of a period characteristic of Russian history, "periods of revolt," which correspond to what in Chinese history is called "periods of contending states." The age of the "periods of revolt" in Russian history

---

this procedure and make it clear that that difference between Roman law and others, except for the comparison between concrete institutions, is effective but secondary. The first and most decisive thing is the way of feeling the law generically and as it is, because this way of feeling is what gives those institutions their full and genuine meaning. The institution of *pater familias*, for example, could exist, and in fact has existed in other laws, but as these other laws, insofar as they were law, were meant in another way, the face of the institution, in spite of the identity of their silhouette or underlying idea, was completely different. Imagine a people who go constantly changing their institutions, who do not see stability as their most important factor, their being, as something on which one *always* can and would count. It is evident that the *pater familias* of that people would not in the least resemble, as a genuine historic reality, the Roman *pater familias*.

This is not the time to set forth the matter in all its generality because it would become too abstract. Using, then, the case of the Roman idea of Law as an example, I would say that it is necessary to distinguish three different levels:

First, the juridical reality lived effectively by the Roman, therefore law as a reality, that is, in the primary full and substantive meaning of the term;

Second, the reflection on the reality of the professional tech-

was the eighteenth century, and the episode of the false Demetrio belongs there. But the "period of revolt" in Greco-Roman civilization begins, according to Toynbee, in the Second Punic War, but for none of the reasons that led us to fix that date as a dividing point in Roman times; it is simply because Rome then enters into war with Greece, as if the tremendous earlier wars between the successors of Alexander and the portions which were taken from the Empire—Egypt, Macedonia, Seleucia— had been nothing but "the turkey's crest."

And here, although I am not going to insist on it, we come to one of those intellectual tricks which are scattered through Toynbee's work; this is the fact that at other times he has no remedy but to recognize that the "period of revolt" in Greece clearly began with the Peloponnesian War, which happened two and a half centuries

---

nical jurists, hence the technical theory of law or jurisprudence which is not juridical reality *sensu stricto;*

Third, the reflection on this jurisprudence which an abstract theory of law gives, that is to say, the so-called philosophy of law.

There were no philosophers in Rome: there was, beginning with Cicero, only a somewhat dull and heavy reception of Greek doctrines. The distance, then, between general definitions which begin with this and then go back and forth, spattering the works of jurisconsuls during the Middle and Lower Empire, and the legal reality expressed in the first statement, is so great that it does not help to conceal it.

This is a matter, then, of creating a new eye in order to see all these problems, penetrating through the theoretic crusts which have fallen over them and making the eye able to contemplate reality itself, which is almost always completely different from all those definitions. The first thing to be seen with this new eye, is that to talk of Right as a reality in itself, is an error *a limine.* The "juridical" aspect of right or of law is *only* one part of its effective reality; its other part is a portion of things in the life of a people which, given the erroneous optic customarily used, seems to have nothing to do with it.

before the war with Hannibal, the Second Punic War. But as he is bent on uniting Greek civilization and Greek history with Roman history in a single civilization, he does not call it Greco-Roman, but another name which I have not mentioned up to now and will never mention because I would then be obliged to a somewhat tempestuous struggle with Toynbee, temporary to be sure, although at the same time it would lead us to discover one of the most genial and valuable things in English life.

According to Toynbee, before those rebellious times the Greek and Romo-Latin peoples lived long centuries of what he calls "formation or development" which correspond in a certain way to what I have described here as a "self-absorbed life," but even earlier than that we found the Hellenic and Latin peoples as primitive peoples, who, coming then from the Euro-Asiatic north, stumbled on the Mediterranean. So that as, in seeking the beginning of our own civilization, we found that it began in a *Völkerwanderung*, with some barbarians of the North who erupted into the Greco-Roman area, so also when the Greco-Roman civilization began, we find some northern barbarians who are now the Hellenic and Italic peoples. We do not know exactly when these latter entered Italy, but like the Hellenic peoples they must have come down to the Mediterranean in successive waves, with long intervals of time between one and another. We do know that the first great Hellenic invasion of the Eastern Mediterranean happened about fourteen hundred years before Christ, and that the second and last invasion, that of the Dorians, which the Greeks called "the return of the Heraclidae," began about 1200 B.C.

What was it that these new barbarians from the north invaded? They invaded a most refined civilization which was there on the Aegean Sea earlier, and which is the one that Toynbee, with his arbitrary way of giving names, calls "Aegean or Minoan." Its geographic figure, compared with that of our civilization and the Greco-Roman, is much smaller. Its center is the Island of Crete, and it extends through the Islands of the Aegean, part of continental Greece, and the edge of Asia Minor including Syria.

I would not like to enter into too many details. Here is how I sum up my idea of what we should know of this Aegean civilization. Of it we have only objects and stones uncovered by careful excavations, but no texts, because even when we have very numerous inscriptions these have shown themselves enormously resistant to all attempts at deciphering them.[3] This very week a prize memoir has just appeared in which it seems that a step forward has been taken in this deciphering; I owe this to Don Benito Gaya, to whom I alluded in an earlier lesson.

The first invasion of the Hellenes into the Aegean world is verified as about 1400 B.C. These newcomers were the oldest Greeks, the Achaeans They burned the most beautiful palaces—Knossos, Gournia, Palaikastro. In 1200 another great destructive wave came down, and this time everything perished. The famous Labyrinth was destroyed. In a very recent book the great Czech philologist Hrozny, who had been able to decipher nothing less than the Hittite cuneiform writing and even the hieroglyphic writing of another Hittite people called the "hieroglyphic Hittites," assures us that the word *labyrinth—labyrinthos—*means precisely "the palace of the sovereigns," "the royal palace"; the place where it was found included the temple of a divinity of the Cretan religion, which was the anthropomorphic bull, the famous Minotaur.

It was known that *labyrinth* was, in fact, a word of

3. This was written before the Linear B discoveries [*Translator's note*].

Hellenic origin, as its root *labrys* indicates; part of the word is also Greek, but not of Greek origin, and it means, for the Greeks themselves, the double axe, an axe which was the supreme religious emblem of the Cretans and at the same time the most important symbol of majesty. Well then, *sovereign*, so far as one can find out, for very complicated reasons, was in Cretan "*taburna*" [Spanish for tavern] or "*laburna*," because in cuneiform apparently the consonant complex *TL* is translated sometimes by *T* and other times by *L*. So Hrozny derived *labyrinth* from *laburna* and the suffix of place, which would indicate the palace of the sovereign.[4]

I have cited this detail simply because it is a novelty and probably not known to anyone, or scarcely anyone, of you, but it would not make sense for us to go on constructing an elemental history of each of the civilizations to which we are going to refer, nor does Toynbee. What we must do is to cling to what is important for Toynbee's doctrine, in this case the Aegean or Minoan civilization. What interests us is only this: we know from the Greek historians that, thanks to their seacoast, the Cretans had enjoyed a certain domination. Island people and sailors, they had made progress in navigation; their ships ruled the seas and permitted them to extend their commerce to regions that were vast and remote. Not only did they reach Greece, but also Sicily and Sardinia. A quarter of a century ago it was thought that they also had arrived—around 1400—at the Mediterranean coasts of Spain. To this was attributed the fact that in the most primitive stages of prehistory there were found glass beads which the Cretans had received from the Egyptians but had learned to imitate for export. To this there also seemed to be attributed the taste of our ancestors—assuming that this is what they were—for certain beautiful

4. B. Hrozny, *Histoire de l'Asie antérieure*, 1947.

decorations which appear in ceramics from Alicante to Narbonne and also in the Balearics, where very much later, Cretan religious objects, their source not known, were found, like the classic heads of a bull with a dove between his consecrated horns.

But in the books of modern Spanish archeologists this is flatly denied. And clearly I have nothing to say in cases like this where it is a matter of things stated by people who know their subject very well—for one must point out, as a positive gain in the last twenty years of Spanish intellectual life, the existence of excellent teams of archeologists, a thing which previously did not exist. There were, it is true, certain individuals. Above all there was Gómez Moreno, whose wisdom about these facts and knowledge of things seems to have had no limit; but there were no teams that were sufficiently complete and well prepared as there are today. Therefore, in cases like this I can do nothing but bow and say no more direct word. Only indirectly would I dare to propose to Spanish archeologists that they might see if it would not make sense to continue their investigations or to revise some of the past ones in the light of the most important fact which has been produced in the last few years in the perspective of the science of history; this is the imperative need to recognize (for abundant facts support this) that the very old civilizations, above all the Mesopotamian and even the oldest of these, the Sumerian, had an expansive influence which was far more important in the whole continental European body than could have been imagined; that is to say, one must run over the distances in the movement of those peoples with respect to what was previously considered impossible.

Having made this observation in a matter in which—I repeat—I am very ignorant, I can only go ahead. We are moving toward what is important for Toynbee.

The primitive Hellenic peoples, that is, the barbarous Hellenes—let us give ourselves for once the pleasure of pronouncing this paradox, "barbarous Hellenes"—destroyed that Cretan maritime power (which the Greeks called *thalassocracy*), that empire of the sea which, according to Toynbee, was a universal state; therefore, in our trip backwards, starting from the Western civilization to which we belong, back through the Greco-Roman civilization until we reach the Aegean, we see repeated, according to Toynbee, the same stages with the same characteristics; this makes him presume—if indeed it needs proof—that societies of this kind called "civilization" always begin with a *Völkerwandung* or invasion of barbarous peoples, or "external proletariat," which produce a chaotic state of some centuries of "interregnum." To these there follow other centuries of formation and development, after which come "times of rebellion"; these, in turn, end when one of the nations that make up this civilization comes to dominate the others, making a universal state, and with it a Pax in which there generates and matures a universal religion originating in the "internal proletariat" of that civilization. The six volumes of Toynbee do nothing but manipulate constantly—and we will see that this is an exasperatingly mechanical method —that bundle of concepts. But that presumption demands proof, and this assumes that we have in view all the civilizations of which we possess information, so as to be able to see whether this process is fulfilled in them.

In a rather summary fashion, Toynbee claims that there have been twenty-one civilizations, neither more nor less. It does not make sense now to enter into a discussion of whether all the presumed civilizations which Toynbee lists and names are actually that or not, because he has taken no great effort to determine this, and it does not make sense for us to oppose to his elegant display a seriousness of method which he does not practice. What is urgent for him is to find himself facing all these civilizations in order to see whether or not the facts in their various historical developments reveal all those stages to which I referred and, above all, those characteristics which to him are the definitive ones of a civilization: that they end in a *Pax* created by a universal state and in a universal church of proletarian origin.

If you put on your work table a series of manuals, each one of which relates the historic vicissitudes of each of these twenty-one civilizations, and manage to find out whether in fact each of them has passed through a *Völkerwanderung*, and so on, and so on, you will have done approximately what Mr. Toynbee did; but do not think he has done much more. What happens is that Mr. Toynbee calls this applying the "empirical method" to history; and when an Englishman thinks that he is going to apply the empirical method to something, he experiences such satisfaction, he feels so happy and secure, that, leaning back in his armchair, he lights his pipe and in the white clouds of rising smoke sees his problem solved. And clearly it is, but certainly not in all cases.

In Toynbee's case, and in that of more than a few English writers of recent years, there is hidden under what is called the "empirical method" the totalitarian resolution that the ideas which the English had previously in their minds shall echo in the facts discovered. So it is in the present case, in which Toynbee comes forth resolved, whether you like it or not, to discover in the Aegean civilization a universal state which was not there. And in view of this he decrees that the almost unarmed thalassocracy of Minos was this universal state. (As the man from Malaga said, "Whether it sticks or not, I am going to paint a parrot on the back of your head.") And this is not a matter of our having a different idea of the universal state than has Toynbee. No; resolved to follow him with utmost docility, we accept his notion, which is neither more nor less than what the Roman Empire shows. Well now, this was the integration of various nations under a single public power; some of those nations were primitive, like Gaul and Spain, others were much more advanced, more civilized, old, rich, and structured, like Rome herself, like Egypt, Greece, and Syria.

When the Greeks talked of the thalassocracy as a reality, it being most remote for them, they understood by that word simply what the word means: "dominion," "empire" if you like, "over the sea"; but they did not have any information, nor have we, nor can Dr. Toynbee have it, that the Aegeans dominated any people, any nation; because, among other things, within their orbit of influence nations did not even exist. Apparently they colonized some of the small Cyclades islands which were uninhabited, or nearly so; those that had people on them were inhabited by the Carian pirates whom the Aegeans abolished in order to clear the sea of piracy. But what one has no information about is of any war or any warlike encounter by the Cretans. Herodotus himself, who notes something of what he heard of the Cretans of his time that alluded to vague wars, shows himself incredulous, and Thucydides, in the first book of his *History*—in that famous part on which perhaps the Institute of the Humanities will comment, word for word, for it is the first scientific expression of the human past and especially of the Hellenic past—Thucydides insists that what the Aegean intervention produced was the possibility for coastal peoples to trade peacefully and to enrich themselves, each for himself.

This tale of what the Cretans achieved indicates that they were not a very dominating people. And, in fact, the Cretans were not warlike. During the greater part of their history their cities and palaces were not surrounded by walls, nor were the people even preoccupied in defending themselves; if there ever was in history a somewhat feminine civilization, that is to say, one that was not pugnacious, it was that of the Aegeans. Certainly they had a wide and vigorous influence, although never very profound, in part of Greece and the coast of Asia Minor, but that influence was obtained not by violence, but by grace. They conquered nobody, but they seduced many people. To put it formally, the Cretan civilization must have been enchanting, and hence its best symbol is its principal goddess, dressed in a long ruffled skirt, in the Andalusian manner, who always appears carrying in her hands and arms, wrapped around her, the serpents that she had charmed.

To consider this Cretan thalassocracy, so soft and so gentle, the equivalent of the Roman Empire, with its imperiousness, its tremendous and inexorable will to command, to call both of them with the same name— *universal state*—is to want to turn out the lights, so that all the cats will become gray. From a certain point of view which does not deprive it of other virtues, Toynbee's book is a strange attempt by means of the gigantic, the pertinacious, and the unpleasant, to turn gray all the cats of history.

But matters become even more difficult when he searches in Aegean history, as preceding the Greco-Roman, the other characteristic sign: a universal religion which would have originated in the internal Aegean proletariat and would have become the firm and fruitful base of Greco-Roman life. But it happens that no one has any information whatsoever as to what the "internal proletariat" of Crete might have been; moveover, the constitutive religions of the Hellenes and the Romans were completely the opposite of the Cretan, and did not come from any proletariat, but from what Toynbee himself, not I, calls the "dominant minority." The Olympic gods are, in fact, the gods of noble warriors and hence are themselves belligerent gods. Toynbee recognizes this, and does not dare to name—this would be an enormity— the Aegean civilization as the maternal ancestor of the Greco-Roman, as one might say that the Greco-Roman civilization is the maternal ancestor of ours or that ours is affiliated with that one.

But as Toynbee is not resolved to surrender to facts, as he cannot state firmly that the Greco-Roman civilization was born as the daughter of the Cretan—that there is between them that relationship which he defines as paternal or maternal and filial—nevertheless, he decides to affirm that the Greco-Roman civilization proceeds from the Aegean; but he adds a question. This question is infinitely English. Interposed as a bumper between the facts and his preconceived idea, the Toynbee query means something like a *gentleman's agreement* between the data and his whimsical conception which allows him to go on quietly smoking his pipe.

Well now, such a query would be admissible if the reasons pro and con whether the Greco-Roman culture could have been derived from the Cretan balanced each other, or even if—although the negative reasons predominated—in the last analysis some weighty reasons should exist to affirm that derivation. But even at a distance this does not happen; in no sense can it be said seriously that the Aegean civilization was the one that engendered the Greco-Roman. In no sense can it be said seriously that the good Cretans were teachers of the Hellenes and the Romans; these good Cretans who were artists, merchants, sailors, dancers, and bullfighters. Therefore this query may be a query, but not a serious one. And I ask you now to note this much against Toynbee—and let it not

become an "if, by chance," an "I have not yet decided"—
when in the last lesson I frame my personal judgment
about his person and his work, you may throw in my
face that I am aggressive, harsh, and exigent.

The truth is that for almost twenty years there has
existed not only in Spain but in the whole world a lack
of shame in the exercise or the pseudo-exercise of intelligence; paradoxically, this coexists with forms of cen-
sorship that are more or less severe, governmental in
some countries, direct and social in others, which becomes the same thing—a lack of shame, I say, that we
must do everything possible to put an end to, because
it is diminishing the Western mind in a most serious way.
Here, in this example, which is a detail, you can see a
representative sample of how an intellect can be out of
shape. Because only to someone who is intellectually not
in good form could it occur to commit such a slip. The
fact is that in the recently published résumé of Toynbee's
work, where he could have taken advantage of the opportunity to correct his major slips, he expresses the
same thing in a way that is even worse, for he says that
the Aegean civilization is *"vaguely linked in parenthood"*
to the Greco-Roman. What does this mean, "vaguely
linked in parenthood"? It is as if we were to say of
someone that he is "vaguely" the father of his sons, a
thing that should be said at a convenient distance from
the father in order to avoid an immediate reprisal. It is,
in fact, a fearful deformity, and I can assure you that in
no German or French book, even of the second or third
class, would you find a similar lack of decorum. Why
does this happen among a people as formidable as the
English, in which there is as much knowledge as there
is anywhere else? It is truly an enigma, which perhaps, if
we had time, we might try—at a distance—to unravel by
managing to say what it means for an Englishman to

write a book; because this is completely different from what it means for a German, a Frenchman, or a Spaniard to write a book.

But for Toynbee's doctrine, the matter itself has a most disastrous aspect. Not being able to state frankly, without question, that the Greco-Roman culture is the child of the Aegean, the former is left without any known origin; the culture that is most important for Toynbee and for us, the model culture, remains without parents, spurious, like an orphan and charity child. And in Toynbee's own doctrine this is inadmissible. For if the Greco-Roman civilization has no precedents, it must then enter into the class of absolutely original civilizations, which do not proceed from any other. For him, there are in Eurasia only two of these, the Mesopotamian or Sumerian and the Egyptian; both of these pose for Toynbee special problems of great interest—this is one of the most interesting parts of his work—in an attempt to find out how one civilization emerges when it is not born from another, when it is not the daughter of another. The fact is that there would not be any way.

This is not the moment to outline more exactly the scientific conduct of a man like Toynbee, observing his manipulations with some attention when he is forced to gather together every religious form he can find in the Aegean world which also appears in Greece. But first, his theory does not demand that; what one would ask would be that he prove that those religious forms which were common in both Greece and the Aegean originated in an "internal proletariat of Crete."

Second—a curious situation—Toynbee could have taken advantage of a great many more events, that is to say, effective religious and other phenomena, which there were in Crete, and which appeared also in Greece. But the fact that he does not know that Cretan civilization

well, or, in general, any other except of course the Greek
and also the Arabian, results in his not noticing this. Outside of being an internationalist—remember my first lesson—as well as being an Anglo-Saxon journalist, he is
badly informed, and, this time, apparently against his
own best interests.

And third, in a certain way all those facts which he
seems not to know would not serve to make a base for
his desire to derive Greek culture from the Aegean, because this is a matter of a gigantic current whose effects
are very deep. These come from very far off, and each
time it appears more clearly—facts and documents continue to show it—that Greek culture comes from the
most primitive culture, from the depths of the Mesopotamian world, where it arrives, as I said before, from
incredible regions.

This, I consider the most important innovation in the
historical perspective of the last quarter of a century.
But that influence is of a type radically different from the
only one which Toynbee admits up to now, the influence
of one civilization determined by another, what he calls
the relationship of paternity and filiality. And that gigantic current of influence is not determined, its limits are
undeterminable because it is in fact properly and strictly
universal. That is to say, there is something more important than that pretended mother-daughter relation
between one civilization and another, and this is the universal influence; this is fatal for Toynbee's doctrine, because he began by stating that the intelligible historical
field, the historical reality which is understood without
moving away from it, is a civilization. But in order to
understand a civilization there is no other course than to
move away from every civilization to a field that is far
more vast. And in fact, although the thing seems incredible, in Book VI, the last one yet published, Toynbee, who

is of course ultimately faithful, hits himself on the head and says, "The Devil"—he does not use that word, but its equivalent—"In the first five volumes of my work I have continued to uphold the idea that the intelligible historic field is a civilization, and now I see that I was wrong, that there are universal influences."

There you have one of the amusing things which are found only in English books, and which can be understood only if one explains what it means for an Englishman to write a book.

When the Aegean civilization began, there were already the two great primary civilizations, the initial Mesopotamian (the Sumerian) and the Egyptian. The Cretans promptly got into contact with them, traded with them, but did not burst upon them or into their area, nor did they try to include these in any universal state. Toynbee does not know what to do with the Aegean civilization, either, and stuttering indecisively, he declares it "vaguely original." In all events we are transferred, as to a court of last instance, to those two civilizations that are even older. The initial Mesopotamian, or Sumerian, puts us in the year 4000 B.C.

Here the historic perspective changes, and this poses for Toynbee a totally new problem, for as this is a civilization that has no precedent, proceeding from no other, he has no choice but to pose to himself in a peremptory fashion the question of how one civilization is born when it is not the daughter of another, when it is, so to speak, born by spontaneous generation. How is it, he says, that after three hundred thousand years with no civilization of this type, this thing should come forth one good day on the banks of the Tigris and the Euphrates, this thing completely new in the planet, which is a civilization?

It seems natural, and it would occur to all of you, to try to derive these civilizations from the preexistent forms of life in primitive societies, which we previously called savage. Never mind that primitive life is not called a civilization, although it is completely impossible to discriminate between where the savage ends and the civilized man begins: but what is beyond question is that those two first civilizations had to be born in continuity with primitive life. And in fact, in Egypt as in Mesopotamia, that primitive past of their inhabitants is of course present in those regions, as the primitive or savage past is of course present in Greece or Rome. As it is present in all of us.

I suggested in an earlier lesson that the human past does not pass away, if by passing away one understands simply ceasing to be; the human past does not end as what is past ends in sectors of the physical world, but it persists throughout the entire present in the peculiar form of having been. It is too often disregarded, I think, that the past, in being properly the past, must be this in a present, must be conserved in a present. Otherwise there would be no past, but simply nothing, pure nonexistence. It is man that conserves this past in the present. Man is an animal that carries destiny within himself, that carries within himself *all* history. There is no definition of man which is less "Darwinian." If I cite certain primitive, therefore savage, things which we do and are, although confining myself solely to things that are evident and without going out of bounds, it is possible that some one of you who perhaps boasts the pretense of not being savage might be disgusted. This would not include me. I am completely convinced of the considerable dose of savagery which there is in me, and which has to be there.

For the truth is that man carries on his shoulders all his human past, including the most primitive; that is to say, he continues to be his past, and thanks to this he is a man. If someone should magically extirpate all this past from any one of us, there would automatically come back into that one the initial semi-gorilla from which we started; a forest-loving tenant dwelling in the trees where he has his home, above infected marshes, and by a hypothesis (note, only hypothesis) which some day I will set forth to you, sick with malaria or some similar ailment, and so forth, and so on. This is not the opportunity to develop the theme, and I even ask that the very few words I have said about it be understood strictly as implying a well-versed knowledge of the present situation in the philogenetic problem of man, which is very different from what existed in the time of Darwin or Haeckel.

The radical separation between civilization and primitive societies, like many other things in Toynbee's work and doctrine, is set forth by him in a very arbitrary manner, without bothering even to give us reasons why he does it. Nevertheless, he has no choice but to recognize also in primitive society the characteristic of an intelligible historical field.

Truth obliges us to make it known that the great progress in historic science during the past fifty years has been due not to philologues and historians *sensu stricto*, but to the ethnologists, archeologists, and economists. Modern ethnology has illumined deep caverns of historic reality that were previously impenetrable, including some in the history of such best-known peoples as those of Greece and Rome. In earlier lessons we have at various times had occasion to collide with this presence of the past in the present. And this idea of wanting to cut the continuity between primitive societies and civilizations can lead Toynbee to no good. Because in this way there is no manner of explaining historically, for historical reasons, therefore with a historical precedent, the origin of primary civilizations like the Egyptian or the Sumerian or the Mesopotamian. Nevertheless, one cannot deny that Toynbee poses this problem with unusual energy; for this we should thank him, and we will see whether his solution succeeds in satisfying us.

The greater part of the twenty-one known civilizations proceed fully or necessarily from six originals, that is, they do not proceed in turn from others. These six are the Sumerian, the Egyptian, the Aegean, the Mayan in Central America, the Inca or Andean in South America, and the Chinese in the extreme Orient, and perhaps—this might be the seventh—the proto-Indian or Mohenjo Daro. And these pose vigorously the problem of their origin. To what is due this most strange phenomenon of the spontaneous outburst of the marvel which a civilization always is?

Although Toynbee recognizes that he has not been able to find "any permanent and fundamental point of difference"—these are his own words—between civilizations and primitive societies, the fact is that he declares the passage from one to the other to be like a mutation, therefore like something fundamental, which consists in that, according to him, while the primitive society is static, civilization is dynamic. Therefore that the genesis of a civilization consists in the fact that a human collectivity which has lived quietly up to a certain moment at that point abandons this peace in order to enter into a phase of movement. But at least, whether it be well or badly founded, this distinction between primitive society and civilization leads Toynbee to propose most urgently the question, Why, after three hundred thousand years of static life, suddenly, six thousand years ago, there should shoot forth that form of mobility in human life which has been called civilization?

If it is well justified that at the time of publication of his first book Toynbee should concede to the human species a longevity on earth of only three hundred thousand years, in successive editions, if he were well informed, he could have repaired such a figure, for various data worth considering apparently converge in making probable the calculation that the presence of man on earth is in the order of a million years. The principal bases of calculation are the periods of the planet's last glaciation.

Well then, what cause could there be why, after those three hundred thousand years of quiet . . . It is an enormity to say three hundred thousand years of *quiet*—hundreds of thousands of years in which apparently nothing happened—when during those years the things most basic for human existence have been invented and erected. How is it, then, that after three hundred thousand years of quiet, there should come forth on a good day, near the Euphrates and the Nile, a prodigious flowering of life, rich, active, and far from quiet, which is called a civilization?

The cause of this must be one of three things: either the appearance of a superior race, or an exceptionally favorable geographic surrounding—land and climate—or a combination of those two factors: the coincidence of a certain race with a certain climate. This is the analysis which Toynbee will make; this leads him to an idea which cannot be said to be his, but which he has undeniably expressed with great energy and effect. In effect, it gives us some light about historical dynamism, on the changes in the human situation, on man's victories and defeats: it is the double category which he entitles "challenge" and "responses." In reality, the first of those two words is not good, because it is one of those words that one finds in every tongue in such an intimate way that it cannot be translated into another language. It is the word *challenge* which means at once "obstacle," "threat," "provocation," "peril," *et cetera.*

But we are going to leave the analysis of all those questions for the moment. We were going to set forth part of Toynbee's thought, but instead, I have given you rest, a rather foolish lesson. I call "foolish" any lesson that lacks dramatic quality. This dramatic quality is not something that the professor adds to the theme, it does not consist in those exaggerations and pathetic details which the professor might want to use and which would be vain, but it consists simply in having understood the theme well; then the dramatic quality springs forth from it, because every scientific theme is a problem, and every problem is a drama, now and forever an intellectual drama, but almost always in addition a drama for the whole man. But if drama goes on too long it gets tiresome. Moreover, I have a certain pride in showing that I too, like any son of any neighbor, can if necessary set forth a lesson which is sufficiently foolish.

X

Review of the previous lesson. The original civilizations. The race factor. The genius of the English. Racism. The empirical method and pure ideas. Challenge-and-response. Man, a fantastic animal.

ACCORDING TO TOYNBEE there have been twenty-one civilizations, counting the present ones. Of these, fifteen were born of others preexistent, with which, according to our author, there was always the precise relationship of daughters to mothers. In order to appreciate the value of this filial relationship one must remember that the new civilization is born amid the destruction by barbarian peoples of a universal state into which the previous one had succeeded in organizing itself; from this universal state the younger one inherits a universal religion which was created within the "internal proletariat" of the older one now in peril of decay. On this religion the daughter civilization is going to live historically, for it finds within itself the residue of the maternal civilization which, in this sense, forms an integrating part of the daughter one.

Note that, if one wants to understand Toynbee, all this must be taken formally, because it is implied in his primary and basic idea that a civilization is the "intelligible historical field"—that is, the historical reality which one can and must understand without moving away from it. Such a conception does not admit, then, that one civilization would receive important influences from another with which it had no parental or filial relationship—those influences which, the other day I called "diffuse" or "universal." This would oblige Toynbee, and in a way it does oblige him, at the end of his published work, to destroy his initial idea of the "intelligible historical field."

Those fifteen filial civilizations transfer us back to six original ones having no precedents, which were born not from others but from themselves. These are the Egyptian; the Sumerian, which is the first Mesopotamian civilization; the Aegean; the Sinic or primitive Chinese, from which the present or Far Eastern China was born; then, that of the Mayas, in Guatemala and Yucatan, in Central America; and the Andean civilization of the Incas in South America.

Toynbee, we said, refuses to derive these originating civilizations from primitive societies, because, in his judgment, the fact of being a civilization means a radical change in human life, which, from being static in primitive society becomes in civilizations a matter of incessant change or movement. It is clear that this imagined static condition of primitive societies is something on which much could be said, but let us leave the subject intact for the moment when I can talk exclusively about primitive life, one of the most moving themes that exist. Probably the difference between a primitive society and a civilization lies not in that fundamental contrast between a presumed static life and a life of movement, but rather in a different rate of acceleration.

The proof of this can be seen in the fact that when one compares one civilization with another, the rate of acceleration differs so much that in one civilization there may be periods of paralysis; Toynbee himself sets up a subclass of civilizations which he calls "detained" and, as this is a secondary theme, we cannot comment on it;

finally, he says that within the same civilization acceleration is different in some periods from what it is in others.
Thus our own, since 1900, has entered into a rhythm of
such speed of change as perhaps has never been on the
planet. And these are not vague value judgments, because
on certain decisive occasions that acceleration can be
measured, and graded by numbers—that is, mathemati-
cally and statistically. Thus, for example with respect to
technical inventions, since 1900 the frequency of those
inventions and therefore their density is such that the
nineteenth century, expressed numerically, seems to have
been standing still. Let us not talk about the earlier ones.
This is one of the things which men of today have not
noted with sufficient care; that the enormous change has
been produced just in these forty recent years. What
happened is that in the nineteenth century—and I do not
say this without reason, for all things are relative—there
was too much talk and there were too many songs in
popular comedies saying that "the sciences move forward
today, which is a barbarity." But the real time when it is
a barbarity, and perhaps has contributed in part to bar-
barization, is now, in our very own century.

In this detail you see that it was not arbitrary on my
part to uphold repeatedly the idea that the new historical
science will have to occupy itself with something more
than paper work in the archives. Apparently it will soon
have to occupy itself with statistics, and statistics cannot
be elaborated except by means of a previous theory that
gives them meaning.

When Toynbee cuts himself off from communication
with primitive societies, he ceases to explain the origin
of two primary civilizations, the Egyptian and the Sumerian, by any reference to a past; therefore with any
historical reason. He is under the necessity of going back
to a hypothesis which is a mixture of geography and

phantasmagoria, because, put that way, the problem, the source from which a civilization springs forth, can be found only in one of these three things—we said this at the end of the previous lesson—either in a superior race which suddenly appears, or in a geographic surrounding which for one reason or another is exceptionally favorable, or in the combination of the two factors—the meeting of a certain race with a certain physical medium.

It is beyond doubt that race cannot be the generating cause of civilization. More than unquestionable, this is unquestioned. It has occurred to nobody to think otherwise, and if this were the only authentic question which the course of his doctrine posed, I would at this moment have dispatched our author with two lines, for the fact that all races except one, the Negro, have engendered civilizations is an exceedingly weighty one; therefore it is not only race by itself which creates a civilization. It is not this that is disputed. Nobody thinks the contrary.

What has been disputed since Gobineau is whether there is any race (or races) which are the only ones capable of creating the most excellent civilization. But neither can this interest Toynbee, because previously the battering of his theory had leveled all the civilizations, even the Greek and the European, at least officially, as well as the Mayan of Guatemala and Yucatan or the Andean of the Incas. Nevertheless he stays with the matter a long time, but clearly not in order to define precisely the strict, scientific notion of race and to elucidate its possible link with the genesis of a civilization. Showing once more that his genuine temperament is not that of an intellectual, a man of science, of theory, or however you want to put it—we will see later what his effective temperament is—he replaced the genuine and scientific question of race and civilization with the journalistic and political question of *racism*, for he, naturally, is furiously antiracist; a fury and an attitude which has no interest at all for those of us who are not racists, but who do not weary ourselves by reading his work for the purpose—which would be morbid—of receiving on ourselves the private secretions of his sympathies and antipathies.

But such is the strange condition of this author that his very perspirations, purely arbitrary, become at times diverting. This is what happens when he talks to us of race and civilization; I will only emphasize certain points. First, Toynbee argues not only that there is no one superior race which would have created *the* civilization—a thing which, as I said, no one pretends—but he argues that race has no importance whatsoever in the formation of the *civilizations*. To demonstrate this he presents a table in which on the one side appear the twenty-one aforesaid civilizations, plus a few which he adds as secondary variants of those, and on the other side the chromatic races, defined by color of skin, which generated them and served them.

The total of civilizations which result from this process is thirty-four; twenty-five of these come from the white race, and only nine from races of other colorations; from these one subtracts, as being expansions of another earlier civilization, the Mexican and the Yucatanian, both coming from the Maya, or vice versa; for there are discussions as to which was the one that influenced the others, but for this discussion it is the same thing, and thus they are reduced to seven.

The natural thing would be that this enormous numerical difference between seven and twenty-five, in favor of the white race, would move this man a bit away from the "empirical method"; but no, it does not, nor does he pay any attention to it. On the other hand, a few pages farther on he presents us with another table, because he is interested in showing how various races have been influential in the formation of almost all civilizations—and now he does not refer solely to the chromatic characteristics of race or to the color of their skins, but to what the anthropologists distinguish today as Nordic, Alpine, Mediterranean, and so on.

From this table one sees—I read his own words—that "two civilizations have been created by the contributions of three different races, nine by the contributions of two different races, and ten by the exclusive effort of a single race;" therefore "more than half of the civilizations which have emerged were created by a mixture of races." By certain summary disquisitions which he wrote in six or seven lines, those ten civilizations, born from a single race, are reduced to a vague smaller number, and then he says triumphantly, "the number of civilizations created by the exclusive effort of a single race becomes, in every case, so relatively minimum that those cases represent exceptions to a prevailing *law*—a law providing that the genesis of civilizations requires contributions from more than one race."

How does this seem to you as a symptom of the mental texture of a thinker? Because note that in those words he commits the following errors one after another: first, he talks of a prevailing law, as if there were scientific laws that were not prevailing; second, he admits exceptions to that law, a thing that happens not with laws, but with mere rules; third, and above all, the man who ends by affirming radically that races are not important in the formation of civilizations, proclaims solemnly, a little farther on, nothing less than an historic law, according to which the normal is that the civilization is born of the contribution of various races.

Well now, I believe that the intervention of various races in the formation of a civilization is a form like any other of the intervention of the principle of race in the genesis of all civilization. Anything else would be like affirming that in making a cocktail, no alcohol intervenes for the reason that several alcohols intervene.

But let us move now to the second point in his way of clarifying the origin of civilization. Here Toynbee reaches the height of absurdity. Racism—which to him is synonymous with a belief in the absolute superiority of one race over the others—proceeds, according to Toynbee, from English Protestantism. With this he shows his impartiality, and that he is not a man who is biased. According to his understanding, the English Protestants were the first to incubate the belief that there is one people which is chosen, superior to the others, and this he had come to believe was England, because he had found that there was a people chosen by God, and this discovery he had made while reading the Old Testament. You see by what a series of caroms on the billiard table of ideas the result appears that anti-Semitism, anti-Judaism, which brought such terrible suffering to the Jews, came as from its originating source out of the Jewish book *par excellence*, the Torah, or Old Testament.

Our Toynbee does not observe that the idea of a people chosen by God is a completely different thing from the idea of race, unless the question is shifted even more grotesquely to assume that God Himself is racist, and that if He has chosen one particular people this is because that people is of a specific race.

It is curious that it never occurs to Toynbee, in whose work there is not a single sharp, perspicacious idea, nor one which is sympathetic to and loving of his own country—a country whose most peculiar way of being, whose surprising history constitutes one of the most suggestive themes for any intelligence that might be intellectually happy and for any heart even halfway impressionable—it never occurs to Toynbee to think that perhaps things might have happened in the opposite way; namely, that because the English people believed almost *a navitate* that they were a people superior to others, this was the reason why he, an Englishman, seeing in the Old Testament talk of a people chosen by God, jumped to the conclusion that his people were the chosen ones, and that England was the authentic Israel. It is well known that for some time, during the Puritan period, the use of Hebrew names for persons who had not a single drop of Jewish blood was very frequent in England. It is clear that this did not affect Toynbee, but that he derived the modern hierarchy of the races solely from the Old Testament; then he adds to that first affirmation the new one that the English were also the first to discover a conscious sense of distance between the races when they had to meet them face to face and live with men of color in their colonies. One does not see how he reconciles this with the unquestionable fact that the people who first and most extensively received and adopted racism—and I am not referring to recent years but to eighty years ago, under the influence of Gobineau—were those of Germany, the only European nation that had no colonies. But the fact is that, putting together the Old Testament and the odor of the Negro or the Hindu, what resulted for Toynbee was racism; therefore when combining Englishman and Bible, or Englishman and Negro, what always appears first is the Englishman. Someone ill-disposed would say here that even without realizing it, Toynbee is so English that he believes the English people were chosen by God to invent everything and to be the origin of everything, of the good and the bad—even of racism. But this would be exceedingly unjust, for in all Toynbee's works, there is not, at least openly, a single word that praises England.

More than that, I note quite the contrary, for I see

something very strange, a coolness toward England, almost a lack of interest in her. And here there begins to appear a little of what I told you that first day we were going to find in the modern Englishman if we cut him open from top to bottom, something very strange which, at first sight, we could, surprised, interpret as if—I affirm nothing, but it is an effect that must be produced in every sensitive reader—as if in the depths of this man there began to ferment a doubt whether it made sense to go on being English. And as this cannot be attributed in the least to trivial motives or to causes of a superficial and topical type, as for instance affiliation with the Communist Party or anything like that, and as we also find something similiar beating in the hearts of others of the best men among the English of today, we have the impression of touching just with a single finger one of the most delicate and perhaps most decisive facts of the present period. We must approach this with scrupulous respect, but at the same time resolved to see it clearly, because perhaps what is beating in that latent state of the spirit is no less than the great secret of the immediate future for all of us. Hence, let it not be a matter of indifference to us, for we have to understand it.

I cannot be more explicit now, or any clearer, but do keep always in mind that the greatest genius of England is not what she thinks with her mind, therefore what her writers or her thinkers think, and even more, in general, what the English say, for it is well known that the English have by custom considered language the most splendid instrument which man possesses for hiding his own thought. The greatest genius of England is not in the brain of England's heads, but in what might be called another brain, in the depths of their being where there functions a strange form of intelligence which is almost pure instinct; or to put inversely, an instinct which has the lucidity of intelligence. Hence, on hearing or reading an Englishman, we ought never to remain content with what is read or heard, but go behind it in order to distinguish what there is back there; the genius of the Englishman is what issues from that almost instinctive depth, which is therefore not to be uttered and at best can only be divined.

Toynbee believes a good explanation of racism to be that combination of the Bible and the colonies, and he judges it sufficient to make known the different conduct which the Catholic colonial peoples, like those of Spain and Portugal, who read the Old Testament less, followed with the indigenous peoples. In effect, in place of exterminating them as the English did at first, or later keeping them humanely at a distance, what our people did was to unite with them and create mixed races. This contrast is beyond question. But I cannot repress my extraordinary sense of strangeness that Toynbee, so sensitive, and with reason, to the atrocious tragedy which racism represents, has no single word for, nor seems even to consider the other tragedy, the tragedy which originates in the widespread existence of mestizos and mulatoes in the countries where they are born—a thing which everyone who has traveled in America and South Africa recognizes.

If I had not promised to set before you Toynbee's doctrine in all its essential architecture, I would stop here to do what he did not do, which is to contemplate from within that generous and human behavior of the Spanish and Portuguese people toward the indigenous peoples, and this would lead me immediately to have to define what seems to me the most basic and evident quality of the Spaniard, which is his most peculiar attitude toward life as such, an attitude completely different from that of all the other Western peoples.

Here in this theme you have one of those pheasants, which I mentioned earlier, that we would have to release and let flutter from one side of the road to the other; I am forbidden to shoot at them because in this course (now so far advanced) I have had to declare an interdiction. The only thing I will add about that different conduct of Catholic colonial countries with primitive peoples when compared with the English conduct, which Toynbee so justly contrasts and emphasizes, is that this section, like his whole book, is a full and almost official symptom of how, since the beginning of the century, Catholicism has begun to take the pulse of Protestantism. This is an unquestionable reality; it is the pure truth—note it that way—and the only thing to be desired is that all the others would be as disposed as I am to recognize the truth whenever it is presented.

Let us go ahead. Toynbee, in order to get down to the bottom (malign, according to him) of what constitutes our period and to shame not only the North Americans, but in general, our whole era, declares that racism, that consciousness of inequality as between the castes of men, was unknown in the West during the Middle Ages and even is still unknown today among some of the Western nations. Certainly, he added, there did exist a form of discrimination in the Middle Ages, but it was founded not on race but on religion.

Is Toynbee sure that the distance felt by the European when confronted by the Moslem, and which he expressed in religious terms, was in fact solely a divergence in religion and not also a hatred as between races? And the periodic slaughterings of Jews in those centuries—were those inspired exclusively by religious differences? It is very unlikely that as this terrible hatred between races has existed in almost all civilizations, it should be lacking in our own, and that it should be necessary for the English in modern days to wear themselves out inventing it. One is suspicious of the fact that caste is expressed in the Hindu word *barna*, which means "color," despite the fact that today the Hindu castes all have the same color, and that therefore this is a matter of very ancient ways of feeling racist before the whole Hindu people had yet been dyed the same tone.

But Toynbee relegates so important a fact to the imperceptible end of a note which is printed in letters that are almost microscopic. And why does Toynbee hide the fact that during the Roman Empire anti-Semitism, anti-Judaism, existed for exactly the same reasons as in our time? Does he not know about that Greek of Alexandria who came face to face with no less a man than Trajan, and shouted at him, "You have your Council of State full of atheist Jews," just as men shout today at Atlee's government or at Truman's? When one really wants to resolve or mitigate the terrible problem of races, is anything to be gained by stating it in this manner, that is, by denying its existence in one place and then attributing its invention to certain others? Is anything to be gained by writing about it with a pen torn from the wing under which an ostrich hides his head in order not to see the truth? I believe, and may I repeat this once more, that anyone who wants truly to solve a problem must begin by seeing it. Do not find it strange that I insist so much on this. It is the most constant question with which we are going to find ourselves in the immediate future.

Because the very people in whose hands, or in whose heads, things move have produced a result in this mania which gives me goose flesh. The matter is very peculiar among English writers of the present day and in some North Americans, who begin by not recognizing the problem with which they are dealing. Exactly the same thing is going to happen with the obvious need for going into a new combination of the nations in larger entities; we are going to begin by believing that nations do not exist, and that some of them have been invented as a form of amusement. In order to throw in the faces of the North Americans their behavior toward the fourteen or fifteen million Negroes (they say officially thirteen million, but this appears to be the only statistic in America which is not exact; there are at least fifteen million of them) that they make use of, Toynbee argues as follows: "During the General War of 1914–18 the negro citizens of the United States who served in the American Army in France were astonished at the social liberality with which the French whites treated the black African subjects of the Republic who served in the French Army, and whose cultural level was much lower than that of the median American negro."

Ought we also not to be astonished—as those Negroes were astonished—that Toynbee tells us this as though it were proof that the French are incapable of feeling toward the Negro what many North Americans feel? To set a Negro free in Tarascan or in Angoulême (as in Quintanar de la Orden or in Daimiel) means a fiesta for the people; but if we should put five million Negroes where people were living quietly in France . . . we should see what would happen. I confess that on reading these things I do not mean to throw blame at anyone, but I do believe it my duty to repeat that when I read these things I get goose flesh.

And here comes the third point in the problem of race and civilization. In the first list to which I referred there is a race—the black race—which has not created any civilization. Hence, I said in the beginning that it was unquestionable and unquestioned that the cause of civilization was not race—this race or that—for all the races except one had created civilizations. Therefore, the real question is the inverse of that: how is it that there was one race which has not been capable of creating a civilization?

Parenthetically, the other day, in order not to seem to be making a charge against Toynbee, this man of the empirical method who does not know what to do with so clear a fact as this and one which he can do no less than recognize as a fact, I did not say that the present theory and methodology of knowledge know perfectly well that the same thing happens to this empirical method as happened to those taxes imposed in Rome; the famous text of a professor in Salamanca says that they began by not existing. There is no empirical method in the sense that Toynbee pretends. All science is constructive, and construction is the opposite of empiricism; therefore, empiricism is contrary to method. The role that facts have in the construction of a theory is something else.

Well then, Toynbee does not yield in the face of so negative a fact. His predilection is for the Negroes, and therefore, he opens for them a credit of unlimited time; recognizing that up to now they have not created any civilization, he affirms that perhaps within thousands of years they will generate one. It is clear that this man, who tells us in a note that he has no faith in English Protestants, apparently has transferred that faith to the Negroes, for faith is needed to state what you have just heard from me. And he takes great care not to recognize, as most of the modern anthropologists do, the Negro race as the oldest of all human races; therefore, the one that up to now has had the most time to wear itself out in inventing a civilization.

Toynbee eliminates geographic surroundings more rapidly as the generator of the decisive moment in the origin of civilization. Here there is, as he finds in the matter of race, no political movement to exploit his skills as journalist and preacher. The naturalist idea, Greek in origin, according to which civilization was born in a climate and a land which are favorable to it, like the other fruits of vegetative life, like the alligator pear in Cuba and the quince in Brazil, is not admissible, for in addition one notes that the same territory has served as cradle for very different civilizations. Toynbee could have taken the matter much more basically, if it were not for his insistence on the absolute separation between primitive societies and civilizations; he could have remembered (if he knows it) an idea, a bit of genius in its very simplicity, which was set forth by Father Teilhard de Chardin. This French Jesuit and anthropologist thinks that in spite of the fact that all efforts to try to find differences in the anatomy and physiology of men from that of the other animals [1] seem to have failed, there is one most simple and purely physical fact which is enough to make one see the unique and separate character that man has, even considered solely from the zoological point of view; this he supports by pointing out that man is the only species capable of living all over the planet.

The idea is of a most elegant simplicity, and an indisputable authenticity. All the other species live assigned to a restricted "habitat," to use this word which the biologists employ; it seems to me a ridiculous word taken from the German, which only uses a Latin word reluctantly. Well then, the gorilla lives in the tropics, but dies in Greenland; man, on the other hand, can live where he pleases, and he arranges his choice so as to live richly under any conditions.

1. I am referring to the time, more than thirty years ago, when Father Teilhard worked on this; later I learned that he has been most recently in China, where he underwent great dangers; this is to note that this idea to which I refer is to be found in a book which has not yet been published (see Father Teilhard de Chardin, *El fenómeno humano* (Madrid: Revista de Occidente, 1960).

But Toynbee, on cutting off continuity with primitive life, cannot benefit from an idea like that of Father Teilhard, nor can he explain the genesis of civilizations in an empirical way as he promised us. His idea is this: that incomparable sprout, *sui generis*, which he calls originary civilization assumes that a people, maintained up to a certain date in the static life of primitive society, explodes suddenly with an energy of creative movement. This supposes, in turn, a new fact which would have caused that change, and this new fact can be no other than an unfavorable shift in geographic surroundings which breaks the established, static adaptation in which they were living; this obliges them to behave in a different manner. The greater part of peoples, faced with such a situation, do not react energetically; on the contrary, they entrust themselves to it and then succumb, or at least deteriorate. This happens with all the present primitive peoples who drag out their decadent existence, still declining in our days. But others, those six that we named earlier, accepted with energy the threat, the contest, the difficulty, the obstacle—in short, what Toynbee calls *challenge*, with the innumerable meanings that this word has in English. They accepted that challenge, obstacle, or difficulty and responded with creative vivacity.

The genesis of an originary human civilization is, then, nothing but a prototypical case of the basic phenomenon of all history which is typically human; the category of relation called threat-and-reply, obstacle-and-reaction, *challenge-and-response*. This category shows clearly and visibly that the viscera of history are drama. Human history has only dramatic entrails, tragic, if you want to call them that. The comic, the humorous are never visceral; they flourish on the outside; they are only skin deep—and this is not intended to deprecate them, but simply to place them. No reality is comic in itself; its aspect, its manifestation, its exterior appearance may be comic, but not its reality. Hence the strange and frightening impression left by the observation I made a few lessons earlier, when I complained that the linguists did not pay more attention to the frequency with which men, in their words and vocabularies, use words which make fun of their own viscera.

The idea, then, that physical surroundings engender a civilization—not directly, not because they are favorable, but just the opposite, for the very reason that they turn unfavorable and hostile, and pose a problem for men—this seems to me an excellent idea which I had stated many years before Toynbee's work appeared, as we will see in the next lessons. But that idea is not empirical; it is completely the opposite, it is a hypothesis, and every hypothesis is a construction, and because of this it is an authentic theory. In so far as they merit that exigent name, ideas are never a mere reception of presumed realities, but they are constructions of possibilities; therefore they are pure bits of imagination, or fine ideas of our own, as Plato of Athens son of Ariston found out once and forever, twenty-four centuries ago; a discovery which, in my understanding, is without possible comparison with any other, the most sublime and efficacious one which has been made up to now on the planet we occupy, and which today, more than ever, constitutes the alpha and omega of every scientific exercise.

And forgive this spurt of philosophic gas which I could not repress.

Toynbee assumes, arbitrarily, that seven thousand years ago no man was living in the valley of the Nile River because it was a marshy jungle obstructed by tangles of water plants; papyrus, reeds, and full of wild beasts—crocodiles, hippopotami, wild bears, leopards, elephants—along with a cloud of aquatic birds, all this representing a landscape very similar to the one that now exists farther down in Egypt at the river of the Gazelles; this was marvelously described by Schweinfurt, who discovered this region in 1850 and who wrote one of the most flavorful books of travel that exist; moreover, he was the first European who ever met a pygmy. Many times I have wanted to try to get this book translated, but without success.

Well then, according to Toynbee, the Hamitic tribes which then inhabited Egypt lived on higher ground on either side of the river, on grassy steppes, with trees scattered here and there, where the hunting of wild animals was easy. This steppe region was a paradise. It was a paradise because, as Toynbee notes, paradise—in Greek, *paradeisos*—is a Persian word which, according to him, means that landscape, that natural region, of tall grasses and trees scattered here and there but not set too thickly; in short, what, as I understand it, geographers call "the steppe." Toynbee suffers, as he so frequently does, from a slight error, for although the word *paradeisos* (this is the way the Greeks pronounce it) was a Persian word, the true meaning of it is not "steppe" but "garden," a place of flowers but also of fruit trees. It is apparently characteristic of certain high regions to create this combination of flower garden and fruit orchard as a place of solace. At least that is what has been the purest, most typical and traditional Castilian garden or orchard. This is what, in the exact meaning of the very beautiful word, is called in Spanish *vergel*. I note this because I am sorry to see that this splendid word has been lost from use, or when it is used, is not given its genuine meaning. A *vergel* is a flower garden together with an orchard of fruit trees.

Well then, things being like that, suddenly the climate changed, the whole region began to dry up, turning the grass-covered steppe into arid and atrocious dry lands which are now the Libyan desert on the west and the

Arabian desert on the east. The animals died, or fled from the new scarcity of food; faced with this change, part of the tribes living there resolved to go down into the valley in order to take advantage of the vein of the Nile. On the other hand, another part followed the line of least resistance, that is to say, they migrated toward the south, which was not yet reached by the drought, in order that they might be able to continue without the slightest change their petrified life in a primitive society which still pursued its elemental existence. But the first group—those who accepted that climactic challenge, that disturbance of the equilibrium which had been their life in the static state of their primitive society—these people reacted by creating new forms of life, which, by demanding a greater effort, represented in turn a new challenge. And this is what became Egyptian civilization.

According to Toynbee, the same thing happened on the banks of the Euphrates with the Sumerians as the founders of Mesopotamian civilization, and also with the first Chinese on the banks of the Yellow River. He sees all those people struggling with new geographic scenarios. They drain the marshes, canalize the rivers, destroy the predators of game, and order labor in the camps. Therefore, by a process of modification, they created for themselves an artificial geographic surrounding.

With this hypothesis, Toynbee merely leans on studies made by the American Huntington, who dedicated his life to a minute study of the possible relation between climate and civilization. His book, of which the title was *Civilization and Climate*, is excellent of its kind, loaded with facts and reasoning, and agreeable to read. Therefore some years ago I made an effort to get it published in Spanish, but as so often happens to me, after having succeeded I was disillusioned to find that almost nobody in our country read it.

Huntington argues that the land-water climate experienced waves of change over long periods, but not so much so that these cannot be perceived within historical chronology. There are periods of flood and periods of drought, and each of these changes means for man a tremendous disturbance. Such great and pathetic happenings always are decanted into great myths, as, for example, the legend of the Flood. It is surprising that there is not a myth of the same dimension which would be the legend of the drought, for one does not fully comprehend as such the book of the Old Testament which tells of the Flood, and also of the wandering life through desert drought, followed by the miracle of the rock from which Moses extracted water.

It is to this theory of Huntington's that Toynbee attaches the turbine of his idea of challenge-and-response, and thinks thus to explain the origin of these first civilizations. But in the Mayan civilization of the Guatemalan reed-land this climatic change is not clear. (I do not know why the English word *jungle* is translated into Spanish, in the title of one of Kipling's famous books, by the phrase "*tierras vírgenes*," when we have had since the sixteenth century the word *junco*, so native despite the fact that the *Dictionary of the Academy* does not carry it.) That theory is still less clear with respect to the genesis of the Incan or Andean civilization, which arose in the formidable and desolate heights of the Andes at a time when no serious climatic change is known. On the other hand, what does appear in all accounts of the genesis of civilizations is that certain peoples in their treatment of land and plant life had previously reached a degree of perfection which well merited the most noble name of agriculture.

In the case of the Mayan civilization the matter has a formal and official character. It is known that the Mayans came down from the mountain ranges of Guatemala and

Honduras to the plains below for the reason that they had already invented the cultivation of corn (maize), which would ray out from there to the whole American continent, coming to be, as it continues to be, the principal food of a good part of other continents. Mayan civilization is built around the idea of corn; therefore that civilization preexisted. In the same way, everything makes one think that the Egyptians, those dwellers on the steppes, on the table land before they went down to the valley of the Nile, were able to accept the challenge of the drought because they were excellent workers and felt themselves capable of putting in order the marshes of the Nile Valley when their highlands were converted into the appalling Libyan desert. The great Lord Bacon said, "Forests are rendered domestic by the plow." In fact it is agriculture that makes this statement possible; that is to say, agriculture was not the origin of civilization, but it preceded civilization. If it makes sense to distinguish between primitive society and civilized or cultivated life, it must be recognized that the origin of culture is agriculture, which gives that word back its etymological meaning.

It is known that our Vives was the first to use the word *culture* in its present meaning, making of farm work a country metaphor for saying *cultura animi*, that is, cultivation of the spirit. We would have it, then, that Egyptians and Sumerians did not create their civilizations *in response* to the challenge of climactic change, but that they were able to accept this change because they were not autochthonous inhabitants of the region near the Euphrates but were newly arrived people who had come from very far away—perhaps the region between Trans-Caucasia, the Caspian Sea, Altai, and Pamir—and who came bringing with them a civilization, including perhaps the knowledge of writing; I do not understand why

Toynbee is silent on this matter, which is so fundamental.

Toynbee's hypothesis, already twisted violently in the case of the Mayas and the Andean people, becomes positively acrobatic when one tries to apply it to the Aegean civilization which arose on the Island of Crete, farthest from the western coast and their nearby islands. How, then, is one to explain this? Toynbee, who never yields to facts, states boldly that the Cretans (something that no one has dared to support) are Hamitic tribes of Africa, like the Egyptians, who replied to the challenge of dessication in a more original manner, accepting a new challenge—that which the sea presented to them. They answered by launching themselves onto the sea. Either one cannot understand this, or does not see the advantages which an island completely unknown to them might have. To assume this would imply that—as I said previously that the Egyptians were great agriculturalists before being Egyptians and going down to the Nile—so the future Cretans while they lived in Africa must have been great sailors—that is, they too already had their civilization. But there is no appearance of this whatsoever.

In the next lesson I will still be touching, in detail, on Toynbee's thesis about the origin of civilizations. But now you will demand, and with reason, that I clearly express my judgment on this doctrine of Toynbee's; while I have, on the one hand, applauded it—a thing which up to now has not been frequent in me with regard to Toynbee's ideas—I shall probably be more gentle about the part which is left to be stated. But if on one side I applauded it, on the other I have amused myself by pulverizing (to use the good work of our apothecary) his doctrine with a relatively minute criticism.

Let us, then, strike a balance. I applauded his idea that the dynamic principle in human history is, in fact, rather like challenge-and-response; but I criticized the use of this idea as an explanation of the genesis of civilizations, first because the facts contradict it, in the sense that in the greater part of the cases there was not that sudden a change in geographic surroundings; second, because even in a case like that of Egypt, where there must have been a challenge, the peoples who responded to this did so because they already possessed a good degree of what Toynbee calls civilization; third, and consequently, because the very statement of the problems, based on assuming that civilization is something *toto caelo* different from primitive life seems to me inacceptable; fourth, because, as we shall soon see, the challenge-response dynamism belongs to human life, and one cannot admit the supposition that it did not act and does not continue to act in the life of primitive societies.

Toynbee imagines that those societies represent a state of equilibrium as between man and his medium. But, then, the result is that civilization also consists in the fact that man would create a new equilibrium before the change in the medium. As usual, he ends by tripping over his own idea. Not only is this a grave error, but it hampers an understanding of history and human destinies to believe that a state of equilibrium in living has ever existed. Such an equilibrium is utopian; one can speak only of a greater or lesser degree of imbalance. Man is essentially an unbalanced animal who, nevertheless, exists; this means that he is not precisely and solely an animal, for to an animal, existing is always equilibrium, or if not, it is ceasing to exist, succumbing. To this paradoxical condition of constitutive lack of balance man owes all his grace and all his disgrace, all his misery and all his splendor. Hence man's origin must be represented by the most anti-Darwinian image there is; this cannot consist, as the people in the seminaries ingenuously and stubbornly think, in separating man from animal—a thing which is completely senseless—

without sufficient courage and intellectual acuteness to take the problem by the horns, but rather like an animal which tries to escape animality, evading it or fleeing from it.

In the face of all Darwinism, man represents the triumph of an animal that is unadapted and unadaptable. Without doubt he will constantly achieve partial adaptations, but each one of them serves him for a new adaptation. But an animal at once unadapted and continuing to live is, from the zoological point of view, a sick animal. Hence, without taking it now as a formal theory, but rather as merely an anti-Darwin, although evolutionist, myth, which tries only to orient our intuition concerning how things could happen, we can, biologically, imagine human origin like this:

According to many modern zoologists the human species is much older than all the tribes of apes. Rather than man descending from monkeys, the monkey apparently descended from man. From the zoological point of view look at this example: the line of evolution of the shift of eyes from the side to the frontal position is what gives the monkey his simian aspect. If you go to the Prado Museum, and enter the room where the Greco portraits are, you will see that one of these, a small portrait of a man with a beard sharper than is usual with Greco, his hair and his beard almost white, looking not like a person that is well but like a miserable one, has his eyes completely on the frontal plane, which gives the man a frankly simian appearance; it is an impression which gives the poor man—one does not know who he is—the aspect of an imbecile. Well then, that species older than the monkeys was a sick species.

Let us, then, imagine man as a sick animal, suffering an illness which I will call *symbolically* malaria because he lived in infected swamps. And that illness, which did not succeed in destroying the species, caused in him an intoxication which produced a cerebral hyperfunctioning; this was the origin of a consequent excessive growth of the cerebral organs which brought with it, in turn, a greater degree of mental hyperfunctioning, the result of which was that man was filled with images and fantasies—in which, as is well known, even the superior animals are so poor; that is to say, he found himself with a whole imaginary world, therefore an interior world, which the animal lacks; an interior world confronting, separate from, and opposing the exterior world. And from then on, this last beast which is the first man has to live at once in two worlds—the one inside and the other outside—and therefore be irremediably and forever unadapted, unbalanced; this is his glory, this is his anguish.

Man is a fantastic animal; he was born of fantasy, he is the son of "the mad woman of the house." And universal history is the gigantic and thousand-year effort to go on putting order into that huge, disorderly, anti-animal fantasy. What we call reason is no more than fantasy put into shape. Is there anything in the world more fantastic than that which is the most rational? Is there anything more fantastic than the mathematical point, and the infinite line, and, in general, all mathematics and all physics? Is there a more fantastic fancy than what we call "justice" and the other thing that we call "happiness"?

We see, then, that even from the zoological point of view, which is the least interesting and—note this—not decisive, a being in such condition can never achieve a genuine equilibrium; we also see something that differs from the idea of challenge-response in Toynbee and, in my judgment, effectively constitutes human life: namely, that no surroundings or change of surroundings can in itself be described as an obstacle, a difficulty, and a challenge for man, but that the difficulty is always relative to the projects which man creates in his imagination, to what he customarily calls his ideals; in short, relative to what man wants to be. This affords us an idea of challenge-and-response which is much deeper and more decisive than the merely anecdotal, adventitious, and accidental idea which Toynbee proposes. In its light, all of human life appears to us as what it is permanently: a dramatic confrontation and struggle of man with the world and not a mere occasional maladjustment which is produced at certain moments.

Next time we will look at this from a much more basic point of view and one antedating all zoology, which, glimpsed only a little after my twentieth year, made me write in those days that what is most valuable in man is his eternal and almost divine discontent, a discontent which is a kind of love without a beloved, and like an ache which we feel in members of our body that we do not have. Man is the only being that misses what he has never had. And the whole of what we miss, without ever having had it, is never what we call happiness. From this one could start a meditation on happiness, an analysis of that strange condition which makes man the only being who is unhappy for the very reason that he needs to be happy. That is, because he needs to be what he is not.

XI

Mr. Toynbee's pieties and the "Numantism" of England. Challenge-and-response continued. General principles and their complement. Two theorems. The human being's lack of definition. Facilities and difficulties. Basic reality. Technique and happiness.

IN THE PREVIOUS LESSON I pointed out that the category "challenge-response," as an equation of energy in the system of history, seemed to me one of Toynbee's most excellent ideas; moreover, he succeeded in setting it forth with splendid skill. But at the same time I opposed his way of understanding and applying it, because this is not sufficient.

Toynbee neither sees it nor thinks about it in its character as something which is genuinely fundamental. He presents it to us as functioning only on the occasion of some very important accident, but an accident which happens occasionally in situations produced in history from time to time; the truth is that the relation of challenge from the surroundings, and response to that challenge, is man's permanent situation, because it is the very substance of human life, at least in its intramundane meaning. Toynbee does not see this, because he is not a philosopher. He does not launch himself on the high sea of ultimate principles; his navigation is purely that of the pilot boat, and this is bad, for to set forth on the high sea of principles, to make philosophy, is always a problematical task, always in good part a failure, but always necessary and always unavoidable.

We saw that in his attempt to explain the particular problem of how the originating civilizations were born, his idea fails. It is true that Toynbee posed the problem so abruptly because he wanted to catch the bull by force. He could not solve it smoothly, and he had to use the strangest stubbornness in the face of facts. In some instances which I adduced in his discussion of racism, we could see the arbitrary character and even the childishness of his resistance to facts, as well as the light quality of his reasoning. It is true that on describing to you Toynbee's thought, according to which racism proceeds from the ways in which English Protestants reacted on meeting color in their colonies, and contrasting this conduct with that which the Spanish and Portuguese peoples followed, I forgot to show how strange I found it that Toynbee was silent on or ignorant of the fact that the word *raza* ("race") comes from the Spanish and Portuguese tongues, perhaps originally from the Portuguese, and that it spread from this to all the others.

But in this, and what I said the other day, I neither had nor have the slightest desire to demonstrate that Mr. Toynbee is not right, for this is a matter of such bulky errors in the management of concepts that it would not be worthwhile to go back over them. My critical operation proposed, inversely, to make it clear quite concretely that Mr. Toynbee does *not try to be right,* for in spite of his abundant knowledge, to which I pay all merited homage, he is not, in the last analysis, a man of reason, of science, of theory. He is a man who believes with the faith of a coal miner in certain philanthropic things which culminate in a strange mysticism about history; and he believes, as one always believes, because he believes. That is proper to the *habitus creditivus* of which the theologians talk, which is all very well, but has nothing to do with theorizing, with thinking, in view of the facts and the reasons.

Here one does not discuss Toynbee's talent, which is great; otherwise it would not make sense for us to devote so much attention to him. What we do is to recognize that his talent is something other than what we foresaw and what was promised us in the beginning of his work. His is not the talent of science, but of belief, of closed faith, and this sets apart that historical mysticism which some call the ethical considerations of history; this also will always be all right as long as it does not include, as a condition, that the historian previously renounce any familiarity with what in fact has happened and is happening in the world. That ethical attitude of the teacher and the preacher, which enchants some people, leads Mr. Toynbee for the moment to the belief that his idea and his attitude will be all that is desired, but it is not enlightening, and with it he seems to be trying to light a small candle on our obscure destinies. Instead of that, what happens is that Mr. Toynbee writes phrases which begin like this: "The militarist Lugalzaggizi" (on hearing this you will assume that this man is some personage of these last years, or at least of the last centuries, and concerning whom one has enough information to understand the cruel and dirty maneuverings which allow us to charge him with militarism). But we go on reading, and we find this: "The militarist Lugalzaggizi, a Sumerian from Uruk, ruled in the year 2677 B.C."

"The devil!" we say to ourselves. "How does Toynbee know that this personage was a militarist when there is scarcely any information about his person and it is only luck if one knows that he existed?" To such extremes does this pedagogical attitude, this misplaced preacher's passion, lead that it makes it impossible for us to understand the man who exercises it. This is what we get from the fact that Mr. Toynbee calls Lugalzaggizi a militarist and adds that he was a Sumerian tyrant of Uruk, using this word *tyrant* in the knowledge that it has long had a bad press, and in spite of knowing, as he very well must, that in the Mesopotamian civilizations there was never tyranny and that the word "tyrant" and the fact of tyranny are specific phenomena of the Aegean and Hellenic worlds.

The word *tyrant* is Greek, but of pre-Hellenic origin; and the institution called "tyranny" was one of those that have created not a few of the most admirable things that have been done among humanity. For example, in Athens, which is beloved of Toynbee, the works of the tyrant Pisistratus, who with perfect consciousness and deliberation had the genial idea of doing something that had never been done on the planet before—of creating a *paideia*, a culture; that culture which Mr. Toynbee and his companions the professors of Oxford so piously adore and to which they pay homage.

Therefore that assertion of ethics, that pedagogic and preacherist attitude which to some people seems a marvel, seems to me—first, a bit ridiculous; second, a bit insolent; and third, very calamitous, for it is the surest way to make certain that some men continue thumbing their noses at others. An arbitrary attitude like that opinion can only provoke a contrary arbitrary attitude, and these bits of arbitrariness are slow secretions which are produced in the brain, in the head, but which soon come down to the fists; whence it might happen that at the end it would be Mr. Toynbee who became the real militarist and not the poor "tyrant" of Uruk who lived five thousand years ago.

These bigotries and this inopportune ethical posture

make one want to tell the well-known tale of the little acolyte who did not know how to play his part in the mass; when the priest pronounced his ritual phrases the lad invariably answered, "Blessed and praised be the most Holy Sacrament." The moment came when the priest, tired of this, turned and said to him "Boy, that is very good, but it has nothing to do with the matter."

But this intellectual fashion of Mr. Toynbee and other present-day English writers is important to you and to me. It is important because Mr. Toynbee is a very influential man in the international policy of England, because he is one of the most representative writers in England, because England exercises an enormous influence on what is happening in the world, and because, as I said the first day (although without proof and only as a reservation which for my own part I needed to make and still reiterate), I believe it to be a great convenience for everybody that England should continue to exercise that influence on the destinies of the world.

If England were not called on to continue exercising that decisive influence, we could drop the question. If, on the other hand, her intellectuals were seriously in earnest, we would not feel impelled to be worried. The worry is that two things come at once: the very powerful efficacy of England and the restless lack of solidity in many of her intellectuals. The coexistence of the two things—the good and the less good—is what recommends that we be on the alert. As for that English power potentiality, I suspect that those are on the wrong track who, because they do not understand history, do not know that in it the same reality may take on very different aspects, including some which, insofar as they are aspects, are contradictory.

In this course it is neither my mission nor my role to enter fully into that matter. On the other hand, I do not think you can consider me an Anglophile. I think I am not a "phile" or a "phobe" of anything, and not because of any admirable virtue, but simply because this does not amuse me. All the "philes" and the "phobes" bore me desperately, like a novel by Ricardo León.[1] Well then, without trying to impress my opinion on anyone—and less in this than in anything else—I am going to state it as briefly as possible, because it concerns a matter which is very important for our existence and which is connected with the world's scientific problem. I think that the greatest thing, in the sense of being the most praiseworthy, which is now happening in the world is how badly the English are eating. As the English have always eaten badly, in the culinary sense, I will avoid the equivocal by making it quite clear that I refer to the slender nutritive value and poor quality of many of their foods,[2] though some others of them continue to be excellent. This, in my judgment, is humanly the most extraordinary thing that is now happening, becauste there is no doubt that they could now be eating approximately the same as they did before, but this would clearly be at the expense of the future, risking the economic, and in general the historic, future of their nation by tricks and subterfuges, eating, in short, the hen that laid the golden egg.

In place of this, the fact that the individuals who make up the English people, without any perceptible loss of quantity, should have accepted scrupulously a drop in the standard of living, restricting their daily existence in an almost intolerable degree without any unusual pressure from their government, and this not with the promise, prospect, or hope that this sacrifice would give back to

1. Ricardo León was a well-known nineteenth-century novelist and essayist (1877–1943) [*Translator's note*].

2. Ortega was talking of the effect of scarcities in England immediately after World War II [*Translator's note*].

England its imperial preponderance over the world, but simply from the conviction that this was unavoidable in order to get through the crudeness of the times and save the English community in the purity of its style for future years; this resolution of spontaneous and resolute national solidarity seems to me one of the most extraordinary examples in history, something that could be called *Numantismo en frio*,[3] to give it a magnificent Iberian name.

What I have just been saying does not contradict what I suggested the other day when I was talking of what, at first sight, seemed to us to be a hint that there was in the depth of certain of the most outstanding English souls a strange feeling that they might begin to doubt whether it made sense to be English. There is no such contradiction between the two suggestions, for it means that the English are beginning, or began some time ago (later I will refer to some old writings of mine in which I announced this)—to believe that England would not continue as it was, that in order to save the existence of the English it was necessary for them to change completely in form and attitudes, and that in this sense, the Englishman was ceasing to be the traditional Englishman.

Over and above that comportment with which English people *think* they can adjust themselves to the external situation, they also retain a supply of energy sufficient to make themselves capable of bringing about a complete transformation in their social structure (on that social structure, and so as not to confuse things, we will for the moment suspend judgment because it is not pertinent to

3. This refers to Numantia, a small town in northern Spain, which rebelled against the Romans in 144 B.C. The Roman general drew six miles of entrenchments around the town and starved it out. It took sixty thousand soldiers and fifteen months to do it. Hence Ortega's complimentary phrase, "cold Numantism," which might be translated "cold Numantic courage" [*Translator's note*].

what we are now saying)—a transformation with which they *think* they can adjust their social body to the internal necessities which the evolution of the times has brought the English. All this reveals that we find ourselves in the presence of one of the great historic events, one which has the most characteristic symptom of a great historic fact; that is to present a completely new figure, not an imitation or a repetition of known and familiar features. When a people does this, it is in full form, a form that is new, and *therefore* complete, and when a people is in full form it has the best guarantees that it will save itself. These guarantees do not, of course, assure success, because nothing human is certain, and less so at a critical point of time like the present one which universal destinies have reached; but do not confuse the worldly circumstances within which England finds herself—which are in fact most difficult—with the state of the English people united in their own being; once more great navigators, the English have again hauled in their mainsails and are sailing close to the wind.

I would almost dare to say that insofar as their collective temper is concerned, the English today are in a form similar to that in which they might have been after Waterloo; indeed, they may be even more so today. What was in better shape at that time was the world around them, England's surroundings—and with this I refer not to external aspects but to what English society suffers internally by finding itself, like everybody else today, in a world torn by the most fundamental crises. Because of this circumstance, while the English temper and inspiration are in full form, this is not true of their intellectuals or even of their institutions, as we are going to see in the next three or four years.

You will understand that I am not at this time going to develop or explain what I just said. That takes time and opportunity. This situation, the present temper of England, I foresaw some time ago; for me, as for anyone interested in the humanities as I am, it was not difficult to glimpse that it was fermenting during the 1920s; this you can prove if you read or now reread, in the *Prologue for the English* published in England in 1937 and afterwards added to my book *The Revolt of the Masses*, the paragraphs devoted to the making of the third British Empire; note that that study of mine went so far as to foresee the attitude of England toward the Spanish war, which deprived me of full freedom to talk. Therefore, reading attentively between the lines, you will find that that third Empire was formed on the base of a methodical pessimism, because even the English foresaw that there would be no freedom of horizons for traditional England and that there was no remedy but to do the inverse of what they had done in the last two centuries—namely, to retire bit by bit from their imperial preponderance.

None of this means that the English retention of Gibraltar seems good to me. On the contrary, if I could have carried out that forbidden development, I would have shown how that retention, the fact that England at that time had not found even the beginning of a way to rectify the Gibraltar situation, is entirely out of character with what I think characterizes the intimate style of the modern Englishman. And note that if I let myself go this far, it is because—having shown earlier that I do not bite my tongue in talking of the English—I ran the risk of leading some of you astray in serious matters. I did not do this, then, not by choice but out of duty; it robbed me of time, and you cannot imagine the anguish I feel on finding myself at the eleventh lesson and seeing that I cannot complete the program which I laid out.

Let us come back to our road. I said that the idea and the formula of "challenge-response" seems magnificent to me, but that Toynbee diminishes it when he refers only to certain heavily dramatic situations, like, for example, the abrupt origin of primary civilizations. The result would be that in the case of a specific change in the climate, for example a specific drought, man would have shown for the first time a capacity to respond to the challenge of his surroundings; this would mean a skill which he had never before shown himself to possess, as if in the tens of thousands of years previous to 7000 B.C., men had not seen changes of all kinds and would not have had to react to many droughts and many floods. But I do not know why Mr. Toynbee concedes to drought the privilege of stimulating man to civilization and does not explain the origin of anything by flood, whereas in the oldest tradition of the Semites who lived in the Near and Middle East, even before the Sumerians—according to Toynbee the creators of the first civilization—there still endures the memory of a great flood and of a group of men who reacted to it, led by a person whom they called Atrichises or Utuapistin, which mean "the most ingenious one," therefore exactly the same meaning as *Sisyphus* in Greek. He is therefore the prototype of one of civilization's heroes, a civilizing hero as was the man whom the Hebrews called Noah, who saved himself in a ship with his family, his followers, and certain animals, and in order to find out whether the waters were ebbing, sent out the birds—the dove, the swallow, the crow. Consequently, this is something that represents a profound memory written in the very souls of those peoples, a very old tradition of which there were Babylonian versions many centuries earlier than the period of Moses. This does not mean that the Bible story necessarily comes from this Sumerian-Acadian tradition; this is a question which from a scientific point of view is still in litigation.[4]

4. When I alluded the other day to the myth of the Flood I referred of course to this Sumerian-Acadian tradition, which was

We saw the lack of "challenge-response" as the basis of the earliest civilizations, even in the case of the Sumerians and the Egyptians. Certainly on referring to the former I forgot to ask you to note the more arbitrary and almost frivolous attitude assumed by Toynbee in the data regarding the question; he assumes that before creating their civilization the Sumerians were already living in the ancient Mesopotamian region near the banks of the Euphrates just as the Egyptians were living near the valley of the Nile before the drought; yet it is well known that the Sumerians were recently arrived folk who came from afar, perhaps from a region lying between the Trans-Caucasus, the Caspian Sea, Attai, and Pamir. Hence they arrived with their good Mongolian lungs already charged with the principles of their civilization, perhaps including (it seems) the oldest writing in the world.

The "challenge-response" principle—note the paradoxes which exist in the most essential structure of the science—though even truer than Toynbee suspects, does not serve to explain the particular fact of the origin of civilizations, any more than it serves to explain any concrete fact. The same thing happens to it as happens to the principle of contradiction, which, although a pure universal principle, does not serve us for anything; we cannot

---

what we were talking about. On what to call that myth, I do not suppose that a basis of reality can be denied. On the contrary. Nothing is myth unless it carries within itself the substance of a real human experience. When this is lacking it is not called a myth but simply "a bit of foolishness." It is a pity and a shame that these observations must be made and these reservations set forth; they ought to not be necessary for people who are even halfway cultured, but I do not know what there is in the intellectual air of Spain today; it seems as though there were suspended in it an ignorance and a demented insipidity which are truly pitiable and which oblige one to take all these grotesque precautions.

derive any other truth from it. Keep in mind this law of thought, that when an idea defines what is in fact a thing, it cannot directly and by itself explain or define the particular modification which may occur in that thing or emanate from it; it needs to be fertilized by other ideas or principles from which come special ideas and laws which, interposed between that most universal idea and the concrete facts, allow the latter to be explained. Most of you will not have understood what I have just said, as I used the proper technical and therefore abstruse terms which correspond to it. But I have already recommended that you be not in the least abashed at failing to understand something I say, because if the fact is shameful, it is so only for me insofar as I do not succeed in having you understand it, as you will shortly do.

My idea of the "challenge-response" principle differs radically from Toynbee's on these two points: human life is not a response on this or that occasion, but in a constitutive and permanent way it is man's having to respond to the difficulties he meets under peril of succumbing, that is to say under peril of there being no human life; second, and vice versa, no circumstance or element in the surroundings, and even less in geographic surrounding alone, exists which in itself can constitute a difficulty for man, unless it be transformed into a difficulty which is relative to the kind of a man who meets it. I am going to explain these two theorems in an order inverse to that in which I stated them, beginning, then, with the second and holding almost exclusively to the facts which Toynbee himself describes and comments on. Toynbee says, for example:

The oil fields of Azerbaijan—an ancient province north of Persia and today called Transcaucasia—originated a challenge to one human society after another, in the form of difficulties in dominating it, before a response to this difficulty eventually arose. The nomads, who are the first inhabitants on the steppes of Azerbaijan of which we have any information, do not seem to have made any use of the mineral riches which gushed forth and leaked out over the pastures used by their herds. The Syrian society which took the place of the nomads in Azerbaijan during the first half of the sixth century B.C., when the Medes dominated the Scyths, did not fail to note the peculiar nautral phenomenon which was present in that remote corner there on the extreme edge of the Syrian world; but during the Syrian administration the Azerbaijan petroleum was used only for religious purposes without taking on any economic character. In fact, some of the most famous wells were enclosed in towers in order that the oil jet might serve the Zoroastrian cult of fire, feeding a perpetual flame at its peak, and even this ritual use of the mineral oil lasted only while the Zoroastrian religion prevailed in the region. When Zoroastrianism gave way to Islam, and the Syrian religion was replaced by the Iranian, its "affiliate," those perpetual flames ceased to burn, and the only use which man had made of mineral oil up to then was abandoned. . . . At the beginning of the nineteenth century Baku was nearly conquered, and this by a Russia which still kept the impetus toward economic Westernization which Peter the Great had given it a century earlier, and in the course of the same century the oil of Baku came to be one of the primary materials and bits of merchandise in the economic system which had come to embrace the whole world and all humanity.

This is how petroleum, which was a difficulty, a worry, an obstacle to the shepherd of the flocks that were the nomad's only wealth, was transmuted into one of the greatest advantages and benefits for contemporary man. To this I add another most recent example. One of the most miserable places on the whole planet has been the eastern end of the Persian Gulf on the coast of Arabia. Here was the independent sheikdom of Kuwait. Well, now, that is today perhaps the wealthiest spot in the whole world, because its recently developed petroleum wells are fantastically rich. Nevertheless, Kuwait is a place where one could hardly live, because up to now there was no way of getting water into the region.

Let us look at another case of variation in geographic reality in a very different situation confronting mankind. Everyone knows that Napoleon was conquered in Russia by "General Winter." It was not the Slavic armies but the snows and the frosts that defended the Muscovites. In 1794–95, when Napoleon invaded Holland, the latter succumbed because it could not use the traditional method, and the only powerful one it had always used for defending itself, which was the flooding of its lands by opening the gates of the dikes near the sea; this time the Dutch could not do this because that winter had been so very hard that the waterways were frozen. So here we have the same cause producing opposite effects.

Nothing material, nothing natural in history is difficult or easy by itself, but at the moment everything is easy or difficult in relation to the state of technique, and technique in turn is a function of life. Because, note, there is not an absolute technique, as you can see in my study *Meditation on Technique;* there is no other technique than that which is relative to what man tries to do by himself. From which we come to a pause, in that the earth, and the particular geographic medium, along with other factors, are pure partial functions of the total figure which human life adopts every hour. For this reason a naturalist historian is impossible. Man is not natural, he has no nature, he is not tied to being a fixed creature, he is infinite in possibilities as God is infinite in actualities. No one can say of what man is not capable in its time and occasion. Not even does talk of the destruction of the planet mean unequivocally the destruction of man, if that destruction of the planet comes when man has been able to reach his possibilities of interplanetary existence. If this, which has always been beyond question, had been said a few years ago by the philosophers who know how to anticipate events, it would have seemed utopian. But within the last few months the first platform to be made outside of terrestrial gravity has been under construction; this means, gentlemen, that the first interplanetary island is actually being fabricated by man.

Toynbee renders his thesis more irritating by affirming that within certain limits one can formulate a law to the effect that the greater the challenge, the difficulty, the more valuable is the response, and he adduces as extreme examples the cases of Venice and Holland. One of these accepts the superlative difficulty of installing itself amid the waters, and the other succeeds in defending its lands beneath the sea by adding earth to them—that is, so to speak, by fabricating its own homeland; the first results in one of the ten most marvelous histories that peoples of the West have ever achieved, and the latter has achieved a level of life and one of the highest forms of supercivilization that has ever existed.

Let us leave Venice aside, and let me say only that I do not see clearly how the challenge of the sea to Holland has been the cause of its admirable civilization. I think that apart from this, and without depreciating it, one must at the moment take account of a factor which is both geographic and historic, that is to say, the human factor: Holland's favorable situation between England, France, and Germany has made of it a cushioned territory between those peoples. These countries have contributed at least as much to sustain Holland as have the Dutch themselves. So we see that the historic meaning of each geographic place is a function of many variables. For example, Spain, without moving from its place, underwent a radical change in its geopolitical or geohistorical history when, in the eighth century, the Moslems cut the Mediterranean horizontally in two, and separated one coast from the other; with this, Spain, which in the last periods of the Roman world had been a Mediterranean country and a passage between Europe and North Africa, was suddenly converted into an extreme promontory of Europe, into a land's end.[5] This is not a vague description; one can be as precise about it as one pleases.[6]

Toynbee says that there are civilizations which save themselves by continuing to live in a place which is undesirable, and hence not wanted by other people, who leave them, isolated in the difficult district, to vegetate in peace. By the very process of fleeing and seizing a piece of country which anyone else would consider impossible, these people save themselves. But is this in fact by accepting the challenge of the surroundings, or is it simply not having any other choice? Do you think it would be an adequate description of what a captain does in a shipwreck to say that he accepts the difficulty of the opportune rock? It seems to me that such a description wanders very far from accuracy. It is known in zoology that the species that are dying out can lengthen the remainder of the life that is left to them by fleeing into the depths of the forests, as the pygmies did; it is to this that they owe

5. Thus, for example, one can report a fact which is not usually examined: few of the great European spectacles have normally been able to come to Madrid for the simple reason that in addition to the expenses of performing in our city they had the cost of the journey in and out; the return trip was fruitless because Spain became the terminus of a dead-end road. And one can be even more precise by seeing which of these spectacles passed, nevertheless, through Barcelona and not through Madrid, for the reason that Barcelona was almost completely on the cyclical line of movement. It would be interesting to follow these companies in their comings and goings.

6. If, as it seems, the West is proceeding at last to the great capitalization of Africa, Spain will recover its ancient position and become again a crossroads as Belgium has been, and continues to be.

their endurance into our own time. The same thing happened to that magnificent animal the okapi, almost unknown forty years ago, which retired to the forests with the pygmy.

Nevertheless—this is curious—Toynbee formally identifies this fugitive conduct which saves those he calls "fossil peoples"—for the peoples who retire pay for their retirement by becoming fossilized—with the conduct of the parents of the first and great civilizations, insofar as, in throwing themselves onto the marshy lands, they remained free from nearby plottings. In this he once again destroys his own principle, for salvation by flight is rendered the same as the heroic creative response. It does not seem, then, that this is the way in which we will reach unequivocal responses. About every place in the planet, about any geographic space of a possible civilization, a thousand things can be said *a priori,* many of them opposed one to the others. This means that that geographic situation, climatic surrounding, is not an element which can be isolated and in itself be considered the determining factor. Hence Toynbee could say the most contradictory things about the same piece of land; the result, as we have seen, is that he destroys his own thesis, because one comes to recognize that in reality every place on the planet is, in turn and successively, both easy and difficult.

This is the pure truth, but Toynbee should have recognized it, and should either have broadened his idea or etched its profile more deeply. Thus he tells us that in ancient Greece, at the dawn of Hellenic history, the rocky and scarcely fertile surface of Attica posed a challenge to the Athenians, which they accepted and, in so doing, created a marvelous civilization. But a few pages later he adds that this also brought them a compensation, because the rocky character of those lands offered no attraction to the terrible Dorian immigrants who therefore laid waste all of Hellas except Attica.

So we see something new: that the decisive fact of a people establishing themselves in a certain region does not simply follow either the theory of challenge posed by climatic change, or the cause which historians always manage so lightly and comfortably, namely, the migration of peoples from place to place for the simple reason that others come and push them out. The Dorians who came —and on this I stay with Toynbee—according to him and to most historians, arrived from the remote Russian steppes, probably from a region near the Black Sea, by way of other more northern peoples. They did not establish themselves in Attica because it did not seem to them agreeable, attractive, because they did not like it. If this is true, as it is, and as Toynbee himself recognizes, this should lead him to construct and establish a new category according to which a people sets itself in a specific terrain not because it challenges them, but because it pleases them. I do not understand why Toynbee does not notice this and set up such a category.

So far as migrations are concerned, I want to say in passing that the present foreign historians who busy themselves with these ancient civilizations give too much weight, as a convenience in explaining them, to the principle of overpopulation. Is it so likely as they accept that in the third millennium before Christ such overpopulation existed in Asia and Africa? I know well that this is a relative matter, depending, in degree, on how techniques progress, but even so, that overflowing of humanity at such dates does not seem conceivable. Would it not be more simple and probable to present an inverse situation —namely, that there were ages in which land was abundant, and that when there is "land beyond," the normal life of peoples is a certain and constant drift, a permanent movement something like the wandering of flocks, as we have recently seen happen with the pioneers of North America? Their progress toward the West was not due to their leaving a super-population behind them, but to the fact that "there was land beyond."

We are going to see that all this complex of my observations was expressed fourteen years before Toynbee's book was published. I said in 1922:

. . . the climatic aridity of the Peninsula does not justify Spain's history. The geographic conditions are a fatality only in the classic sense of *fata ducunt, non trahunt:* "the fates direct, they do not pull along." Perhaps there is no better way of expressing the kind of influence that physical surrounding, the "medium," has on the animal and especially on man. The land influences man, but in what manner? Man, like every vital organism, is a reactive being. This means that the modification produced in him by some fact outside himself is never simply an effect that follows a cause. The "medium" is not the cause of our acts, but only an excitant; our acts are not the effect of the "medium" but a free response, an automatic reaction.

Fortunately the biologists are becoming convinced that the idea of cause and effect is not applicable to vital phenomena, and that in their place it is necessary to make use of this other pair of concepts: stimulus and reaction. The difference between one category and the other is very clear. One cannot talk of effect except when one phenomenon reproduces in a new form what there was in another, which is the cause. *Causa aequat effectum.* The impulse which puts into motion a billiard ball brings to pass, after the first shock, movement of another ball to which that impulse passes. No one has ever seen the second billiard ball move faster than the first. On the other hand, the movement of a hand in the air is enough to move a squadron of cavalry to break into a gallop. The vital reaction is an effect constantly disproportionate to its cause; therefore it is not an effect.

It was, then, a mistake to seek the "causes" of historic events which are definitely biological events. Strictly speaking, the only cause which is active in the life of a man, of a people, of a period is that man, that people, that period. To put it another way, historical reality is automatic, it causes itself. In comparison with the influence which we Spaniards have had on ourselves, the influence of climate is strictly something to be disdained.

Fata ducunt, non trahunt. The earth has an influence on man, but man is a reactive being whose reaction can in turn transform the earth. The dryness of the earth acts on him, producing in him thirst and drowsiness. If a man is strong, he will know how to react, dotting the wasteland with wells and imposing on himself a vigorous positive discipline which conquers the laziness of the muscles. So that the place where the influence of the earth on man is most notable is in the influence of man on the earth.

Certainly there are places on the planet which are not inhabitable. Life in them is impossible; but by the same token, they are not influential in life. There where life can be only minimally positive, the organic being reacts on the "medium" and transforms it in accord with his vital potency. . . .

The landscape does not determine historic destinies causally, inexorably. Geography does not drag history along; it only incites it. The arid land which surrounds us is not a fatality to us, but a problem before us. Each people found itself with a problem posed by the territory to which it arrived, and solved that problem in its own way, some good, others bad. The results of that solution are visible in the present landscapes.

It is necessary, then, to invert the terms. Geographic data is very important for history; but in a sense opposite to the one that Taine gave it. One cannot make use of it as a cause which explains the character of a people, but on the contrary, as a symptom and symbol of this character. Each race carries in its primitive soul an ideal of landscape which it tries to realize within the geographic frame of the surroundings. Castile is terribly arid because the Castilian man is arid. Our race has accepted the surrounding dryness by feeling it related to the interior steppe of the Castilian soul. As within the individual the element which reveals him best is the character of the women he chooses, so there are few things that declare the condition of a people more subtly than the landscape they accept.

I will be told that at times the geographic face is so adverse to the desires of a race that all its reactions in an attempt to transform it will be vain. Certainly, but then there is produced in history the curious phenomenon of migration which means exactly the refusal to accept a landscape and the pilgrim desire for a country that is dreamed of, a land of promise which every strong race promises itself.[7]

And a little later I insisted on the thesis, including this about the migrations:

The terrain does not in itself determine history. There is a factor which we might call "the historic inspiration of the peoples" which cannot be explained zoologically. And that factor is the decisive one in a people's destinies. With the same geographic and even anthropological material there may be produced different histories. There is in addition another phenomenon of great importance, the migration of peoples. The autochthonous condition is always problematical and utopian. In fact we do not know more in history than that peoples who have set themselves in motion and then settled themselves temporarily—"temporarily" in terms of thousands of years, at times—in one place on the planet, have there created this history. If we then cling to the strictness of events, what is important to understand is *why* a people which displaced itself will suddenly stop and identify itself with a landscape. It is like a man who moves forward among a group of women and suddenly stops, caught by one of them.

It is vain to take refuge, as is customary, in utilitarian considerations, in facts. One must end by recognizing an affinity between the soul of a people and the style of its landscape. Hence one fastens on this—because he likes it. For me, then, there is a symbolic relation between nation and territory. Peoples migrate in search of their ideal landscape, which, in the secret depths of their soul, has been promised them by God. The promised land is a promised landscape.[8]

7. "Temas de viaje," Chapter III, *Historia y geografía* (*Obras completas*, vol. II).

8. "En el centenario de Hegel," Chapter III, *Historia y geografía* (*Obras completas*, vol. V).

Now you see that many years before Toynbee began to write his book, the interpretation of the relations between man and the land had been thought out in Castile as challenge-and-response—that is to say, the earth acts upon man, not directly causing his actions, but indirectly posing problems for him. But at the same time you will have noted the basic radical difference which exists between the two methods of understanding it. Toynbee starts from a purely physical fact, from one element in the surroundings, and believes that in itself it can constitute a difficulty for any man, whoever he be. I, on the other hand, start from the man and say that the project of existence, the peculiar idea or ideal of life which a people carries within itself, in each of its stages, oppresses the surroundings; it is under the outline of that determined pressure that the geographic surroundings also take on a determined profile of difficulty. But one must add that this is also a profile of facility. There is no need to emphasize the former exclusively. There is no need to dramatize further.

The challenge of the surrounding cannot be only a challenge; it cannot be pure difficulty, but it is also, in one measure or another, facility. Without certain facilities akin to what a certain man wants to be, he would succumb; then there would be no history. Each geographic space, insofar as it is a space for a possible history, is, I said, a function of many variables. For the moment, of the state of the technique. But this state of the technique, I said, depends in turn on the figure of the entire life. Therefore, one must always count, first, on what kind of man you have. When the first missionaries explained the Christian doctrine to the Eskimos and described to them the felicities of beatitude in Paradise, the Eskimos asked, "But are there seals in Paradise?"

And as the missionaries answered that there were none,

the Eskimos shook their worried heads and said, "Then the Christian heaven will not do for the Eskimos. Because what does an Eskimo do without seals?"

This joke—for it is a joke that Heine tells, founded, perhaps, on a story told by some missionary—expresses gracefully the effective and permanent situation of man in respect to his surroundings, not in the other life, but in this one.

As I announced and promised in the previous lesson, one must reach all these questions from a much more fundamental and decisive point of view and one that antedates such biological and zoological considerations. Thus, when I proposed to you a myth or an imaginary picture of how man emerges from among the animals and begins to be something different, that is, begins to be man, I added that apart from its being only a myth, the question of the zoological position, the philogenetic problem of man, is secondary and not in the least decisive. What I firmly believe is that what characterizes man is his extreme abundance of imagination, which is so scarce in other species; therefore, that man is a fantastic animal and that universal history is the gigantic, continuous, and insistent effort to go, little by little, putting some order into the crazy fantasy. The history of reason is the history of the stages through which the domestication of our disorderly imagining has gone. There is no other way than to understand how that refining of the human mind has continued to be produced.

If one assumes that that full faculty of reasoning existed in the beginning, one does not understand how it lost so much time in manifesting its effectiveness. But biology, like this which was psychological, is concerned with particular and therefore secondary points of view; they consist in occupations to which man dedicates himself when he finds himself living. All the special sciences surge within, and by reason of the fundamental and primary perspective which is the simple fact of living. In this all of them have their origin, their basis and their justification; and by the same token they transfer us, as to a court of final instance, to the basic reality which is our life—human life, which is always and for the moment the life of each one of us. And if I call basic this reality which is my life, it is not because I consider my life a unique reality, or even a superior reality, but simply because it is for me the root of all the other things which, because they are to me that kind of realities, must appear or announce themselves in some manner within my own life. God himself, in order to be God to me, must reveal Himself to me, manifest Himself, epiphanize Himself to me in some manner in the trembling and resounding spaces which constitute my life.

Well now, it is important to say of this fundamental phenomenon only that it consists primarily in the simple fact that man finds himself having to be, to exist, in an element different from him, an element which is alien to him, in a circumstance or medium which one customarily calls the "world," and which, in order to simplify, we, too, will call "the world." Evidently, living is for the moment the finding which each of us makes of his own person; then of others, different in person from every other; then of something else different from him—the world. The world would not exist for me, I would not take it into consideration, it would not be a world for me, if it did not oppose me, did not resist and limit my desires, therefore hamper my intention to be what I am.

The world is, then, first of all—I do not say more or less, but most of all—resistance to me. It is the hostile thing, and therefore something other than I. The primordial relation between man and world becomes clear without more than going back rapidly over the three unique suppositions which can be made: First, that the world might be pure facility; therefore, that it would consist in pure conveniences for man, as optimists, for example the rationalist philosophers of the eighteenth century, have thought from time to time. Second, that the world might consist in hostility, only in hostility, in pure difficulty for man; this supposition is what, without recognizing it, Toynbee assumes. And third, that the world would be a combined system of things that are easy and those that are difficult.

The second supposition, that of the world as hostility, is at once eliminated because, in a world which was one of absolute difficulty, human life would be impossible. Man would *ipso facto* succumb.

The first supposition is also impossible, but the reason for this is more interesting. If I should want now to advance rectilineally, and this table, all by itself, as if divining my wish, should move back or let me pass through it, I would not distinguish it from myself. In order to distinguish it I must collide with it, must feel that it resists me. Then, if as in that supposition that the table yields, the same thing should happen with all the rest of the world because it is made up (as in the hypothesis) of pure facilities, the world would be not a world at all, but merely a prolongation of myself: it would be like my own body, it would be me. Therefore, in order to be a world to me, the world must consist in resistances, in difficulties; it must oppose itself to me. Remember what it undoubtedly costs a child to learn (at the cost of bruises and the experience of colliding with furniture) that his body does not reach to the horizon, that he has frontiers and limitations; that his person ends in a certain place, and that at that point there begins another thing which is alien and stubborn.

Living, in the sense of "finding ourselves amid what resists us" is what differentiates basically the meaning which the world has when referring to man and when referring to God. Because for God, living, being is not existing in a world. He who created the world made it for man, and it is man's world. God finds no resistance, and nothing that opposes Him. God has no world. The one He creates is for man, it is not God's world. Hence God has no frontiers, no limits. He is unlimited, infinite. For God, living is floating within Himself, without anything or anybody before Him or against Him. From this comes that most terrible and majestic attribute of God— His capacity to be, to exist in the most absolute solitude. That the cold of this tremendous, transcendent solitude does not freeze God is a measure of the promise of ignition, of the fire that resides within Him.

Hence the profound meaning of the mystery of the Incarnation, in which God, by a specific, concrete act of His will—allow me to say that this is divinely paradoxical —resolved to make Himself human, that is, to undertake and to suffer the experience of living in the world, of ceasing to be alone, and of accompanying man. It is one of the sides of *cur Deus homo*, of the reason why God made himself man.

A world which consisted in pure ease, pure facilities, would not be a world to us; it would be a paradise. And paradise is a surrounding which makes our desires real, which does not oppose us in anything. Therefore, strictly speaking it is not a surrounding at all; it is indistinguishable from the person who lives in it. Only when the angel with the flaming sword threw Adam and Eve out of Paradise did they begin to have human life in the natural meaning of the term, for what the angel did then was to put Adam and Eve into the world. That is to say, in what was resistant, hostile to, and other than they themselves. Here is a theme which I believe to be new, and which I offer to the theologians as long as those theologians get all possible beauty and precision from these questions. I ask this: before the act of sin, finding themselves in *statu innocentiae*, what was the relation between Adam and Paradise? How did he distinguish it from himself, it being, as we see—this is understood always in the order of natural thinking—such that it could not be a surrounding for Adam, as is the world for us? From the natural point of view, Adam would have had to feel as if Paradise were the same as his own, universal body.

Man, we said the other day, is perennially unadapted and inadaptable. Hence he collides with the world, and therefore he has a world. Because the world does not exist except as it is an obstacle. Therefore man's conduct would be inverse to that of the other animals: they adapt themselves to the medium; what he does is to adapt the medium to his person. In these circumstances, man's destiny implies energetic and continual force—having to adapt this world to his constitutive essential needs which are precisely those for which he is an unadapted one. He has, then, to force himself to transform this world which does not coincide with him, which is strange to him, which therefore is not his. He must transform it into another world in which his desires will be fulfilled. Because man is a system of desires which in this world are impossible. So to create another world of which it can be said that it is his world, the idea of a world that coincides with desire, is what is called happiness. Man feels himself unhappy, and for that very reason his destiny is happiness. Well now, for transforming this world into the world which can be his and with which he can coincide, he has no other instrument than technique, and physics is the possibility of an unlimited technique. From this we come to recognize that physics is the organ of human happiness and that the renewal of this science has, in human affairs, been the most important event in universal history.[9]

9. See the author's *Meditation on Technique* to which he alluded [*Translator's note*].

XII

The trajectory followed. The substance.
Being and the reform of intelligence.
The superficial character of French
existentialism. The three great concepts
in Toynbee's thought. The paradox of
the Roman state. Roman Law and
concord. Modern law and the *desiderata*.
The parable of the man and the bear.

WE FIND OURSELVES come to the last lesson. We have
reached it without major stumblings. Let us now take
account of our main trajectory. We have tried to set
forth and submit to critical examination Professor Toynbee's doctrine of history, which he developed in the literary super-stronghold of his work, with the six motors of
its six huge volumes.

Toynbee's doctrine begins by asking itself what the
true subject of history is, or, to put it another way, what
reality it is that has *its* own history, and therefore a history can be made out of it. A partial reality such (according to Toynbee) as a nation is, England, for example, will have a partial history, a piece or fragment of
history which, being a fragment, is no more intelligible
than a mere piece of a phrase. The true historical subject,
according to Toynbee, must be an entire, compact reality,
which can be understood from within itself and without
moving away from it. This, according to our author, does

not happen to the societies which are nations, but it does happen to societies of another type, broader societies in which many nations live joined together like members that integrate an organism. These societies, which are based on themselves, autarchic, sufficient unto themselves, and explaining themselves from within themselves— Toynbee calls these civilizations. Toynbee believes himself to be a man of the empirical method, but the fact is that, without realizing it, Mr. Toynbee is, in philosophic matters, a man of enchanting and paradisaical innocence. Without realizing it, intent on proclaiming the true historic subject which may be autarchic and sufficient and is explained within itself, he does nothing but postulate the least empirical idea that exists in the world: the Aristotelian idea of substance, which is the metaphysical idea *par excellence.*

Aristotle also says literally that the true real subject is substance, and this because it is autarchic, sufficient, and able to be understood from within itself.

That anti-Aristotelian, Descartes, is no more than a faithful disciple of Aristotle when he too defines substance as the sufficient being, as "that which does not want or have need for any other thing in order to exist." Toynbee, who is the *bourgeois gentilhomme* of philosophy, and who talks in Aristotelian and Cartesian terms without being aware of it, suspects even less that after twenty-five centuries of intellectual experiences, we have forced ourselves to abandon the interpretation of reality as substance, and we are holding our heads in an attempt to see if we can succeed in recognizing, as one inevitably notes, that all intramundane reality is the opposite, is the needy, deficient being which is not sufficient unto itself, which is in want and nevertheless exists.

The thing seems acrobatically paradoxical and ultra-difficult to understand, because our mental habits since the European nations were born have been formed under the rule of Greek discipline, and the Greeks (except for Heraclitus) thought the opposite: in one way or another, they thought that reality is the sufficient being, the underlying self. Well, now, we have no choice but to think in another way, because as the Greeks, perhaps with the unique exception of Heraclitus, thought that reality is the being that is sufficient in itself, they were convinced optimists; and that intellectual optimism for which the being, simply because it is, must be sufficient, compact, perfect, therefore good, has been handed down to us first by the Scholastics and then by their enemies the Humanists; for on this point, which is fundamental, the two brother enemies coincide. This suspicious coincidence was due to the fact that the Scholastics, in place of holding to the authentic Christian inspiration, gave themselves up to ways of thinking that originated in Hellenic paganism and renounced the creation of a philosophy which would be Christian in itself and not only in its application to philosophy.

That authentically Christian philosophy would have been enormously more profound than the Greek, but it would not have been optimistic, for in the first chapter of Genesis, God, after creating all the things of this world, recognizes that they were *valde bona*, exceedingly good, after the sin; and the root of Christianity is the consciousness of sin, that is, man recognizing himself and everything around him as needful of salvation. After the sin, I say, man and the world, converted into a mere natural reality, ceased to be *valde bona* and were converted into in-valids, decrepit creatures who went limping. Hence Christianity—I have already reminded you—gives this world a definition which is more serious and more profound than all the definitions of Greek philosophy, a simple geographic definition, when it tells us that this world is "a vale of tears."

And the curious thing is that those among you for whom I feel a profound sympathy, who have been especially instructed and educated in that philosophy which is called Christian, will be the first, although recognizing the truth of the phrase, to judge that for me to call it a definition can only be in jest. Because a definition is what Aristotle said was a definition, and as they have been incrusted with that mummified and archaic notion, they do not know it to be notorious that Aristotle had rather deficient notions of what a definition was; those notions have been admirable in their time, and not only then, for Aristotle is truly one of the four or five prodigious heads which have been in the world, truly what one can call heads, and not the honorary paperweights that the rest of us customarily carry on our shoulders. Well, then, these Christian philosophers among you think that that was not a definition; while we think in all seriousness that that Christian saying about the world is the only form of definition which the ultimate realities can tolerate.

There you have the present vicissitude; there you have the way things have turned; and if we, out of purely philosophic necessities (apart from other reasons), find ourselves reliving the Christian intuition of reality at root, and forced to see how we can manage to think of reality as it demands, as an indigent being, therefore a being which, at once is, and does not cease to be; this means that for the first time European man transcends intellectually the magic circle traced by Greek discipline, by classic traditions. This reason recommends the creation of an Institute of the Humanities in which these ideas may be studied and investigated far beyond humanism and the classic tradition; these latter will continue to be closely examined, but not in the classic way. On the contrary, they will be greatly enriched.

I invite you to pay attention to what I have just been saying and not pass it by, for it is a serious matter and of great importance. It treats of nothing less than the most profound reform in intelligence and in ideas about man and the world that has been attempted since the luminous times of Greece. All the sciences, and, more importantly, most of the disciplines of Western man, live, in the last instance, on the idea of being which predominated in Greece. Consequently a radical reform in the idea of being, however little may be achieved, brings with it a basic renewal in all the sciences and all the human disciplines. This attempt is the only great promise which rises above today's horizon, and it constitutes the only probability that many problems hitherto insoluble, having to be reframed in a totally different form, may within the new perspective receive some solution.

But I do not ask or desire anyone to abandon the traditional positions of thought in which he finds himself; nor would I dissuade him from those positions in order to accept this project of reform of intelligence at its root simply because it is new. I do ask, on the other hand, that you manage calmly and serenely to understand it enough to judge it, rather than closing your minds to it completely and foolishly. I ask, in short, that you do not react to what is a great idea as roughly and carelessly as is customary in our country.

Now we can say formally that for Toynbee the civilizations are the subjects or substances that make up history. So that—whatever is talked of in history, for example, the biography of a person—one is always talking about a civilization; Western civilization, or Greek civilization, or Egyptian civilization. Toynbee's immediate step is to try to determine what attributes in the enormous mass of historic facts allow us to recognize which of their convolutions are built into the figure of the civilization.

Starting from the four that are now existent, and going

back to the past, Toynbee believes he can establish the list of those characteristics or symptoms distinctive of a civilization. The greater part of these, he thinks, proceed, in their existence, in this form: they begin with a Völkerwanderung, a migration of barbarous people, the "external proletariat," who destroy a preexistent universal state in an earlier civilization; they then inherit from that civilization a universal religion created by an "internal proletariat" of the conquered state. This is followed by centuries of chaos, after which come slow and peaceful centuries of formation. These are then interrupted by centuries of revolt which end in one of those nations subjugating the other, and then creating the atrocious awkwardness of a public power by itself, which is the universal state, a *Pax* from whence surges, as if gushing from its deep proletarian breasts, a universal religion. These are the filial or derived civilizations, but these date back to six original and primary civilizations which do not inherit from any earlier one.

Many times I have had to repeat this series of concepts, of stages through which, according to Toynbee, all civilizations except the original ones pass, and I have had to do it because it is the vertebral column of his entire doctrine. In it, as you will note, is a question which stands out above all the others: Is this the origin of civilizations? But this question is in turn bifurcated, because the origin of the derived civilizations is different from that of the primary or originating ones. This basic origin is, for Toynbee, abrupt, though he does not call it so; he considers this manner of setting it forth to be the most natural thing in the world.

We have devoted several lessons to his way of explaining this sudden origin and to his way of thinking about this question. We saw the role, too negative and confused, which, according to Toynbee, the "race" factor plays in this question; we saw what the geographic surroundings and real (or hypothetical) changes represent as a challenge which the earth launches and to which groups of heroic men respond with the creation of one civilization or another. This led us to analyze in depth the first and most important category within Toynbee's doctrine, the idea of "challenge-response," giving reasons in which I showed what are the coincidences and what the differences as between his thought and mine. In order to clarify this difference I had no choice but to raise the veil of a fundamental philosophy which starts with human life, and whose basic and primary phenomenon, more evident and basic, shows us man *perpetually and constitutively* in combat, compromised, *engagé* to struggle with the world, which more or less resists him, limits him, and denies his intention to be what he has to be.

And as everything in this course, including that which at first appears most adventitious, is rigorously systematic, this brief immersion in the reality which is our life (the life of each one of us) afforded us certain views about some transcendental problems, problems concerning God, man, and happiness. It now allows us—but without stopping—to get a glimpse of the reason which makes me consider the so-called existentialist philosophy an error *a limine*, that is, from the start. This philosophy, with a delay of twenty years in Germany and twenty-five years with respect to Spain, is now fashionable to the point of epidemic in Paris. For according to this, the result would be that for man to vow his life to an enterprise, that is, to engage himself, is a special act, and one specially thought out so that at a certain moment he must make up his mind about it—as if living were not always his own living and if he himself were not already vowed, *engagé*, which is the word the existentialists use.

One forgets too often that if man lives it is because he

accepts living; he might very well not accept it. It is not, then, that finding himself alive he must *s'engager*, or vow himself, but that the simple act of living is an inexorable, unavoidable constitutive matter of being already *engagé*, or vowed. Compared with this basic and primary *engagement* or contract which simple living is, all other vows— secondary and special—are superficial, even frivolous, as one sees by doing no more than looking them in the face.

Let Jean-Paul Sartre, whom I admire because—say what you like, he has a great talent—let me say to him that the things in which he has been saying that he was recently *"engagé"* (in the last six months, because we have seen him change frequently) are insipid and lacking in taste, the wormiest subjects now moving through the streets. And if a man of great talent says or does tasteless things, the fault is not his, but that of the erroneous doctrine in which he finds himself.

Here you see how existentialism, with respect to *engagement*, commits exactly the same error as Toynbee with respect to the idea of challenge-and-response; namely, it takes the matter in secondary and superficial forms and zones instead of seeing it in the depth of its constitutive and transcendent value.

But the question of the origin of civilizations presents another appearance when one considers those that are filial and derived. These are born, we said, after a migration of new peoples, who erupt into a universal state where they find a universal church. These three concepts —Völkerwanderung or the migration of peoples, universal state, and universal religion—are the three fundamental concepts of Toynbee's thought. But the surprising thing is that he never occupies himself seriously, and a bit in depth, in telling us what is the content of those concepts, despite the fact that their names appear on almost every page of his book. It should be noted that Toynbee does the same thing with all the most acute and decisive problems. About migrations, as his work goes on, he tells us less each time they are mentioned, until at the end he chooses to put a note at the foot of a page saying that he will treat the subject in that part of his work which has not yet been published.

In the last instance he does well to behave timidly about migrations, because this is really a very fragile, brittle subject, and, despite its being a historical phenomenon of the first order, it has not yet been analyzed in structure and consistence. When one finds historians with the unquestionable fact that a people have migrated, they simply assume, without thinking themselves obliged to prove the effectiveness of their assumption, that other peoples came along and pushed the first ones out; this moves them to imagine a third people who push out the second, and so on *ad infinitum*. One wants to say to the historians, as the street people say, "no shoving."

Well then, in order to justify these pushings, the historians take refuge in the concept of overpopulation; this is hardly probable in such ancient periods of history, yet it is a fact that this concept of overpopulation is frequently employed as a matter of general utility. Is it so likely as they assert that toward the year 5000 or 4500 B.C. the Russian steppes, Asia Minor, or the north of Africa were in truth so overpopulated? I know well that everything is relative in terms of the degree of progress of techniques, but even so, the existence of overpopulation in those dawnings of historic times seems to me hardly comprehensible. Neither the formation of languages nor the growth of myths nor, in general, the many forms of modes of living of men then existent in protohistory can be explained unless one assumes that human groups lived very far from each other, that the meeting between strange groups was relatively unlikely, and that the fact of such a meeting remained driven into their memories like one of the great tales.

Would it not be simpler and more probable to think that in those days the land was abundant? And where there is land "over there," the normal life of peoples would probably consist in a sure and incessant drift, in a constant mobility rather like that of moving herds, as we have seen happen recently with the pioneers of North America. The advance of those Americans, most of them immigrants, toward the west was not due to their leaving an overpopulated condition behind them, but simply to the fact that there was land ahead. More than this, when a people finds itself in a geographic zone where there is land ahead, more land than it may need, it responds to that land in a perfectly characteristic human fashion which has occurred before in a strict and potentially historical sense. Such peoples are not in history. When there is more than enough land, it is geography which commands, and it takes the form of a real paradise which certain human groups have been able to enjoy. That is what is called the colonial man, a theme of the first order, and also of enormous interest.[1] Perhaps some day, in the Institute of the Humanities, we will study this for a while, because I have gathered considerable data on it.

I am ashamed not to have studied colonial man in the libraries of the world, a man who has existed in every civilization, in each with his own particular characteristics; he becomes a man totally different from metropolitan man, but this is something that those who talk too lightly and ingenuously of our American sons completely ignore. I have not been able to undertake this task because not only would one have to travel greatly and compare both old cities and the oldest ones; one would have

1. See the author's *Meditation on a Young People, Obras completas,* vol. VIII.

to have gone to Australia; to New Zealand; to the newest-born of the English colonies, which is Rhodesia. But this means a great deal of traveling for a man like me, who takes even a streetcar only when he must.

On this theme of the migrations, although referring to a very primitive period, I remember having written some years ago a few very brief paragraphs. I said:

I keep an ancient image in my mind. It is in Castile. A straw-colored field with a red splash of blood, the blood of a wounded bull who just went by. A little later, on the lonely horizon, another bull appeared which crossed the torrid area and sniffed at the liquid stain, still warm. The animal's eye lit up. His body trembled, and shivered from muzzle to tail; he pawed the earth and raised his neck toward heaven with a loud bawling. The animal's almost electric manner of reacting to the vital traces of another of his kind made a profound impression on me. Apparently when one life meets in space another life—or simply its vestiges—there is always induced a kind of current, a frantic spurt of vitality—that is to say, life is magnified when another life enters its presence.

With man the same thing happens. Here we are, moving about through the great, immovable emptiness which land and vegetation deposit on the earth. Suddenly a bird breaks its flight at our feet. We tremble. In the distance a man appears. The emptiness established by botanical elements is suddenly inhabited by an ingredient which is not quiet. And we in this age are thoroughly accustomed to the proximity of a neighbor. What such a thing would have meant in other times! You have been told that in the dawning of our species man was a rare animal. Minute human groups wandered over the immense geological scenery. Now and then, with long intervals in between, there occurred the terrible happening: one group of men in the universe met another group of men. This encounter must have stirred fabulous tremblings! What ardors, what terrors, what prolonged trepidation this shock of one group of men experiencing the passing image of other men must have left in their imaginations! [2]

2. ("Prologue to an Edition of his Works," in *Obras completas*, vol. VI.)

But let us leave this matter of emigrations—now that Toynbee himself transfers it to a part of his work which is still unpublished. There remain the universal state and the universal church. Neither are these two important realities in his thought treated in depth and seriously, though he applies them mechanically to all civilizations. He calls anything a universal state or a universal church, up to the point where one need only list the historic facts which he describes with those names to produce an effect that might be genuinely comic.

I said earlier that the reality which inspired in Toynbee the idea of the universal state was the Roman Empire. He would be right if he gave us an idea or an analysis of what the Roman Empire was; but the result of his notion is that the Spanish viceregal state in Peru is also a universal state, and I confess that to jump from the Roman Empire to the viceregal state in Peru and identify them one with the other takes more acrobatic agility than I possess. This is why I thought it necessary in this case—under pain of doing no more than skate or slide across the spaces of history—to present schematically an internal vision of what the Roman Empire was, so that you would have a more concrete image of it.

This vision, which I think the most condensed and lucid of the explanations up to now, was presented in a couple of lessons. It obliged us to retrace a model which has no parallel in the whole human past: the evolution, over a length of time, of the supreme power in a people or a nation, in Rome. The process begins with the intermittent and elemental power of the occasional emperor, which then achieves a maturity without par in the primary and authentic legitimacy; this is followed by a secondary and partial legitimacy; to come finally to that atrocious awkwardness of unconsecrated public power, absolute and absolutely illegitimate, which is the Roman

Empire. And this is the paradox presented by that reality, which was the most illustrious state that ever existed in the world.

It was a pity that we could not study this entire process, following it through its deepest strata—namely, how the Romans felt about Law—those Romans who were not Greek philosophers nor their disciples. Law was like a reality that they lived, and not like a definition of the theoreticians which they called law. I could only allude to this with vague words. I said that Law, for the Roman, was not law because it was just, but the reverse; the just is just because it is law.

With this somewhat sybilline formula I tried to state two things at once: first, that justice, in the vague ethical sense which the word wears predominantly for us today, has nothing to do with what the Roman, who was only a Roman and not a disciple of the Greeks, called law. Second, that law was a form of behavior dowered by society with inexorable force to which the individual could surely go back and depend on because he was sure that it would be acknowledged *and it was not going to be changed between night and morning*. What that form of behavior had in it of Right, for the Roman, was not its particular content—that was secondary.

The Roman juridical institutions were concretely what they were, but they could have been completely different and possessed, nonetheless, the essence of Law that was essentially Roman, namely, the formal character of invariable force of whose fulfillment and permanence the individual could be sure. This was vital to them because life—we forget it too often, we do a great deal to forget it, yet it is true—life is in essence insecurity. I said this in 1914, in my *Meditations on Quixote*. We are unsure, including a doubt as to whether or not each of us will be existing tomorrow; but much more insecure as to what will happen with the various elements of our life: health, fortune, luck, love, sorrow, pleasure . . . At the same time man needs to be certain of some dimension in his life, even to know to what, in it, he can cling, in order to confront with *brio* the problematical rest of it. For the Romans, Law was this certainty. Thanks to the fact that they were secure in their Law, the citizen of Rome could sink his heels into it confidently, make himself firm in it, and at peace; feeling himself defended, so to speak, at the rear, he could without trepidation, shock, or neurosis seek ways and means to conduct himself in order to be a man with dignity, in order to develop his personal life seriously and with integrity, and to shape himself a character that would be compact and energetic. In short, to be a Roman. That genial sensibility which made him see his rights, his law, above all feel Law effectively as something at once inexorable and invariable, was what must have been able to make the Romans the great people they were.

On the other hand, there was perhaps no one less preoccupied with that vague thing which we irresponsibly call justice. For the same reason that the Romans knew very well, in the light of a surprising intuition, that within what is human there is no form of conduct that in any final and absolute way can be considered superior to the rest, no form of conduct to which the rest would therefore have to submit and even to annul themselves, so they knew, for example, that there neither is nor can have been anything which is absolutely what we today call justice, and which tomorrow will seem to us injustice.

What did the Romans do? They dowered with absolute, rigid, unchangeable, and inescapable characteristics a figure of comportment—let us say it deliberately with some exaggeration, so that the thing is clearer—they dowered with those absolute, rigid, invariable characteristics *any* figure of comportment whatsoever. And this is the authentic meaning of the Roman Law and, in the end, the authentic meaning of all law. The concrete profile of Roman juridical institutions—legal procedures, national power, property, inheritance, and so on—were not derived from any assumed idea of law, but from simple inveterate usage, or from compromises between struggling social groups.

Ordinarily, the line of that profile of the juridical institutions marks exactly the line of the dynamic equilibrium between struggling social forces; therefore what the figure of the institution, its profile does is to define a compromise, an accord. Roman institutions, like all Roman history, did not live on extrajuridical justice, but on political concord. All Roman history turns about the concept of concord; when it functions with its broadest characteristics it is called *concordia ordinis*, the coming to agreement of the different social classes. A great lesson which we might well learn and could also explain to men, but it is not explained to them with evidence and vigor.

According to this image which I propose to you, not that you may accept it but that you may meditate on it, these two notes appear to us as the two essentials of what law was for the Romans: first, it was to be, in principle, immutable; second, it was not to be a command of any personal will, but to be that which is established, or what is the same thing, the Law. First, customary, immemorial law; then the statutory, new laws, which arose out of preexistent laws that determined how new laws could be made; but without ever being an order that emanated from a personal authority.

For the Roman, rights and law are the contrary of *imperium*, the contrary of all authoritarianism. The act of *imperium*, practiced by part of the judicial magistracy, intervenes only in the interstices, in the gaps in law—such are the *decreta*, the interdicts; that is to say, authority, insofar as it is authority and *imperium*, and not objective and impersonal law, intervenes only when Law is lacking. This was law, and the law is that which is established, that which has always been there; that which one knows from the time he was born that he can resort to, and cling to, because it has been there for a long time and it is unchangeable.

Law is, then, properly and in substance *lex lata*, law already made, law that was already there, concerned with rights already existent. Then and only then, secondarily, comes *lex ferenda*, new law, law which is going to be made, but to be made according to a previous law made earlier, one which already existed and which determines the procedure. To put it in schematized but ideally exaggerated form so as to make a strong impact on your minds, I would say that Law, for the Roman, is what cannot be made, just as a cosmic law—the law of gravity, for example—cannot be made. And this in consideration of the fact that if law can be made, it can also be unmade; it will therefore be mutable, unstable, and insecure. Therefore I said that law is the stable thing, that which is established.

Here is the source of and the reason for the famous Roman conservatism in the matter of law and rights. It is not that they resisted modification of it just as far as possible because they were conservative, but on the contrary, the Roman was a conservative in juridical matters because he knew, he felt as no one before him, what law *is*. In essence, it is that which cannot be reformed, which cannot be varied. Nevertheless, the necessities of collective life make it obligatory to introduce modifications, and therefore reforms. But the attitude which is adopted in the face of this inescapable need to reform the law is what defines the attitude toward Right, that which Right is for a people and for a period. The Roman reformed his law slowly, with great reluctance, drop by drop, and never destroying the structural torso of his institutions, so that the Roman's consciousness that Right is for him unreformable is best made manifest in his very manner of reforming his Law.

As in so many other things, the English in their attitude toward law and rights greatly resemble the Romans. And hence Lévy-Ullman, in his magnificent book *Système juridique de l'Angleterre* (of which I think that only one volume has been published), says, with respect to the juridical order, that there does not exist in England "any bar between the present and the past." Positive rights go back in history without interruption to time immemorial. English Right is a *historical* right. Juridically speaking, there is no "ancient English Law" because "in England all law is present and actual, no matter what may be its period" (Vol. I, pp. 38–39).

Contrast the Roman and the English attitude toward law with that of the continental European peoples over the last two centuries. About 1750 in France, and half a century later in the other nations, there arose a mania of believing that Law is Law *because* and *if* it is just, where *just* means certain desiderata of a moral and ethical, utopian and mystical order, in themselves totally foreign to law as such. But as the law that was there, the stable and established law, had not been made with the fundamental and primary purpose of being just, but as a resultant of political and social struggles, as a precipitate of practical experiences of and for the fact of common living, the result was that the existent law was converted into the law which must be reformed. And as all reform will, in practice, make the ideal of extrajuridical justice real only insufficiently, and, moreover, as this ideal, like everything vague and finally arbitrary, will vary constantly, one reform will tend to be followed more and more quickly by another, and we end with the idiocy of believing that the law is what must be incessantly reformed, therefore modified and provided with substitutes.

From the timid and cautious reform which the Roman or the Englishman saw himself forced to make against his will, we come, on the Continent, especially after 1789, to the reform of reform itself, to reformism as the primary attitude toward the law. There can be no more basic turnabout or inversion in the way of thinking about law, for since then, law ceases to be in essence that which is stable, established, invariable, and always there, and is converted by definition into what *must* be reformed, therefore what must be ended and a substitute provided. Thus Law becomes what there will be tomorrow when the new, just law is made, but by the same token what never is today, for what there is today serves only to invite us to find a substitute for it. Thus law is the *lex ferenda* which turns against the *lex lata* and destroys it.

And in fact, since that date, in a process daily more intense and speeded, the law, whose mission it is to be one of the quiet and secure things on which man can count and to which he knows he can hold, has been transformed into the most unstable, fluctuating, and insecure thing. From being *terra firma*, on which one can plant one's feet, it has become a fluid element on which one can only go falling, decaying. In these last twenty years it has reached its final extremes. All the great peoples have contributed to destroying all rights and now nobody *has* any rights because there is no Law. There being none, this and that institution of private law stay like floating islands; the integral architecture of the juridical system being broken, they are degraded to being mere insubstantial regulations. It is of no use that the part of the civil code which prescribes about property continues to function today, because nobody knows that it is going to be tomorrow. It is of no account that the Penal Code goes on working slowly when no one knows if what he is doing today, which has always been considered correct, is not going to be converted—thanks to a law passed tomorrow and made retroactive—from a good act to a transgression and a crime.

When I, the citizen of a neutral country, found myself in Argentina, also a neutral country, and received my letters visaed by a British censor posted on the island of Trinidad—in the delicious blue of the Caribbean Sea—I felt a sense of fear. It did not, of course, matter to me that the English censors should take on themselves the labor of committing an impertinence by inspecting the letters that my children wrote me from Spain; what frightened me was to see that even a people like the English were collaborating *au fond* in the destruction of the last and least right that remained—the right to be neutral.

About this conduct of the great countries toward the neutrality of the smaller ones I must write very soon, for it is a theme with many appendages and seriously shameful. "*Tu quoque!*" I said in my mind to England; now the revolutionaries of so-called justice and the authoritarians of order have annihilated almost every right there was in the world, and here another country, like England neither revolutionary nor authoritarian, comes to give the last push to the small bit that is left! Certain circumstances of pure chance have made it possible that in some countries there still remains an appearance or a film of rights in the daily life of citizens; taking advantage of this, they attack those in which even that appearance has been lost.

But I have nothing to do with politics, nor is anything that I am saying political, but it is enormously more profound and serious than all of politics. Therefore I call attention in the most express fashion to the fact that I neither defend those who are attacked nor censure the attackers, insofar as what they say in their attacks signifies political strategy. But I do say to those who ostentatiously emphasize that an appearance of Right is still subsisting in the laws of their country, "Let us leave politics for a moment, and all the insincerities which have always constituted politics, all political statements, and go to the truth of things, which in this case is ultra-grave; on this phase of truth, you know very well that this apparent residue of Law in your country, compared with what it used to be, is today a mere appearance—that this juridical film you exalt is a mere film, behind which there does not exist in your country any compact mass of will for rights which would defend and sustain it. And you know just as well that any serious conflict which might arise nowadays in your country will come to nothing, with the soap-bubble pomp to which law and right have been reduced."

I am not speaking now especially—or even principally —for Spain. I made it clear in my first lesson that after fifteen years of almost total silence I was now renewing my public activity, although strictly of an intellectual order—as an activity going out from Spain. So my anguished cry goes from here to the powerful ones of the earth in order that they may be fully conscious of the enormity they have committed, and are committing, in destroying the element of rights in human affairs. One does not know that humanity ever, except for certain fugitive instants of chaos—and never throughout the whole world—has been able to live without law. But now this seems to be merely an extra item in the clock of human life. We will see if those gentlemen succeed in making the delicate clock which is humanity continue to run without it.

Rights are what cannot be reformed—nevertheless, from time to time reforms have to be introduced. Someone will tell us that this is a contradiction, and I answer at once, "You are right, completely right. It is an atrocious contradiction, but it is not mine, I am not the one that contradicts myself, it is reality itself, and the fault is not mine that it is that way, because I neither made rights or law, nor did I create the Universe. What happens is that you, immobilized by a philosophic tradition already in a coma, continue to believe that reality cannot in itself be contradictory, because you go on thinking that it is the sufficient being, complete, perfect, and best. But this only convinces me the more that the elaboration of a philosophy which is radically new and free from Hellenism and confused clamor must be undertaken."

What I have said is only in anticipation of what we will have to say more in depth in a course to be called "Man and People," wherein I propose to analyze in depth certain elemental, basic phenomena which involve human society. There we will see what the collectivity is, as I told you earlier, and what the reality of the individual within it; what customs are, uses, abuses, the useless; what public power is; what is the State, man's rights, authority; what is language, and what public opinion. In short, what, in a precise sense, it is of which everybody talks at all hours, without ever having the least clear idea of what it is, namely, the "collective soul." Then and only then will we be given power to cast a fruitful glance on the particular case of that collective soul which is *española* ("Spanishist") as compared to the other collective souls of other nations. And I say "Spanishist," because I cannot accommodate myself to the erudite term *hispani-*

dad, which has been functioning in these last years, a term which from the point of view of the Castilian language seems to me an error, for the correct Castilian phrase is to speak, for example, of a man who comes of good Vizcayan family, or a good *Castilian*, which would let us say, "*española*." [3] On the other hand, *hispanidad* is a mannered word, taken from a Latinism which the Italians recently originated, for they were the first to talk of *italianidad*, and in my judgment a bit vulgarly.

We will talk more formally of Law in Rome and in the absolute; but I was eager not to neglect this occasion in order to begin a campaign—not political, but practical. For the first time after so many years I come back to cry aloud in the desert. Because this is the mission of the intellectual who is truly a prophet—to cry in the desert. The greatest of the prophets, Isaiah, made it notable, of course, when he spoke of himself as the voice of one "crying in the wilderness." Because the mission of the intellectual is to be the man who, from his desert, his basic solitude—and man is only man amid his truth, only himself when he is alone—cries aloud to others and invites them to enter each into his own solitude. Isaiah's verse says it in the clearest way: "Vox clamantis in deserto: Parate viam Domini, rectas facite in solitudine semitas Dei nostri." [4]

If we examine the phrase "voice of one who cries aloud in the wilderness," we see the nourishing marrow that it encloses without more than taking apart each of its terms and asking ourselves, What is pure crying aloud, What pure voice, What pure desert! That voice, which is only voice—the rest has no importance, does not exist—cries

3. This invented word of Ortega's is awkward both in Spanish and in any English invention which sits among his phrases [*Translator's note*].

4. Isaiah 40:3.

aloud in the wilderness, "Prepare ye the way of the Lord, make straight in the desert a highway for our Lord," and desires to follow God—*in solitudine*—in his solitude. When man stays alone, truly alone, *ipso facto*, God appears. So that he is staying alone with God.

The universal destruction of Rights cries aloud to Heaven; therefore it had to cry aloud so urgently. By dint of talking about *justice*, the *jus*, the Law, the Right has been done away with, because its essence, which is inexorability and invariability, has not been respected. Reforming the Law, making it unstable, movable, has strangled it. When I wrote *The Revolt of the Masses*, when I prepared the articles which were to be put together in one volume a quarter of a century ago, I saw how this catastrophe was germinating, and I tried in my book to describe it and formulate it.

From that date up to now, what has happened? The saddest and most extreme fulfillment of the prophecies. From then on we do not see the creation of any Right, but on the contrary we are present almost exclusively at an end of the Rights that were. Among the many formulae which I used then to define this terrible phenomenon, I would like to remind you of the most humble of all, the case of the gypsy who goes to confess to the priest: as the priest asks him about the Commandments of the Law of God, the gypsy answers, "Look, Father, I was going to learn them, but then I heard a rumor that they were going to be done away with."

Today, Law is only the rumor that something is going to be done away with, and all on account of what is called justice. For the Roman, there was no other justice than that of the judge, the intrajuridical judge; hence I said that the just was just because it was Law. It is justice that Law produces and creates, but not that vague and irresponsible thing that is talked about in newspaper editorials and in speeches at meetings, which, making the Law unstable, makes what was *terra firma* under men's feet into mush; and when that point of support is lacking, what can man do but fall? No longer can he fix himself on that firm ground which was the Right, the Law, and from which he could try to make a life with dignity. Now man's rights are shapeless, and man falls; I have never seen anyone fall from the seventh story, and while falling, know how to do so with dignity. All falling is a process of going to pieces. The destruction of the Right can produce nothing on the part of man but a growing vileness, and this, with this word, I prophesied to Europe a quarter of a century ago. Once more, as always happens, the best has been the enemy of the good, and because of this desire for what is presumed to be justice, but I think that what has been happening, inspired by many men of good faith for the love of men, is the destroying of many of the best human things.

It is the fable of the bear and the man. The bear is the friend of man and man lies down close to him to take a siesta. The bear watches, and guards his slumber. Suddenly a fly lights on the man's forehead. This, given his friendship with the man, the bear cannot abide, and he resolves to kill the fly. He aims a blow at the man's forehead and does away with the fly, but he also flattens the face of his friend the man. Many things pretending to be utopian, of which no one has had a moment's doubt, are in practice Aesopian stories of the man and the bear.

I come to this final page full of remorse, and I feel like a culprit because I have not known how to complete the initial program fully. Of Toynbee's doctrine I have not been able to explain more than the first part, though that required the most abstract amount of explanation. Now I can say that some of these lectures, good or bad, are the most dense, most concentrated that have ever been given anywhere. Good or bad, the important thing is their density, for this is what defends my behavior. We have not, I think, wasted time in wordiness, nor have we amused ourselves with poetic gaiety. For my part, I have withheld all my reverberating and pointed adjectives and the poor fragile images which at times amuse me. In the depths of my mind, I heard them growling, bleating, bawling, moaning to be freed, but I behaved myself inexorably.

Now I have nothing more to say to you except to express my hope that we will all meet again.